THE COMPLETE PLAYS OF SEAN O'CASEY

THE COMPLETE PLAYS OF
SEAN O'CASEY

Volume Two

THE SILVER TASSIE
WITHIN THE GATES
THE STAR TURNS RED

M
MACMILLAN

ISBN 0 333 37367 7

First published 1949 by
MACMILLAN LONDON LIMITED
London and Basingstoke

Associated companies in Auckland, Dallas, Delhi, Dublin, Hong Kong, Johannesburg, Lagos, Manzini, Melbourne, Nairobi, New York, Singapore, Tokyo, Washington and Zaria

Reprinted 1950, 1952, 1958

Reissued 1984 as *Volume Two* of *The Complete Plays of Sean O'Casey*

Printed in Hong Kong

Contents

THE SILVER TASSIE

A Tragi-Comedy in Four Acts

STAGE VERSION

TO

EILEEN

WITH THE YELLOW DAFFODILS

IN THE GREEN VASE

NOTES

THE Croucher's make-up should come as close as possible to a death's head, a skull; and his hands should show like those of a skeleton's. He should sit somewhere *above* the group of Soldiers; preferably to one side, on the left, from view-point of audience, so as to overlook the Soldiers. He should look languid, as if very tired of life.

The group of Soldiers — Scene Two — should enter in a close mass, as if each was keeping the other from falling, utterly weary and tired out. They should appear as if they were almost locked together.

The Soldiers' last response to the Staff Wallah's declaration, namely, " To the Guns ! " should have in these three words the last high notes of " The Last Post ".

The song sung at the end of the play should be given to the best two (or one) singers in the cast. If, on the other hand, there be no passable singer among the players, the song should be omitted.

Perhaps a more suitable Spiritual than " Sweet Chariot " would be chosen for Harry to sing. For instance, " Keep Inchin' Along ", or " Keep Me from Sinkin' Down ".

The Chants in the play are simple Plain Song. The first chant is given in full as an example of the way in which they are sung. In the others, the dots . . . indicate that the note preceding them should be sustained till the music indicates a change. There are three parts in each chant; the Intonation; the Meditation; and the Ending. After a little practice, they will be found to be easy to sing. The Soldiers having the better voices should be selected to intone the chants, irrespective of the numbers allotted to them as characters in the book of the play.

CHARACTERS IN THE PLAY
(As they appear)

SYLVESTER HEEGAN
MRS. HEEGAN, *his wife*
SIMON NORTON
SUSIE MONICAN
MRS. FORAN
TEDDY FORAN, *her husband*
HARRY HEEGAN, D.C.M., *Heegan's son*
JESSIE TAITE
BARNEY BAGNAL
THE CROUCHER
1ST SOLDIER
2ND SOLDIER
3RD SOLDIER
4TH SOLDIER
THE CORPORAL
THE VISITOR
THE STAFF WALLAH
1ST STRETCHER-BEARER
2ND STRETCHER-BEARER
1ST CASUALTY
2ND CASUALTY
SURGEON FORBY MAXWELL
THE SISTER OF THE WARD

———

ACT I.—Room in Heegan's home.
ACT II.—Somewhere in France (*later on*).
ACT III.—Ward in a Hospital (*a little later on*).
ACT IV.—Room in Premises of Avondale Football Club
          (*later on still*).

ACT I

The eating, sitting, and part sleeping room of the Heegan family. A large window at back looks on to a quay, from which can be seen the centre mast of a steamer, at the top of which gleams a white light. Another window at right looks down on a side street. Under the window at back, plump in the centre, is a stand, the legs gilded silver and the top gilded gold; on the stand is a purple velvet shield on which are pinned a number of silver medals surrounding a few gold ones. On each side of the shield is a small vase holding a bunch of artificial flowers. The shield is draped with red and yellow ribbons. To the left of the stand is a bed covered with a bedspread of black striped with vivid green. To the right of the stand is a dresser and chest of drawers combined. The fireplace is to the left. Beside the fireplace is a door leading to a bedroom, another door which gives access to the rest of the house and the street, on the right. At the corner left is a red coloured stand resembling an easel, having on it a silver-gilt framed picture photograph of Harry Heegan in football dress, crimson jersey with yellow collar and cuffs and a broad yellow belt, black stockings, and yellow football boots. A table on which are a half-pint bottle of whisky, a large parcel of bread and meat sandwiches, and some copies of English illustrated magazines.

Sylvester Heegan and Simon Norton are sitting by the fire. Sylvester Heegan is a stockily built man of sixty-five; he has been a docker all his life since first the muscles of his arms could safely grip a truck, and even at sixty-five the steel in them is only beginning to stiffen.

Simon Norton is a tall man, originally a docker too, but by a little additional steadiness, a minor effort towards self-education,

*a natural, but very slight superior nimbleness of mind, has risen
in the Company's estimation and has been given the position
of checker, a job entailing as many hours of work as a docker,
almost as much danger, twice as much responsibility, and a
corresponding reduction in his earning powers.   He is not so
warmly, but a little more circumspectly dressed than Sylvester,
and in his manner of conduct and speech there is a hesitant
suggestion of greater refinement than in those of Sylvester, and a
still more vague indication that he is aware of it.   This timid
semi-conscious sense of superiority, which Simon sometimes forgets,
is shown frequently by a complacent stroking of a dark beard
which years are beginning to humiliate.   The night is cold, and
Simon and Sylvester occasionally stretch longingly towards the
fire.   They are fully dressed and each has his topcoat and hat
beside him, as if ready to go out at a moment's notice.   Susie
Monican is standing at the table polishing a Lee-Enfield rifle with
a chamois cloth ; the butt of the rifle is resting on the table.   She
is a girl of twenty-two, well-shaped limbs, challenging breasts,
all of which are defiantly hidden by a rather long dark blue skirt
and bodice buttoning up to the throat, relieved by a crimson scarf
around her neck, knotted in front and falling down her bosom
like a man's tie.   She is undeniably pretty, but her charms are
almost completely hidden by her sombre, ill-fitting dress, and the
rigid manner in which she has made her hair up declares her
unflinching and uncompromising modesty.   Just now she is
standing motionless, listening intently, looking towards the door
on right.*

*Mrs. Heegan is standing at the window at right, listening
too, one hand pulling back the curtain, but her attention, taken
from the window, is attracted to the door.   She is older than
Sylvester, stiffened with age and rheumatism ; the end of her
life is unknowingly lumbering towards a rest : the impetus
necessity has given to continual toil and striving is beginning to
slow down, and everything she has to do is done with a quiet*

mechanical persistence. Her inner ear cannot hear even a faint echo of a younger day. Neither Sylvester nor Simon has noticed the attentive attitude of Mrs. Heegan or Susie, for Sylvester, with one arm outstretched crooked at the elbow, is talking with subdued intensity to Simon.

Sylvester. I seen him do it, mind you. I seen him do it.

Simon. I quite believe you, Sylvester.

Sylvester. Break a chain across his bisseps ! [*With panto-mime action*] Fixes it over his arm . . . bends it up . . . a little strain . . . snaps in two . . . right across his bisseps !

Susie. Shush you, there !
   [*Mrs. Heegan goes out with troubled steps by door. The rest remain still for a few moments.*

Sylvester. A false alarm.

Simon. No cause for undue anxiety ; there's plenty of time yet.

Susie [*chanting as she resumes the polishing of gun*] :
   Man walketh in a vain shadow, and disquieteth him-
      self in vain :
   He heapeth up riches, and cannot tell who shall
      gather them.
   [*She sends the chant in the direction of Sylvester and Simon, Susie coming close to the two men and sticking an angry face in between them.*

Susie. When the two of yous stand quiverin' together on the dhread day of the Last Judgment, how will the two of yous feel if yous have nothin' to say but " he broke a chain across his bisseps " ? Then the two of you'll know that the wicked go down into hell, an' all the people who forget God !

[*She listens a moment, and leaving down the rifle, goes out by door left.*

Sylvester. It's persecutin', that tambourine theology of Susie's. I always get a curious, sickenin' feelin', Simon, when I hear the Name of the Supreme Bein' tossed into the quietness of a sensible conversation.

Simon. The day he won the Cross Country Championship of County Dublin, Syl, was a day to be chronicled.

Sylvester. In a minor way, yes, Simon. But the day that caps the chronicle was the one when he punched the fear of God into the heart of Police Constable 63 C under the stars of a frosty night on the way home from Terenure.

Simon. Without any exaggeration, without any exaggeration, mind you, Sylvester, that could be called a memorable experience.

Sylvester. I can see him yet [*he gets up, slides from side to side, dodging and parrying imaginary blows*] glidin' round the dazzled Bobby, cross-ey'd tryin' to watch him.

Simon [*tapping his pipe resolutely on the hob*]. Unperturbed, mind you, all the time.

Sylvester. An' the hedges by the road-side standin' stiff in the silent cold of the air, the frost beads on the branches glistenin' like toss'd-down diamonds from the breasts of the stars, the quietness of the night stimulated to a fuller stillness by the mockin' breathin' of Harry, an' the heavy, ragin' pantin' of the Bobby, an' the quickenin' beats of our own hearts afraid, of hopin' too little or hopin' too much.

[*During the last speech by Sylvester, Susie has come in with
a bayonet, and has commenced to polish it.*

Susie. We don't go down on our knees often enough ;
that's why we're not able to stand up to the Evil One :
we don't go down on our knees enough. . . . I can
hear some persons fallin' with a splash of sparks into
the lake of everlastin' fire. . . . An account of every
idle word shall be given at the last day.

[*She goes out again with rifle.*

Susie [*bending towards Simon and Sylvester as she goes*]. God
is listenin' to yous ; God is listenin' to yous !

Sylvester. Dtch, dtch, dtch. People ought to be forcibly
restrained from constantly cannonadin' you with the
name of the Deity.

Simon. Dubiety never brush'd a thought into my mind,
Syl, while I was waitin' for the moment when Harry
would stretch the Bobby hors dee combaa on the
ground.

Sylvester [*resuming his pantomime actions*]. There he was
staggerin', beatin' out blindly, every spark of energy
panted out of him, while Harry feinted, dodg'd, side-
stepp'd, then suddenly sail'd in an' put him asleep
with . . .

Simon. A right-handed hook to the jaw !
Sylvester. A left-handed hook to the jaw ! } [*together*].

Sylvester [*after a pause*]. A left-handed hook to the jaw,
Simon.

Simon. No, no, Syl, a right-handed hook to the jaw.

[*Mrs. Foran runs quickly in by the door with a frying-pan
in her hand, on which is a steak. She comes to the fire,*

*pushing, so as to disturb the two men. She is one of the
many gay, careworn women of the working-class.*

Mrs. Foran [*rapidly*]. A pot of clothes is boilin' on the fire
above, an' I knew yous wouldn't mind me slappin' a
bit of a steak on here for a second to show him, when
he comes in before he goes away, that we're mindful of
his needs, an' I'm hopeful of a dream to-night that
the sea's between us, not lookin' very haggard in the
mornin' to find the dream a true one. [*With satisfied
anticipation*]

For I'll be single again, yes, I'll be single again ;
An' I eats what I likes, . . . an' I drinks what I
likes,
An' I likes what I likes, when I'm——
[*Stopping suddenly*] What's the silence for ?

Sylvester [*slowly and decidedly*]. I was at the fight, Simon,
an' I seen him givin' a left-handed hook to the jaw.

Mrs. Foran. What fight ?

Simon [*slowly and decidedly*]. I was there too, an' I saw him
down the Bobby with a right-handed hook to the jaw.

Mrs. Foran. What Bobby ?   [*A pause.*

Sylvester. It was a close up, an' I don't know who'd know
better if it wasn't the boy's own father.

Mrs Foran. What boy . . . what father ?

Sylvester. Oh, shut up, woman, an' don't be smotherin'
us with a shower of questions.

Susie [*who has entered on the last speech, and has started to
polish a soldier's steel helmet*]. Oh, the miserableness of
them that don't know the things that belong unto
their peace. They try one thing after another, they try

everything, but they never think of trying God. [*Coming nearer to them.*] Oh, the happiness of knowing that God's hand has pick'd you out for heaven. [*To Mrs. Foran*] What's the honey-pot kiss of a lover to the kiss of righteousness and peace ?

> [*Mrs. Foran, embarrassed, goes over to window.*

Susie [*turning to Simon*]. Simon, will you not close the dandy door of the public-house and let the angels open the pearly gates of heaven for you ?

Sylvester. We feel very comfortable where we are, Susie.

Susie. Don't mock, Sylvester, don't mock. You'd run before a great wind, tremble in an earthquake, and flee from a fire ; so don't treat lightly the still, small voice calling you to repentance and faith.

Sylvester [*with appeal and irritation*]. Oh, do give over worryin' a man, Susie.

Susie. God shows His love by worrying, and worrying, and worrying the sinner. The day will come when you will call on the mountains to cover you, and then you'll weep and gnash your teeth that you did not hearken to Susie's warning. [*Putting her hands appealingly on his shoulders*] Sylvester, if you pray long enough, and hard enough, and deep enough, you'll get the power to fight and conquer Beelzebub.

Mrs. Foran. I'll be in a doxological mood tonight, not because the kingdom of heaven'll be near me, but because my husband'll be far away, and tomorrow [*singing*] :

I'll be single again, yes, single again ;
An' I goes where I likes, an' I does what I likes,
An' I likes what I likes now I'm single again !

C.P.—II

Simon. Go on getting Harry's things ready, Susie, and defer the dosing of your friends with canticles till the time is ripe with rest for them to listen quietly.

[*Simon and Sylvester are very self-conscious during Susie's talk to them. Simon empties his pipe by tapping the head on the hob of the grate. He then blows through it. As he is blowing through it, Sylvester is emptying his by tapping it on the hob ; as he is blowing it Simon taps his again ; as Simon taps Sylvester taps with him, and then they look into the heads of the pipes and blow together.*

Susie. It must be mercy or it must be judgement : if not mercy today it may be judgement tomorrow. He is never tired of waiting and waiting and waiting ; and watching and watching and watching ; and knocking and knocking and knocking for the sinner — you, Sylvester, and you, Simon — to turn from his wickedness and live. Oh, if the two of you only knew what it was to live ! Not to live leg-staggering an' belly-creeping among the pain-spotted and sin-splashed desires of the flesh ; but to live, oh, to live swift-flying from a holy peace to a holy strength, and from holy strength to a holy joy, like the flashing flights of a swallow in the deep beauty of a summer sky.

[*Simon and Sylvester shift about, self-conscious and uneasy.*

Susie [*placing her hand first on Simon's shoulder and then on Sylvester's*]. The two of you God's elegant swallows ; a saved pair ; a loving pair strong-wing'd, freed from the gin of the snarer, tip of wing to tip of wing, flying fast or darting swift together to the kingdom of heaven.

Simon [*expressing a protecting thought to Sylvester*]. One of the two of us should go out and hunt back the old woman from the perishing cold of watching for the return of Harry.

Sylvester. She'll be as cold as a naked corpse, an' unstinted watchin' won't bring Harry back a minute sooner. I'll go an' drive her back. [*He rises to go*] I'll be back in a minute, Susie.

Simon [*hurriedly*]. Don't bother, Syl, I'll go ; she won't be farther than the corner of the street ; you go on toasting yourself where you are. [*He rises*] I'll be back in a minute, Susie.

Mrs. Foran [*running to the door*]. Rest easy the two of you, an' I'll go, so as to give Susie full time to take the sin out of your bones an' put you both in first-class form for the kingdom of heaven.   [*She goes out.*

Susie. Sinners that jeer often add to the glory of God : going out, she gives you, Sylvester, and you, Simon, another few moments, precious moments — oh, how precious, for once gone, they are gone for ever — to listen to the warning from heaven.

Simon [*suddenly*]. Whisht, here's somebody coming, I think ?

Sylvester. I'll back this is Harry comin' at last.
          [*A pause as the three listen.*

Sylvester. No, it's nobody.

Simon. Whoever it was 's gone by.

Susie. Oh, Syl, oh, Simon, don't try to veil the face of God with an evasion. You can't, you can't cod God. This may be your last chance before the pains of hell encompass the two of you. Hope is passing by ;

salvation is passing by, and glory arm-in-arm with her. In the quietness left to you go down on your knees and pray that they come into your hearts and abide with you for ever. . . . [*With fervour, placing her left hand on Simon's shoulder and her right hand on Sylvester's, and shaking them*] Get down on your knees, get down on your knees, get down on your knees and pray for conviction of sin, lest your portion in David become as the portion of the Canaanites, the Amorites, the Perizzites and the Jebusites !

Sylvester. Eh, eh, Susie ; cautious now — you seem to be forgettin' yourself.

Simon. Desist, Susie, desist. Violence won't gather people to God. It only ingenders hostility to what you're trying to do.

Sylvester. You can't batter religion into a man like that.

Simon. Religion is love, but that sort of thing is simply a nullification of religion.

Susie. Bitterness and wrath in exhortation is the only hope of rousing the pair of yous into a sense of coming and everlasting penalties.

Sylvester. Well, give it a miss, give it a miss to me now. Don't try to claw me into the kingdom of heaven. An' you only succeed in distempering piety when you try to mangle it into a man's emotions.

Simon. Heaven is all the better, Susie, for being a long way off.

Sylvester. If I want to pray I do it voluntarily, but I'm not going to be goaded an' goaded into it.

Susie. I go away in a few days to help to nurse the

wounded, an' God's merciful warnings may depart
along with me, then sin 'll usher the two of you into
Gehenna for all eternity.   Oh, if the two of you could
only grasp the meaning of the word eternity !   [*Bending
down and looking up into their faces*] Time that had no
beginning and never can have an end — an' there you'll
be — two cockatrices creeping together, a desolation,
an astonishment, a curse and a hissing from everlasting
to everlasting.   [*She goes into room.*

Sylvester. Cheerful, what !   Cockatrices — be-God, that's
a good one, Simon !

Simon. Always a trying thing to have to listen to one
that's trying to push the kingdom of God into a
reservation of a few yards.

Sylvester. A cockatrice !   Now where did she manage to
pick up that term of approbation, I wonder ?

Simon. From the Bible.   An animal somewhere mentioned in the Bible, I think, that a serpent hatched out
of a cock's egg.

Sylvester. A cock's egg !   It couldn't have been the egg
of an ordinary cock.   Not the male of what we call a
hen ?

Simon. I think so.

Sylvester. Well, be-God, that's a good one !   You know
Susie'll have to be told to disintensify her soul-
huntin', for religion even isn't an excuse for saying
that a man 'll become a cockatrice.

Simon. In a church, somehow or other, it seems natural
enough, and even in the street it's alright, for one
thing is as good as another in the wide-open ear of the

air, but in the delicate quietness of your own home it, it——

Sylvester. Jars on you !

Simon. Exactly !

Sylvester. If she'd only confine her glory-to-God business to the festivals, Christmas, now, or even Easter, Simon, it would be recommendable ; for a few days before Christmas, like the quiet raisin' of a curtain, an' a few days after, like the gentle lowerin' of one, there's nothing more . . . more——

Simon. Appropriate. . . .

Sylvester. Exhilaratin' than the singin' of the Adestay Fidellis.

Simon. She's damned pretty, an' if she dressed herself justly, she'd lift some man's heart up, an' toss down many another. It's a mystery now, what affliction causes the disablement, for most women of that kind are plain, an' when a woman's born plain she's born good. I wonder what caused the peculiar bend in Susie's nature ? Narrow your imagination to the limit and you couldn't call it an avocation.

Sylvester [*giving the head of his pipe a sharp, quick blow on the palm of his hand to clear it*]. Adoration.

Simon. What ?

Sylvester. Adoration, Simon, accordin' to the flesh. . . . She fancied Harry and Harry fancied Jessie, so she hides her rage an' loss in the love of a scorchin' Gospel.

Simon. Strange, strange.

Sylvester. Oh, very curious, Simon.

Simon. It's a problem, I suppose.

Sylvester. An inconsolable problem, Simon.

[*Mrs. Foran enters by door, helping in Mrs. Heegan, who is pale and shivering with cold.*

Mrs. Heegan [*shivering and shuddering*]. U-u-uh, I feel the stream of blood that's still trickling through me old veins icifyin' fast ; u-uh.

Mrs. Foran. Madwoman, dear, to be waitin' out there on the quay an' a wind risin' as cold as a stepmother's breath, piercin' through your old bones, mockin' any effort a body would make to keep warm, an' [*suddenly rushing over to the fireplace in an agony of dismay, scattering Simon and Sylvester, and whipping the frying-pan off the fire*] — The steak, the steak ; I forgot the blasted steak an' onions fryin' on the fire ! God Almighty, there's not as much as a bead of juice left in either of them. The scent of the burnin' would penetrate to the street, an' not one of you'd stir a hand to lift them out of danger. Oh, look at the condition they're in. Even the gospel-gunner couldn't do a little target practice by helpin' the necessity of a neighbour. [*As she goes out*] I can hear the love for your neighbours almost fizzlin' in your hearts.

Mrs. Heegan [*pushing in to the fire, to Simon and Sylvester*]. Push to the right and push to the left till I get to the fosterin' fire. Time eatin' his heart out, an' no sign of him yet. The two of them, the two of my legs is numb . . . an' the wind's risin' that'll make the sea heave an' sink under the boat tonight, under shaded lights an' the submarines about. [*Susie comes in, goes over to window, and looks out.*] Hours ago the football match must have been over, an' no word of him yet, an' all drinkin' if they won, an' all drinkin' if they lost ; with Jessie hitchin' on after him, an' no one thinkin' of me an' the maintenance money.

Sylvester. He'll come back in time ; he'll have to come back ; he must come back.

Simon. He got the goals, Mrs. Heegan, that won the last two finals, and it's only fair he'd want to win this, which'll mean that the Cup won before two——

Sylvester [*butting in*]. Times hand runnin'.

Simon. Two times consecutively before, makin' the Cup the property of the Club.

Sylvester. Exactly !

Mrs. Heegan. The chill's residin' in my bones, an' feelin's left me just the strength to shiver. He's overstayed his leave a lot, an' if he misses now the tide that's waitin', he skulks behind desertion from the colours.

Susie. On Active Service that means death at dawn.

Mrs. Heegan. An' my governmental money grant would stop at once.

Susie. That would gratify Miss Jessie Taite, because you put her weddin' off with Harry till after the duration of the war, an' cut her out of the allowance.

Sylvester [*with a sickened look at Simon*]. Dtch, dtch, dtch, the way the women wag the worst things out of happenings ! [*To the women*] My God Almighty, he'll be back in time an' fill yous all with disappointment.

Mrs. Heegan. She's coinin' money workin at munitions, an' doesn't need to eye the little that we get from

Harry ; for one evening hurryin' with him to the pictures she left her bag behind, an' goin' through it what would you think I found ?

Susie. A saucy book, now, or a naughty picture ?

Mrs. Heegan. Lion and Unicorn standin' on their Jew ay mon draw. With all the rings an' dates, an' rules an' regulations.

Simon. What was it, Mrs. Heegan ?

Mrs. Heegan. Spaced an' lined ; signed an' signatured ; nestlin' in a blue envelope to keep it warm.

Sylvester [*testily*]. Oh, sing it out, woman, an' don't be takin' the value out of what you're goin' to tell us.

Mrs. Heegan. A Post Office Savings Bank Book.

Sylvester. Oh, hairy enough, eh ?

Simon. How much, Mrs. Heegan ?

Mrs. Heegan. Pounds an' shillings with the pence missin' ; backed by secrecy, an' security guaranteed by Act of Parliament.

Sylvester [*impatiently*]. Dtch, dtch. Yes, yes, woman, but how much was it ?

Mrs. Heegan. Two hundred an' nineteen pounds, sixteen shillings, an' no pence.

Sylvester. Be-God, a nice little nest egg, right enough !

Susie. I hope in my heart that she came by it honestly, and that she remembers that it's as true now as when it was first spoken that it's harder for a camel to go through the eye of a needle than for a rich person to enter the kingdom of heaven.

Simon. And she hidin' it all under a veil of silence, when there wasn't the slightest fear of any of us bein' jealous of her.

> [*A tumult is heard on the floor over their heads, followed by a crash of breaking delf. They are startled, and listen attentively.*

Mrs. Heegan [*breaking the silence*]. Oh, there he's at it again. An' she sayin' that he was a pattern husband since he came home on leave, merry-making with her an' singin' dolorously the first thing every mornin'. I was thinkin' there'd be a rough house sometime over her lookin' so well after his long absence . . . you'd imagine now, the trenches would have given him some idea of the sacredness of life !

> [*Another crash of breaking delfware.*

Mrs. Heegan. An' the last week of his leave she was too fond of breakin' into song in front of him.

Sylvester. Well, she's gettin' it now for goin' round heavin' her happiness in the poor man's face.

> [*A crash, followed by screams from Mrs. Foran.*

Susie. I hope he won't be running down here as he often does.

Simon [*a little agitated*]. I couldn't stay here an' listen to that ; I'll go up and stop him : he might be killing the poor woman.

Mrs. Heegan. Don't do anything of the kind, Simon ; he might down you with a hatchet or something.

Simon. Phuh, I'll keep him off with the left and hook him with the right. [*Putting on his hat and coat as he goes to the door.*] Looking prim and careless 'll astonish him. Monstrous to stay here, while he may be killing the woman.

Mrs. Heegan [*to Simon as he goes out*]. For God's sake mind yourself, Simon.

Sylvester [*standing beside closed door on right with his ear close to one of the panels, listening intently*]. Simon's a tidy little man with his fists, an' would make Teddy Foran feel giddy if he got home with his left hook. [*Crash.*] I wonder is that Simon knockin' down Foran, or Foran knockin' down Simon ?

Mrs. Heegan. If he came down an' we had the light low, an' kept quiet, he might think we were all out.

Sylvester. Shush. I can hear nothin' now. Simon must have awed him. Quiet little man, but when Simon gets goin'. Shush ? No, nothin' . . . Something unusual has happened. O, oh, be-God !

[*The door against which Sylvester is leaning bursts suddenly in. Sylvester is flung headlong to the floor, and Mrs. Foran, her hair falling wildly over her shoulders, a cut over her eye, frantic with fear, rushes in and scrambles in a frenzy of haste under the bed. Mrs. Heegan, quickened by fear, runs like a good one, followed by Susie, into the room, the door of which they bang after them. Sylvester hurriedly fights his way under the bed with Mrs. Foran.*]

Mrs. Foran [*speaking excitedly and jerkily as she climbs under the bed*]. Flung his dinner into the fire — and started to smash the little things in the room. Tryin' to save the dresser, I got a box in the eye. I locked the door on him as I rushed out, an' before I was half-way down, he had one of the panels flyin' out with — a hatchet !

Sylvester [*under the bed — out of breath*]. Whythehell

didn'tyou sing out beforeyousent thedoor flyin' inon-
top o' me !

Mrs. Foran. How could I an' I flyin' before danger to
me — life ?

Sylvester. Yes, an'you'vegot meinto a nice extremity now !

Mrs. Foran. An' I yelled to Simon Norton when he had
me — down,   but the boyo only ran the faster out of
the — house !

Sylvester. Oh, an' the regal like way he went out to
fight !   Oh, I'm findin' out that everyone who wears
a cocked hat isn't a Napoleon !

  [*Teddy Foran, Mrs. Foran's husband, enters by door, with
  a large, fancy, vividly yellow-coloured bowl, ornamented
  with crimson roses, in one hand and a hatchet in the
  other.   He is big and powerful, rough and hardy.   A man
  who would be dominant in a public-house, and whose
  opinions would be listened to with great respect.   He is
  dressed in khaki uniform of a soldier home on leave.*

Teddy. Under the bed, eh ?   Right place for a guilty
conscience.   I should have thrown you out of the
window with the dinner you put before me.   Out
with you from under there, an' come up with your
husband.

Susie [*opening suddenly door right, putting in her head, pulling it back and shutting door again*]. God is looking at
you, God is looking at you !

Mrs. Foran. I'll not budge an inch from where I am.

Teddy [*looking under the bed and seeing Sylvester*]. What are
you doin' there encouragin' her against her husband ?

Sylvester. You've no right to be rippin' open the poor
woman's life of peace with violence.

Teddy [*with indignation*]. She's my wife, isn't she ?

Mrs. Foran. Nice thing if I lose the sight of my eye with the cut you gave me !

Teddy. She's my wife, isn't she ？ An' you've no legal right to be harbourin' her here, keepin' her from her household duties. Stunned I was when I seen her lookin' so well after me long absence. Blowin' her sighin' in me face all day, an' she sufferin' the tortures of hell for fear I'd miss the boat !

Sylvester. Go on up to your own home ; you've no right to be violatin' this place.

Teddy. You'd like to make her your cheery amee, would you ？ It's napoo, there, napoo, you little pip-squeak. I seen you an' her goin' down the street arm-in-arm.

Sylvester. Did you expect to see me goin' down the street leg-in-leg with her ?

Teddy. Thinkin' of her Ring-papers instead of her husband. [*To Mrs. Foran*] I'll teach you to be rippling with joy an' your husband goin' away ! [*He shows the bowl.*] Your weddin' bowl, look at it ; pretty, isn't it ？ Take your last eyeful of it now, for it's goin' west quick !

Susie [*popping her head in again*]. God is watching you, God is watching you !

Mrs. Foran [*appealingly*]. Teddy, Teddy, don't smash the poor weddin' bowl.

Teddy [*smashing the bowl with a blow of the hatchet*]. It would be a pity, wouldn't it ？ Damn it, an' damn you. I'm off now to smash anything I missed, so that you'll have a gay time fittin' up the little home again by the time your loving husband comes back. You can come an' have a look, an' bring your mon amee if you like.

[*He goes out, and there is a pause as Mrs. Foran and Sylvester peep anxiously towards the door.*

Sylvester. Cautious, now cautious ; he might be lurking outside that door there, ready to spring on you the minute you show'd your nose !

Mrs. Foran. Me lovely little weddin' bowl, me lovely little weddin' bowl !

[*Teddy is heard breaking things in the room above.*

Sylvester [*creeping out from under the bed*]. Oh, he is gone up. He was a little cow'd, I think, when he saw me.

Mrs. Foran. Me little weddin' bowl, wrapp'd in tissue paper, an' only taken out for a few hours every Christmas — me poor little weddin' bowl.

Susie [*popping her head in*]. God is watching — oh, he's gone !

Sylvester [*jubilant*]. Vanished ! He was a little cow'd, I think, when he saw me.

[*Mrs. Heegan and Susie come into the room.*

Mrs. Foran. He's makin' a hash of every little thing we have in the house, Mrs. Heegan.

Mrs. Heegan. Go inside to the room, Mrs. Foran, an' if he comes down again, we'll say you ran out to the street.

Mrs. Foran [*going into room*]. My poor little weddin' bowl that I might have had for generations !

Susie [*who has been looking out of the window, excitedly*].

They're comin', they're comin' : a crowd with a concertina ; some of them carrying Harry on their
shoulders, an' others are carrying that Jessie Taite too,
holding a silver cup in her hands. Oh, look at the
shameful way she's showing her legs to all who like
to have a look at them !

Mrs. Heegan. Never mind Jessie's legs — what we have to
do is to hurry him out in time to catch the boat.

[*The sound of a concertina playing in the street outside has
been heard, and the noise of a marching crowd. The
crowd stop at the house. Shouts are heard — " Up the
Avondales ! " ; " Up Harry Heegan and the Avondales ! "   Then steps are heard coming up the stairs,
and first Simon Norton enters, holding the door cere-
moniously wide open to allow Harry to enter, with his
arm around Jessie, who is carrying a silver cup joyously,
rather than reverentially, elevated, as a priest would
elevate a chalice. Harry is wearing khaki trousers, a
military cap stained with trench mud, a vivid orange-
coloured jersey with black collar and cuffs. He is twenty-
three years of age, tall, with the sinewy muscles of a
manual worker made flexible by athletic sport. He is a
typical young worker, enthusiastic, very often boisterous,
sensible by instinct rather than by reason. He has gone
to the trenches as unthinkingly as he would go to the
polling booth. He isn't naturally stupid ; it is the
stupidity of persons in high places that has stupefied him.
He has given all to his masters, strong heart, sound lungs,
healthy stomach, lusty limbs, and the little mind that
education has permitted to develop sufficiently to make all
the rest a little more useful. He is excited now with the
sweet and innocent insanity of a fine achievement, and the
rapid lowering of a few drinks.*

[*Jessie is twenty-two or so, responsive to all the animal impulses of life. Ever dancing around, in and between the world, the flesh, and the devil. She would be happy climbing with a boy among the heather on Howth Hill, and could play ball with young men on the swards of the Phœnix Park. She gives her favour to the prominent and popular. Harry is her favourite : his strength and speed has won the Final for his club, he wears the ribbon of the D.C.M. It is a time of spiritual and animal exaltation for her.*

[*Barney Bagnal, a soldier mate of Harry's, stands a little shyly near the door, with a pleasant, good-humoured grin on his rather broad face. He is the same age as Harry, just as strong, but not so quick, less finely formed, and not so sensitive ; able to take most things quietly, but savage and wild when he becomes enraged. He is fully dressed, with topcoat buttoned on him, and he carries Harry's on his arm.*

Harry [*joyous and excited*]. Won, won, won, be-God ; by the odd goal in five. Lift it up, lift it up, Jessie, sign of youth, sign of strength, sign of victory !

Mrs. Heegan [*to Sylvester*]. I knew, now, Harry would come back in time to catch the boat.

Harry [*to Jessie*]. Leave it here, leave it down here, Jessie, under the picture, the picture of the boy that won the final.

Mrs. Heegan. A parcel of sandwiches, a bottle of whisky, an' some magazines to take away with you an' Barney, Harry.

Harry. Napoo sandwiches, an' napoo magazines : look at the cup, eh ? The cup that Harry won, won by the odd goal in five ! [*To Barney*] The song that the little Jock used to sing, Barney, what was it ? The little Jock we left shrivellin' on the wire after the last push.

Barney. " Will ye no come back again ? "

Harry. No, no, the one we all used to sing with him, " The Silver Tassie ". [*Pointing to cup*] There it is, the Silver Tassie, won by the odd goal in five, kicked by Harry Heegan.

Mrs. Heegan. Watch your time, Harry, watch your time.

Jessie. He's watching it, he's watching it — for God's sake don't get fussy, Mrs. Heegan.

Harry. They couldn't take their beatin' like men. . . . Play the game, play the game, why the hell couldn't they play the game ? [*To Barney*] See the President of the Club, Dr. Forby Maxwell, shaking hands with me, when he was giving me the cup, " Well done, Heegan ! " The way they yell'd and jump'd when they put in the equalizing goal in the first half !

Barney. Ay, a fluke, that's what it was ; a lowsey fluke.

Mrs. Heegan [*holding Harry's coat up for him to put it on*]. Here, your coat, Harry, slip it on while you're talkin'.

Harry [*putting it on*]. Alright, keep smiling, don't fuss. [*To the rest*] Grousing the whole time they were chasing the ball ; an' when they lost it, " Referee, referee, offside, referee . . . foul there ; ey, open your eyes, referee ! "

Jessie. And we scream'd and shout'd them down with " Play the game, Primrose Rovers, play the game ! "

Barney. You ran them off their feet till they nearly stood still.

Mrs. Foran [*has been peeping twice in timidly from the room and now comes in to the rest*]. Somebody run up an' bring Teddy down for fear he'd be left behind.

Sylvester [*to Harry*]. Your haversack an' trench tools, Harry ; haversack first, isn't it ?

Harry [*fixing his haversack*]. Haversack, haversack, don't rush me. [*To the rest*] But when I got the ball, Barney, once I got the ball, the rain began to fall on the others. An' the last goal, the goal that put us one ahead, the winning goal, that was a-a-eh-a stunner !

Barney. A beauty, me boy, a hot beauty.

Harry. Slipping by the back rushing at me like a mad bull, steadying a moment for a drive, seeing in a flash the goalie's hands sent with a shock to his chest by the force of the shot, his half-stunned motion to clear, a charge, and then carrying him, the ball and all with a rush into the centre of the net !

Barney [*enthusiastically*]. Be-God, I did get a thrill when I seen you puttin' him sittin' on his arse in the middle of the net !

Mrs. Foran [*from the door*]. One of yous do go up an' see if Teddy's ready to go.

Mrs. Heegan [*to Harry*]. Your father 'll carry your kit-bag, an' Jessie 'll carry your rifle as far as the boat.

Harry [*irritably*]. Oh, damn it, woman, give your wailin' over for a minute !

Mrs. Heegan. You've got only a few bare minutes to spare, Harry.

Harry. We'll make the most of them, then. [*To Barney*]

Out with one of them wine-virgins we got in " The Mill in the Field ", Barney, and we'll rape her in a last hot moment before we set out to kiss the guns !

[*Simon has gone into room and returned with a gun and a kit-bag. He crosses to where Barney is standing.*]

Barney [*taking a bottle of wine from his pocket*]. Empty her of her virtues, eh ?

Harry. Spill it out, Barney, spill it out. . . . [*Seizing Silver Cup, and holding it towards Barney*] Here, into the cup, be-God. A drink out of the cup, out of the Silver Tassie !

Barney [*who has removed the cap and taken out the cork*]. Here she is now. . . . Ready for anything, stripp'd to the skin !

Jessie. No double-meaning talk, Barney.

Susie [*haughtily, to Jessie*]. The men that are defending us have leave to bow themselves down in the House of Rimmon, for the men that go with the guns are going with God.

[*Barney pours wine into the cup for Harry and into a glass for himself.*]

Harry [*to Jessie*]. Jessie, a sup for you. [*She drinks from the cup.*] An' a drink for me. [*He drinks.*] Now a kiss while our lips are wet. [*He kisses her.*] Christ, Barney, how would you like to be retreating from the fairest face and [*lifting Jessie's skirt a little*] — and the trimmest, slimmest little leg in the parish ? Napoo, Barney, to everyone but me !

Mrs. Foran. One of you go up, an' try to get my Teddy down.

Barney [*lifting Susie's skirt a little*]. Napoo, Harry, to every-one but——

Susie [*angrily, pushing Barney away from her*]. You khaki-cover'd ape, you, what are you trying to do ? Man-handle the lassies of France, if you like, but put on your gloves when you touch a woman that seeketh not the things of the flesh.

Harry [*putting an arm round Susie to mollify her*]. Now, Susie, Susie, lengthen your temper for a passing moment, so that we may bring away with us the breath of a kiss to the shell-bullied air of the trenches. . . . Besides, there's nothing to be ashamed of — it's not a bad little leggie at all.

Susie [*slipping her arm round Harry's neck, and looking defiantly at Barney*]. I don't mind what Harry does ; I know he means no harm, not like other people. Harry's different.

Jessie. You'll not forget to send me the German helmet home from France, Harry ?

Susie [*trying to rest her head on Harry's breast*]. I know Harry, he's different. It's his way. I wouldn't let anyone else touch me, but in some way or another I can tell Harry's different.

Jessie [*putting her arm round Harry under Susie's in an effort to dislodge it*]. Susie, Harry wants to be free to keep his arm round me during his last few moments here, so don't be pulling him about !

Susie [*shrinking back a little*]. I was only saying that Harry was different.

Mrs. Foran. For God's sake, will someone go up for Teddy, or he won't go back at all !

Teddy [*appearing at door*]. Damn anxious for Teddy to go back ! Well, Teddy's goin' back, an' he's left everything tidy upstairs so that you'll not have much trouble sortin' things out. [*To Harry*] The Club an' a crowd's waitin' outside to bring us to the boat before they go to the spread in honour of the final. [*Bitterly*] A party for them while we muck off to the trenches !

Harry [*after a slight pause, to Barney*]. Are you game, Barney ?

Barney. What for ?

Harry. To go to the spread and hang the latch for another night ?

Barney [*taking his rifle from Simon and slinging it over his shoulder*]. No, no, napoo desertin' on Active Service. Deprivation of pay an' the rest of your time in the front trenches. No, no. We must go back !

Mrs. Heegan. No, no, Harry. You must go back.

Simon,
Sylvester, } [*together*]. You must go back.
and Susie

Voices of crowd outside. They must go back !
                    [*The ship's siren is heard blowing.*

Simon. The warning signal.

Sylvester. By the time they get there, they'll be unslinging the gangways !

Susie [*handing Harry his steel helmet*]. Here's your helmet, Harry.   [*He puts it on.*

Mrs. Heegan. You'll all nearly have to run for it now !

Sylvester. I've got your kit-bag, Harry.

Susie. I've got your rifle.

Simon. I'll march in front with the cup, after Conroy with the concertina.

Teddy. Come on : ong, avong to the trenches !

Harry [*recklessly*]. Jesus, a last drink, then ! [*He raises the Silver Cup, singing*] :
 Gae bring to me a pint of wine,
 And fill it in a silver tassie ;

Barney [*joining in vigorously*] :
 . . . . a silver tassie.

Harry :
 That I may drink before I go,
 A service to my bonnie lassie.

Barney :
 . . . . bonnie lassie.

Harry :
 The boat rocks at the pier o' Leith,
 Full loud the wind blows from the ferry ;
 The ship rides at the Berwick Law,
 An' I must leave my bonnie Mary !

Barney :
 . . . . . . leave my bonnie Mary !

Harry :
 The trumpets sound, the banners fly,
 The glittering spears are ranked ready ;

Barney :
 . . . glittering spears are ranked ready ;

Harry :
    The shouts of war are heard afar,
    The battle closes thick and bloody.

Barney :
    . . . . . . closes thick and bloody.

Harry :
    It's not the roar of sea or shore,
    That makes me longer wish to tarry,
    Nor shouts of war that's heard afar —
    It's leaving thee, my bonnie lassie !

Barney :
    . . leaving thee, my bonnie lassie !

Teddy. Come on, come on.
                    [*Simon, Sylvester, and Susie go out.*

Voices outside :
    Come on from your home to the boat ;
    Carry on from the boat to the camp.
    [*Teddy and Barney go out. Harry and Jessie follow ; as
    Harry reaches the door, he takes his arm from round Jessie
    and comes back to Mrs. Heegan.*

Voices outside. From the camp up to the lines to the
trenches.

Harry [*shyly and hurriedly kissing Mrs. Heegan*]. Well, goodbye, old woman.

Mrs. Heegan. Goodbye, my son.
    [*Harry goes out. The chorus of " The Silver Tassie ",
    accompanied by a concertina, can be heard growing fainter
    till it ceases. Mrs. Foran goes out timidly. Mrs. Heegan
    pokes the fire, arranges the things in the room, and then
    goes to the window and looks out. After a pause, the loud*

and long blast of the ship's siren is heard. The light on the masthead, seen through the window, moves slowly away, and Mrs. Heegan with a sigh, " Ah dear ", goes over to the fire and sits down. A slight pause, then Mrs. Foran returns to the room.

Mrs. Foran. Every little bit of china I had in the house is lyin' above in a mad an' muddled heap like the flotsum an' jetsum of the seashore !

Mrs. Heegan [*with a deep sigh of satisfaction*]. Thanks be to Christ that we're after managin' to get the three of them away safely.

Act II

In the war zone : a scene of jagged and lacerated ruin of what was once a monastery. At back a lost wall and window are indicated by an arched piece of broken coping pointing from the left to the right, and a similar piece of masonry pointing from the right to the left. Between these two lacerated fingers of stone can be seen the country stretching to the horizon where the front trenches are. Here and there heaps of rubbish mark where houses once stood. From some of these, lean, dead hands are protruding. Further on, spiky stumps of trees which were once a small wood. The ground is dotted with rayed and shattered shell holes. Across the horizon in the red glare can be seen the criss-cross pattern of the barbed wire bordering the trenches. In the sky sometimes a green star, sometimes a white star, burns. Within the broken archway to the left is an arched entrance to another part of the monastery, used now as a Red Cross Station. In the wall, right, near the front is a stained-glass window, background green, figure of the Virgin, white-faced, wearing a black robe, lights inside making the figure vividly apparent. Further up from this window is a life-size crucifix. A shell has released an arm from the cross, which has caused the upper part of the figure to lean forward with the released arm outstretched towards the figure of the Virgin. Underneath the crucifix on a pedestal, in red letters, are the words : PRINCEPS PACIS. *Almost opposite the crucifix is a gunwheel to which Barney is tied. At the back, in the centre, where the span of the arch should be, is the shape of a big howitzer gun, squat, heavy underpart, with a long, sinister barrel now pointing towards the front at an angle of forty-five degrees. At the base of the gun a piece of wood is placed on which is chalked,* HYDE PARK CORNER. *On another piece of wood*

35

near the entrance of the Red Cross Station is chalked, NO HAWKERS OR STREET CRIES PERMITTED HERE. *In the near centre is a brazier in which a fire is burning. Crouching above, on a ramp, is a soldier whose clothes are covered with mud and splashed with blood. Every feature of the scene seems a little distorted from its original appearance. Rain is falling steadily ; its fall worried now and again by fitful gusts of a cold wind. A small organ is heard playing slow and stately notes as the curtain rises.*

After a pause, the Croucher, without moving, intones dreamily :

Croucher. And the hand of the Lord was upon me, and carried me out in the spirit of the Lord, and set me down in the midst of a valley.

And I looked and saw a great multitude that stood upon their feet, an exceeding great army.

And he said unto me, Son of man, can this exceeding great army become a valley of dry bones ?

[*The music ceases, and a voice, in the part of the monastery left standing, intones :* Kyr . . . ie . . . e . . . eleison. Kyr . . . ie . . . e . . . eleison, *followed by the answer :* Christe . . . eleison.

Croucher [*resuming*]. And I answered, O Lord God, thou knowest. And he said, prophesy and say unto the wind, come from the four winds a breath and breathe upon these living that they may die.

[*As he pauses the voice in the monastery is heard again :* Gloria in excelsis Deo et in terra pax hominibus bonae voluntatis.

Croucher [*resuming*]. And I prophesied, and the breath came out of them, and the sinews came away from them, and behold a shaking, and their bones fell asunder, bone from his bone, and they died, and the exceeding great army became a valley of dry bones.

[*The voice from the monastery is heard, clearly for the first half of the sentence, then dying away towards the end :* Accendat in nobis Dominus ignem sui amoris, et flammam aeternae caritatis.

[*A group of soldiers come in from fatigue, bunched together as if for comfort and warmth. They are wet and cold, and they are sullen-faced. They form a circle around the brazier and stretch their hands towards the blaze.*

1st Soldier. Cold and wet and tir'd.

2nd Soldier. Wet and tir'd and cold.

3rd Soldier. Tir'd and cold and wet.

4th Soldier [*very like Teddy*]. Twelve blasted hours of ammunition transport fatigue !

1st Soldier. Twelve weary hours.

2nd Soldier. And wasting hours.

3rd Soldier. And hot and heavy hours.

1st Soldier. Toiling and thinking to build the wall of force that blocks the way from here to home.

2nd Soldier. Lifting shells.

3rd Soldier. Carrying shells.

4th Soldier. Piling shells.

1st Soldier. In the falling, pissing rine and whistling wind.

2nd Soldier. The whistling wind and falling, drenching rain.

3rd Soldier. The God-dam rain and blasted whistling wind.

1st Soldier. And the shirkers sife at home coil'd up at ease.

2nd Soldier. Shells for us and pianos for them.

3rd Soldier. Fur coats for them and winding-sheets for us.

4th Soldier. Warm.

2nd Soldier. And dry.

1st Soldier. An' 'appy.   [*A slight pause.*

Barney. An' they call it re-cu-per-at-ing !

1st Soldier [*reclining near the fire*]. Gawd, I'm sleepy.

2nd Soldier [*reclining*]. Tir'd and lousey.

3rd Soldier [*reclining*]. Damp and shaking.

4th Soldier [*murmuringly, the rest joining him*]. Tir'd and lousey, an' wet an' sleepy, but mother call me early in the morning.

1st Soldier [*dreamily*]. Wen I thinks of 'ome, I thinks of a field of dysies.

The Rest [*dreamily*]. Wen 'e thinks of 'ome, 'e thinks of a field of dysies.

1st Soldier [*chanting dreamily*] :
    I sees the missus paryding along Walham Green,
    Through the jewels an' silks on the costers' carts,
    Emmie a-pulling her skirt an' muttering,
    " A balloon, a balloon, I wants a balloon ",
    The missus a-tugging 'er on, an' sying,
    " A balloon, for shime, an' your father fighting :
    You'll wait till 'e's 'ome, an' the bands a-plying ! "
                                        [*He pauses.*

[*Suddenly*] But wy'r we 'ere, wy'r we 'ere — that's wot we wants to know !

2nd Soldier. God only knows — or else, perhaps, a red-cap.

1st Soldier [*chanting*] :
   Tabs'll murmur, 'em an' 'aw, an' sy : " You're 'ere because you're
   Point nine double o, the sixth platoon an' forty-eight battalion,
   The Yellow Plumes that pull'd a bow at Crecy,
   And gave to fame a leg up on the path to glory ;
   Now with the howitzers of the Twenty-first Division,
   Tiking life easy with the Army of the Marne,
   An' all the time the battered Conchie squeals,
   ' It's one or two men looking after business ' "

3rd Soldier. An' saves his blasted skin !

1st Soldier [*chanting*]. The padre gives a fag an' softly whispers :
   " Your king, your country an' your muvver 'as you 'ere."
   An' last time 'ome on leave, I awsks the missus :
   " The good God up in heaven, Bill, 'e knows,
   An' I gets the seperytion moneys reg'lar."
                                    [*He sits up suddenly.*
   But wy'r we 'ere, wy'r we 'ere, — that's wot I wants to know ?

The Rest [*chanting sleepily*]. Why 's 'e 'ere, why 's 'e 'ere — that's wot 'e wants to know !

Barney [*singing to the air of second bar in chorus of "Auld Lang Syne"*]. We're here because we're here, because we're here, because we're here !

[*Each slides into an attitude of sleep — even Barney's head droops a little. The Corporal, followed by the Visitor, appears at back. The Visitor is a portly man with a rubicund face ; he is smiling to demonstrate his ease of mind, but the lines are a little distorted with an ever-present sense of anxiety. He is dressed in a semi-civilian, semi-military manner — dark worsted suit, shrapnel helmet, a haversack slung round his shoulder, a brown belt round his middle, black top boots and spurs, and he carries a cane. His head is bent between his shoulders, and his shoulders are crouched a little.*]

Visitor. Yes, to-morrow, I go a little further. Penetrate a little deeper into danger. Foolish, yes, but then it's an experience ; by God, it's an experience. The military authorities are damned strict — won't let a . . . man . . . plunge !

Corporal. In a manner of speakin', sir, only let you see the arses of the guns.

Visitor [*not liking the remark*]. Yes, no ; no, oh yes. Damned strict, won't let a . . . man . . . plunge ! [*Suddenly, with alarm*] What's that, what was that ?

Corporal. Wha' was what ?

Visitor. A buzz, I thought I heard a buzz.

Corporal. A buzz ?

Visitor. Of an aeroplane.

Corporal. Didn't hear. Might have been a bee.

Visitor. No, no ; don't think it was a bee. [*Arranging helmet with his hands*] Damn shrapnel helmet ; skin tight ; like a vice ; hurts the head. Rather be, without.

it ; but, regulations, you know.   Military authorities damn particular — won't let a . . . man . . . plunge !

Visitor [*seeing Barney*]. Aha, what have we got here, what have we got here ?

Corporal [*to Barney*]. 'Tshun !   [*To the Visitor*] Regimental misdemeanour, sir.

Visitor [*to Barney*]. Nothing much, boy, nothing much ?

Barney [*chanting softly*] :
    A Brass-hat pullin' the bedroom curtains
    Between himself, the world an' the Estaminay's
        daughter,
    In a pyjama'd hurry ran down an' phon'd
    A Tommy was chokin' an Estaminay cock,
    An' I was pinch'd as I was puttin' the bird
    Into a pot with a pint of peas.

Corporal [*chanting hoarsely*] :
    And the hens all droop, for the loss has made
    The place a place of desolation !

Visitor [*reprovingly, to the Corporal*]. Seriously, Corporal, seriously, please.   Sacred, sacred : property of the citizen of a friendly State, sacred.   On Active Service, serious to steal a fowl, a cock.   [*To Barney*] The uniform, the cause, boy, the corps.   Infra dignitatem, boy, infra dignitatem.

Barney. Wee, wee.

Visitor [*pointing to reclining soldiers*]. Taking it easy, eh ?

Corporal. Done in ; transport fatigue ; twelve hours.

Visitor. Um, not too much rest, corporal.   Dangerous.

Keep 'em moving much as possible.   Too much rest —
bad.   Sap, sap, sap.

Corporal [*pointing to the left*]. Bit of monastery left intact.
Hold services there ; troops off to front line.   Little
organ plays.

Visitor. Splendid.   Bucks 'em up.   Gives 'em peace.
     [*A Staff Officer enters suddenly, passing by the Visitor with
     a springing hop, so that he stands in the centre with the
     Visitor on his right and the Corporal on his left.   He is
     prim, pert, and polished, superfine khaki uniform, gold
     braid, crimson tabs, and gleaming top boots.   He speaks
     his sentences with a gasping importance.*

Corporal [*stiffening*]. 'Shun !   Staff !

Soldiers [*springing to their feet — the Croucher remains as he is,
     with a sleepy alertness*]. Staff !   'Shun !

Corporal [*bellowing at the Croucher*]. Eh, you there : 'shun !
Staff !

Croucher [*calmly*]. Not able.   Sick.   Privilege.   Excused
duty.

Staff Wallah [*reading document*] :
          Battery Brigade Orders, F.A., 31 D 2.

Units presently recuperating, parade eight o'clock P.M.
Attend Lecture organised by Society for amusement
     and mental development, soldiers at front.
Subject : Habits of those living between Frigid Zone
     and Arctic Circle.
Lecturer : Mr. Melville Sprucer.
Supplementary Order : Units to wear gas masks.
As you were.
     [*The Staff Wallah departs as he came with a springing hop.*

*The Visitor and the Corporal relax, and stroll down
towards the R.C. Station.   The soldiers relax too, seeking
various positions of ease around the fire.*

Visitor [*indicating R.C. Station*]. Ah, in here.   We'll just
pop in here for a minute.   And then pop out again.
      [*He and the Corporal go into the R.C. Station.   A
      pause.*

1st Soldier [*chanting and indicating that he means the Visitor by
looking in the direction of the R.C. Station*] :
      The perky bastard's cautious nibbling
      In a safe, safe shelter at danger queers me.
      Furiously feeling he's up to the neck in
      The whirl and the sweep of the front-line fighting.

2nd Soldier [*chanting*] :
      In his full-blown, chin-strapp'd, shrapnel helmet,
      He'll pat a mug on the back and murmur,
      " Here's a stand-fast Tauntonshire before me ",
      And the mug, on his feet, 'll whisper " yessir ".

3rd Soldier [*chanting*] :
      Like a bride, full-flush'd, 'e'll sit down and listen
      To every word of the goddam sermon,
      From the cushy-soul'd, word-spreading, yellow-
          streaked dud.

Barney [*chanting*]. Who wouldn't make a patch on a
      Tommy's backside.   [*A pause.*

1st Soldier. 'Ow long have we been resting 'ere ?

2nd Soldier. A month.

3rd Soldier. Twenty-nine days, twenty-three hours and
[*looking at watch*] twenty-three minutes.

4th Soldier. Thirty-seven minutes more'll make it thirty days.

Croucher :

    Thirty days hath September, April, June, and November —

    November — that's the month when I was born — November.

    Not the beginning, not the end, but the middle of November.

    Near the valley of the Thames, in the middle of November.

    Shall I die at the start, near the end, in the middle of November ?

1st Soldier [*nodding towards the Croucher*]. One more scrap, an' 'e'll be Ay one in the kingdom of the bawmy.

2nd Soldier. Perhaps they have forgotten.

3rd Soldier. Forgotten.

4th Soldier. Forgotten us.

1st Soldier. If the blighters at the front would tame their grousing.

The Rest. Tame their grousing.

2nd Soldier. And the wounded cease to stare their silent scorning.

The Rest. Passing by us, carried cushy on the stretchers.

3rd Soldier. We have beaten out the time upon the duck-board.

4th Soldier. Stiff standing watch'd the sunrise from the firestep.

2nd Soldier. Stiff standing from the firestep watch'd the sunset.

3rd Soldier. Have bless'd the dark wiring of the top with curses.

2nd Soldier. And never a ray of leave.

3rd Soldier. To have a quiet drunk.

1st Soldier. Or a mad mowment to rustle a judy.

> [*3rd Soldier takes out a package of cigarettes ; taking one himself he hands the package round. Each takes one, and the man nearest to Barney, kneeling up, puts one in his mouth and lights it for him. They all smoke silently for a few moments, sitting up round the fire.*

2nd Soldier [*chanting very earnestly and quietly*] :
> Would God I smok'd an' walk'd an' watch'd th'
> Dance of a golden Brimstone butterfly,
> To the saucy pipe of a greenfinch resting
> In a drowsy, brambled lane in Cumberland.

1st Soldier :
> Would God I smok'd and lifted cargoes
> From the laden shoulders of London's river-way ;
> Then holiday'd, roaring out courage and movement
> To the muscled machines of Tottenham Hotspur.

3rd Soldier :
> To hang here even a little longer,
> Lounging through fear-swell'd, anxious moments ;
> The hinderparts of the god of battles
> Shading our war-tir'd eyes from his flaming face.

Barney :
> If you creep to rest in a clos'd-up coffin,
> A tail of comrades seeing you safe home ;

Or be a kernel lost in a shell exploding —
It's all, sure, only in a lifetime.

All Together :
Each sparrow, hopping, irresponsible,
Is indentur'd in God's mighty memory ;
And we, more than they all, shall not be lost
In the forgetfulness of the Lord of Hosts.

[*The Visitor and the Corporal come from the Red Cross Station.*]

Visitor [*taking out a cigarette case*]. Nurses too gloomy. Surgeons too serious. Doesn't do.

Corporal. All lying-down cases, sir. Pretty bad.

Visitor [*who is now standing near the crucifix*]. All the more reason make things merry and bright. Lift them out of themselves. [*To the soldiers*] See you all to-morrow at lecture ?

1st Soldier [*rising and standing a little sheepishly before the Visitor*]. Yessir, yessir.

The Rest. Yessir, yessir.

The Visitor. Good. Make it interesting. [*Searching in pocket*]. Damn it, have I none ? Ah, saved.

[*He takes a match from his pocket and is about to strike it carelessly on the arm of the crucifix, when the 1st Soldier, with a rapid frightened movement, knocks it out of his hand.*]

1st Soldier [*roughly*]. Blarst you, man, keep your peace-white paws from that !

2nd Soldier. The image of the Son of God.

3rd Soldier. Jesus of Nazareth, the King of the Jews.

1st Soldier [*reclining by the fire again*]. There's a Gawd knocking abaht somewhere.

4th Soldier. Wants Him to be sending us over a chit in the shape of a bursting shell.

The Visitor. Sorry put it across you. [*To Corporal*] Too much time to think. Nervy. Time to brood, brood ; bad. Sap. Sap. Sap. [*Walking towards where he came in*] Must return quarters ; rough and ready. Must stick it. There's a war on. Cheerio. Straight down road instead of round hill : shorter ?

Corporal. Less than half as long.

The Visitor. Safe ?

Corporal. Yes. Only drop shells off and on, cross roads. Ration party wip'd out week ago.

The Visitor. Go round hill. No hurry. General Officer's orders, no unnecessary risks. Must obey. Military Authorities damned particular — won't let a . . . man . . . plunge !

[*He and the Corporal go off. The soldiers in various attitudes are asleep around the fire. After a few moments' pause, two Stretcher-Bearers come in slowly from left, carrying a casualty. They pass through the sleeping soldiers, going towards the Red Cross Station. As they go they chant a verse, and as the verse is ending, they are followed by another pair carrying a second casualty.*

1st Bearers [*chanting*] :
    Oh, bear it gently, carry it softly —
    A bullet or a shell said stop, stop, stop.
    It's had it's day, and it's left the play,
    Since it gamboll'd over the top, top, top.
    It's had its day and it's left the play,
    Since it gamboll'd over the top.

2nd Bearers [*chanting*] :
    Oh, carry it softly, bear it gently —
    The beggar has seen it through, through, through.
    If it 'adn't been 'im, if it 'adn't been 'im,
    It might 'ave been me or you, you, you.
    If it 'adn't been 'im, if it 'adn't been 'im,
    It might 'ave been me or you.

Voice [*inside R.C. Station*]. Easy, easy there ; don't crowd.

1st Stretcher-Bearer [*to man behind*]. Woa, woa there, Bill, 'ouse full.

Stretcher-Bearer [*behind, to those following*]. Woa, woa ; traffic blocked.

                [*They leave the stretchers on the ground.*

The Wounded on the Stretchers [*chanting*] :
    Carry on, carry on to the place of pain,
    Where the surgeon spreads his aid, aid, aid.
    And we show man's wonderful work, well done,
    To the image God hath made, made, made,
    And we show man's wonderful work, well done,
    To the image God hath made !

    When the future hours have all been spent,
    And the hand of death is near, near, near,
    Then a few, few moments and we shall find
    There'll be nothing left to fear, fear, fear,
    Then a few, few moments and we shall find
    There'll be nothing left to fear.

    The power, the joy, the pull of life,
    The laugh, the blow, and the dear kiss,
    The pride and hope, the gain and loss,
    Have been temper'd down to this, this, this,
    The pride and hope, the gain and loss,
    Have been temper'd down to this.

1st Stretcher-Bearer [*to Barney*]. Oh, Barney, have they liced you up because you've kiss'd the Colonel's judy ?

Barney. They lit on me stealin' Estaminay poulthry.

1st Stretcher-Bearer. A hen ?

2nd Stretcher-Bearer. A duck, again, Barney ?

3rd Stretcher-Bearer. A swan this time.

Barney [*chanting softly*] :
    A Brass-hat pullin' the bedroom curtains
    Between himself, the world an' the Estaminay's
       daughter,
    In a pyjama'd hurry ran down and phon'd
    A Tommy was chokin' an Estaminay cock ;
    An' I was pinch'd as I was puttin' the bird
    Into a pot with a pint of peas.

1st Stretcher-Bearer. The red-tabb'd squit !

2nd Stretcher-Bearer. The lousey map-scanner !

3rd Stretcher-Bearer. We must keep up, we must keep up the morale of the awmy.

2nd Stretcher-Bearer [*loudly*]. Does e' eat well ?

The Rest [*in chorus*]. Yes, 'e eats well !

2nd Stretcher-Bearer. Does 'e sleep well ?

The Rest [*in chorus*]. Yes, 'e sleeps well !

2nd Stretcher-Bearer. Does 'e whore well ?

The Rest [*in chorus*]. Yes, 'e whores well !

2nd Stretcher-Bearer. Does 'e fight well ?

The Rest [*in chorus*]. Napoo ; 'e 'as to do the thinking for the Tommies !

Voice [*from the R.C. Station*]. Stretcher Party — carry on !
> [*The Bearers stoop with precision, attach their supports to the stretchers, lift them up and march slowly into the R.C. Station, chanting.*

Stretcher-Bearers [*chanting*] :
> Carry on — we've one bugled reason why —
> We've 'eard and answer'd the call, call, call.
> There's no more to be said, for when we are dead,
> We may understand it all, all, all.
> There's no more to be said, for when we are dead,
> We may understand it all.
> [*They go out, leaving the scene occupied by the Croucher and the soldiers sleeping around the fire. The Corporal re-enters. He is carrying two parcels. He pauses, looking at the sleeping soldiers for a few moments, then shouts.*

Corporal [*shouting*]. Hallo, there, you sleepy blighters ! Number 2, a parcel ; and for you, Number 3. Get a move on — parcels !
> [*The Soldiers wake up and spring to their feet.*

Corporal. For you, Number 2. [*He throws a parcel to 2nd Soldier.*] Number 3.
> [*He throws the other parcel to 3rd Soldier.*

3rd Soldier [*taking paper from around his parcel*]. Looks like a bundle of cigarettes.

1st Soldier. Or a pack of cawds.

4th Soldier. Or a prayer book.

3rd Soldier [*astounded*]. Holy Christ, it is !

The Rest. What ?

3rd Soldier. A prayer book !

4th Soldier. In a green plush cover with a golden cross.

Croucher. Open it at the Psalms and sing that we may be saved from the life and death of the beasts that perish.

Barney. Per omnia saecula saeculorum.

2nd Soldier [*who has opened his parcel*]. A ball, be God !

4th Soldier. A red and yellow coloured rubber ball.

1st Soldier. And a note.

2nd Soldier [*reading*]. To play your way to the enemies' trenches when you all go over the top. Mollie.

1st Soldier. See if it 'ops.
  [*The 2nd Soldier hops the ball, and then kicks it from him. The Corporal intercepts it, and begins to dribble it across the stage. The 3rd Soldier tries to take it from him. The Corporal shouts " Offside, there ! " They play for a few minutes with the ball, when suddenly the Staff-Wallah springs in and stands rigidly in centre.*

Corporal [*stiff to attention as he sees the Staff-Wallah*]. 'Shun. Staff !
  [*All the soldiers stiffen. The Croucher remains motionless.*

Corporal [*shouting to the Croucher*]. You : 'shun. Staff !

Croucher. Not able. Sick. Excused duty.

Staff-Wallah [*reading document*] :
  Brigade Orders, C/X 143. B/Y 341. Regarding gasmasks. Gas-masks to be worn round neck so as to lie in front 2½ degrees from socket of left shoulder-

blade, and 2¾ degrees from socket of right shoulder-blade, leaving bottom margin to reach ¼ of an inch from second button of lower end of tunic. Order to take effect from 6 A.M. following morning of date received. Dismiss !

[*He hops out again, followed by Corporal.*

1st Soldier [*derisively*]. Comprenneemoy.

3rd Soldier. Tray bong.

2nd Soldier [*who is standing in archway, back, looking scornfully after the Staff-Wallah, chanting*] :
    Jazzing back to his hotel he now goes gaily,
    Shelter'd and safe where the clock ticks tamely.
    His backside warming a cushion, downfill'd,
    Green clad, well splash'd with gold birds redbeak'd.

1st Soldier :
    His last dim view of the front-line sinking
    Into the white-flesh'd breasts of a judy ;
    Cuddling with proud, bright, amorous glances
    The thing salved safe from the mud of the trenches.

2nd Soldier :
    His tunic reared in the lap of comfort,
    Peeps at the blood-stain'd jackets passing,
    Through colour-gay bars of ribbon jaunty,
    Fresh from a posh shop snug in Bond Street.

Croucher :
    Shame and scorn play with and beat them,
    Till we anchor in their company ;
    Then the decorations of security
    Become the symbols of self-sacrifice.

[*A pause.*

2nd Soldier :

> A warning this that we'll soon be exiles
> From the freedom chance of life can give,
> To the front where you wait to be hurried breath-
>   less,
> Murmuring how, how do you do, to God.

3rd Soldier :

> Where hot with the sweat of mad endeavour,
> Crouching to scrape a toy-deep shelter,
> Quick-tim'd by hell's fast, frenzied drumfire
> Exploding in flaming death around us.

2nd Soldier :

> God, unchanging, heart-sicken'd, shuddering,
> Gathereth the darkness of the night sky
> To mask His paling countenance from
> The blood dance of His self-slaying children.

3rd Soldier :

> Stumbling, swiftly cursing, plodding,
> Lumbering, loitering, stumbling, grousing,
> Through mud and rain, and filth and danger,
> Flesh and blood seek slow the front line.

2nd Soldier :

> Squeals of hidden laughter run through
> The screaming medley of the wounded —
> Christ, who bore the cross, still weary,
> Now trails a rope tied to a field gun.

> [*As the last notes of the chanting are heard the Corporal comes
> rapidly in ; he is excited but steady ; pale-faced and
> grim.*

Corporal. They attack. Along a wide front the enemy
attacks. If they break through it may reach us even
here.

Soldiers [*in chorus as they all put on gas-masks*]. They attack.
  The enemy attacks.

Corporal. Let us honour that in which we do put our
  trust.

Soldiers [*in chorus*] :
    That it may not fail us in our time of need.

    [*The Corporal goes over to the gun and faces towards it,
    standing on the bottom step. The soldiers group around,
    each falling upon one knee, their forms crouched in a
    huddled act of obeisance. They are all facing the gun with
    their backs to the audience. The Croucher rises and joins
    them.*

Corporal [*singing*] :
    Hail cool-hardened tower of steel emboss'd
    With the fever'd, figment thoughts of man ;
    Guardian of our love and hate and fear,
    Speak for us to the inner ear of God !

Soldiers :
    We believe in God and we believe in thee.

Corporal :
    Dreams of line, of colour, and of form ;
    Dreams of music dead for ever now ;
    Dreams in bronze and dreams in stone have gone
    To make thee delicate and strong to kill.

Soldiers :
    We believe in God and we believe in thee.

Corporal :
    Jail'd in thy steel are hours of merriment
    Cadg'd from the pageant-dream of children's play ;
    Too soon of the motley stripp'd that they may sweat
    With them that toil for the glory of thy kingdom.

Soldiers :

> We believe in God and we believe in thee.

Corporal :

> Remember our women, sad-hearted, proud-fac'd,
> Who've given the substance of their womb for
>   shadows ;
> Their shrivel'd, empty breasts war tinselléd
> For patient gifts of graves to thee.

Soldiers :

> We believe in God and we believe in thee.

Corporal :

> Dapple those who are shelter'd with disease,
> And women labouring with child,
> And children that play about the streets,
> With blood of youth expiring in its prime.

Soldiers :

> We believe in God and we believe in thee.

Corporal :

> Tear a gap through the soul of our mass'd enemies ;
> Grant them all the peace of death ;
> Blow them swiftly into Abram's bosom,
> And mingle them with the joys of paradise !

Soldiers :

> For we believe in God and we believe in thee.

> [*The sky has become vexed with a crimson glare, mixed with
>   yellow streaks, and striped with pillars of rising brown
>   and black smoke. The Staff-Wallah rushes in, turbulent
>   and wild, with his uniform disordered.*

Staff-Wallah :

> The enemy has broken through, broken through,
>   broken through !
> Every man born of woman to the guns, to the guns.

Soldiers :

To the guns, to the guns, to the guns !

Staff-Wallah :

Those at prayer, all in bed, and the swillers drinking
deeply in the pubs.

Soldiers :

To the guns, to the guns.

Staff-Wallah :

All the batmen, every cook, every bitch's son that
hides
A whiff of courage in his veins,
Shelter'd vigour in his body,
That can run, or can walk, even crawl —
Dig him out, dig him out, shove him on —

Soldiers :

To the guns !

[*The Soldiers hurry to their places led by the Staff-Wallah
to the gun. The gun swings around and points to the
horizon ; a shell is swung into the breech and a flash
indicates the firing of the gun, searchlights move over the
red glare of the sky ; the scene darkens, stabbed with
distant flashes and by the more vivid flash of the gun
which the Soldiers load and fire with rhythmical movements while the scene is closing. Only flashes are seen ;
no noise is heard.*

Act III

The upper end of an hospital ward. At right angles from back wall are two beds, one covered with a red quilt and the other with a white one. From the centre of the head of each bed is an upright having at the top a piece like a swan's neck, curving out over the bed, from which hangs a chain with a wooden cross-piece to enable weak patients to pull themselves into a sitting posture. To the left of these beds is a large glass double-door which opens on to the ground : one of the doors is open and a lovely September sun, which is setting, gives a glow to the garden.

Through the door two poplar trees can be seen silhouetted against the sky. To the right of this door is another bed covered with a black quilt. Little white discs are fixed to the head of each bed : on the first is the number 26, on the second 27, and on the third 28. Medical charts hang over each on the wall. To the right is the fireplace, facing down the ward. Farther on, to the right of the fire, is a door of a bathroom. In the corner, between the glass door and the fire, is a pedestal on which stands a statue of the Blessed Virgin ; under the statue is written, "Mater Misericordiae, ora pro nobis". An easy-chair, on which are rugs, is near the fire. In the centre is a white, glass-topped table on which are medicines, drugs, and surgical instruments. On one corner is a vase of flowers. A locker is beside the head, and a small chair by the foot of each bed. Two electric lights, green shaded, hang from the ceiling, and a bracket light with a red shade projects from the wall over the fireplace. It is dusk, and the two lights suspended from the ceiling are lighted. The walls are a brilliant white.

Sylvester is in the bed numbered " 26 " ; he is leaning upon his elbow looking towards the glass door.

57

Simon, sitting down on the chair beside bed numbered " 27 ", is looking into the grounds.

Sylvester [*after a pause*]. Be God, isn't it a good one !

Simon. Almost, almost, mind you, Sylvester, incomprehensible.

Sylvester. To come here and find Susie Monican fashion'd like a Queen of Sheba.   God moves in a mysterious way, Simon.

Simon. There's Surgeon Maxwell prancing after her now.

Sylvester [*stretching to see*]. Heads together, eh ? Be God, he's kissing her behind the trees !   Oh, Susannah, Susannah, how are the mighty fallen, and the weapons of war perished !

> [*Harry Heegan enters crouched in a self-propelled invalid chair ; he wheels himself up to the fire. Sylvester slides down into the bed, and Simon becomes interested in a book that he takes off the top of his locker. Harry remains for a few moments beside the fire, and then wheels himself round and goes out as he came in ; Sylvester raises himself in the bed, and Simon leaves down the book to watch Harry.*

Sylvester. Down and up, up and down.

Simon. Up and down, down and up.

Sylvester. Never quiet for a minute.

Simon. Never able to hang on to an easy second.

Sylvester. Trying to hold on to the little finger of life.

Simon. Half-way up to heaven.

Sylvester. And him always thinking of Jessie.

Simon. And Jessie never thinking of him.

> [*Susie Monican, in the uniform of a V.A.D. nurse, enters the ward by the glass door. She is changed, for it is clear that she has made every detail of the costume as attractive as possible. She has the same assertive manner, but dignity and a sense of importance have been added. Her legs, encased in silk stockings, are seen (and shown) to advantage by her short and smartly cut skirt. Altogether she is now a very handsome woman. Coming in she glances at the bed numbered 28, then pauses beside Sylvester and Simon.*

Susie. How is Twenty-eight ?

Simon and Sylvester [*together*]. Travelling again.

Susie. Did he speak at all to you ?

Sylvester. Dumb, Susie, dumb.

Simon. Brooding, Susie ; brooding, brooding.

Sylvester. Cogitatin', Susie ; cogitatin', cogitatin'.

Susie [*sharply, to Sylvester*]. It's rediculous, Twenty-six, for you to be in bed. The Sister's altogether too indulgent to you. Why didn't you pair of lazy devils entice him down to sit and cogitate under the warm wing of the sun in the garden ?

Sylvester. Considerin' the low state of his general health.

Simon. Aided by a touch of frost in the air.

Sylvester. Thinkin' it over we thought it might lead——

Simon. To him getting an attack of double pneumonia.

Sylvester and Simon [together]. An' then he'd go off like —
[*they blow through their lips*] poof — the snuff of a
candle !

Susie. For the future, during the period you are patients
here, I am to be addressed as " Nurse Monican ", and
not as " Susie ". Remember that, the pair of you,
please.
[*Harry wheels himself in again, crossing by her, and, going
over to the fire, looks out into grounds.*

Susie [irritatedly, to Sylvester]. Number Twenty-six, look
at the state of your quilt You must make an effort to
keep it tidy. Dtch, dtch, dtch, what would the Matron
say if she saw it !

Simon [with a nervous giggle]. He's an uneasy divil, Nurse
Monican.

Susie [hotly, to Simon]. Yours is as bad as his, Twenty-
seven. You mustn't lounge on your bed ; it must be
kept perfectly tidy [*she smoothes the quilts*]. Please don't
make it necessary to mention this again. [*To Harry*]
Would you like to go down for a little while into
the garden, Twenty-eight ?
[*Harry crouches silent and moody.*

Susie [continuing]. After the sober rain of yesterday it is
good to feel the new grace of the yellowing trees, and
to get the fresh smell of the grass.
[*Harry wheels himself round and goes out by the left.*

Susie [to Sylvester as she goes out]. Remember, Twenty-six,
if you're going to remain in a comatose condition,
you'll have to keep your bed presentable.   [*A pause.*

Sylvester [mimicking Susie]. Twenty-six, if you're going to remeen in a comatowse condition, you'll have to keep your bed in a tidy an' awdahly mannah.

Simon. Dtch, dtch, dtch, Twenty-seven, it's disgriceful. And as long as you're heah, in the capacity of a patient, please remember I'm not to be addressed as " Susie ", but as " Nurse Monican ".

Sylvester. Twenty-seven, did you tike the pills the doctah awdahed ?

Voice of Susie, left. Twenty-six !

Sylvester. Yes, Nurse ?

Voice of Susie. Sister says you're to have a bawth at once ; and you, Twenty-seven, see about getting it ready for him.   [*A fairly long pause.*

Sylvester [*angrily*]. A bawth : well, be God, that's a good one ! I'm not in a fit condition for a bath !
                                          [*Another pause.*

Sylvester [*earnestly, to Simon*]. You haven't had a dip now for nearly a week, while I had one only the day before yesterday in the late evening : it must have been you she meant, Simon.

Simon. Oh, there was no dubiety about her bellowing out Twenty-six, Syl.

Sylvester [*excitedly*]. How the hell d'ye know, man, she didn't mix the numbers up ?

Simon. Mix the numbers up ! How could the woman mix the numbers up ?

Sylvester. How could the woman mix the numbers up ! What could be easier than to say Twenty-six instead of

Twenty-seven ?   How could the woman mix the numbers up !   Of course the woman could mix the numbers up !

Simon. What d'ye expect me to do — hurl myself into a bath that was meant for you ?

Sulvester. I don't want you to hurl yourself into anything ; but you don't expect me to plunge into a bath that maybe wasn't meant for me ?

Simon. Nurse Monican said Twenty-six, and when you can alter that, ring me up and let me know.
   [*A pause ;   then Simon gets up and goes toward bathroom door.*

Sylvester [*snappily*]. Where are you leppin' to now ?

Simon. I want to get the bath ready.

Sylvester. You want to get the bawth ready !   Turn the hot cock on, and turn the cold cock on for Number Twenty-six, mixin' them the way a chemist would mix his medicines — sit still, man, till we hear the final verdict.
   [*Simon sits down again.   Susie comes in left, and, passing to the door leading to grounds, pauses beside Simon and Sylvester.*

Susie [*sharply*]. What are the two of you doing ?   Didn't I tell you, Twenty-six, that you were to take a bawth ; and you, Twenty-seven, that you were to get it ready for him ?

Sylvester [*sitting brightly up in bed*]. Oh, just goin' to spring up, Nurse Monican, when you popped in.

Susie. Well, up with you, then, and take it. [*To Simon*]
You go and get it ready for him.
                    [*Simon goes into the bathroom.*

Sylvester [*venturing a last hope as Susie goes towards the entrance
   to grounds*]. I had a dip, Nurse, only the day before
   yesterday in the late evening.

Susie [*as she goes out*]. Have another one now, please.
     [*The water can be heard flowing in the bathroom, and a light
       cloud of steam comes out by the door which Simon has left
       open.*

Sylvester [*mimicking Susie*]. Have another one, now, please !
   One to be taken before and after meals. The delicate
   audacity of the lip of that one since she draped her
   shoulders with a crimson cape !
     [*Simon appears and stands leaning against the side of the
       bathroom door.*

Simon [*gloating*]. She's steaming away now, Sylvester, full
   cock.

Sylvester [*scornfully, to Simon*]. Music to you, the gurgling
   of the thing, music to you. Gaugin' the temperature
   for me. Dtch, dtch, dtch [*sitting up*], an hospital's the
   last place that God made. Be damn it, I wouldn't let
   a stuffed bird stay in one !

Simon. Come on, man, before the hot strength bubbles out
   of it.

Sylvester [*getting out of bed*]. Have you the towels hot an'
   everything ready for me to spring into ?

Simon [*with a bow*]. Everything's ready for your enjoyment, Sir.

Sylvester [*as he goes towards the bathroom*]. Can't they be content with an honest to God cleanliness, an' not be tryin' to gild a man with soap and water.

Simon [*with a grin, as Sylvester passes*]. Can I do anything more for you, Sir ?

Sylvester [*almost inarticulate with indignation, as he goes in*]. Now I'm tellin' you, Simon Norton, our cordiality's gettin' a little strained !

> [*Harry wheels himself in, goes again to the fireplace, and looks into grounds. Simon watches him for a moment, takes a package of cigarettes from his pocket and lights one.*

Simon [*awkwardly, to Harry*]. Have a fag, Harry, oul' son ?

Harry. Don't want one ; tons of my own in the locker.

Simon. Like me to get you one ?

Harry. I can get them myself if I want one. D'ye think my arms are lifeless as well as my legs ?

Simon. Far from that. Everybody's remarking what a great improvement has taken place in you during the last few days.

Harry. Everybody but myself.

Simon. What with the rubbing every morning and the rubbing every night, and now the operation to-morrow as a grand finally, you'll maybe be in the centre of the football field before many months are out.

Harry [*irritably*]. Oh, shut up, man ! It's a miracle I want — not an operation. The last operation was to give life to my limbs, but no life came, and again I felt the horrible sickness of life only from the waist up. [*Raising his voice*] Don't stand there gaping at me, man.

Did you never before clap your eyes on a body dead from the belly down ? Blast you, man, why don't you shout at me, " While there's life there's hope ! "

[*Simon edges away to his corner. Susie comes in by the glass door and goes over to the table.*

Harry [*to Susie*]. A package of fags. Out of the locker. Will you, Susie ?

[*Susie goes to Harry's locker, gets the cigarettes and gives them to him. As he lights the cigarette, his right arm gives a sudden jerk.*

Susie. Steady. What's this ?

Harry [*with a nervous laugh*]. Barred from my legs it's flowing back into my arms. I can feel it slyly creeping into my fingers.

Voice of Patient, out left [*plaintively*]. Nurse !

Susie [*turning her head in direction of the voice*]. Shush, you Twenty-three ; go asleep, go asleep.

Harry. A soft, velvety sense of distance between my fingers and the things I touch.

Susie. Stop thinking of it. Brooding checks the chance of your recovery. A good deal may be imagination.

Harry [*peevishly*]. Oh, I know the different touches of iron [*he touches the bed rail*] ; of wood [*he touches the chair*] ; of flesh [*he touches his cheek*] ; and to my fingers they're giving the same answers — a feeling of numb distance between me and the touches of them all.

Voice of Patient, out left. Nurse !

Susie. Dtch, dtch. Go asleep, Twenty-three.

Voice, out left. The stab in the head is worse than ever, Nurse.

Susie. You've got your dose of morphia, and you'll get no more. You'll just have to stick it.

> [*Resident Surgeon Forby Maxwell enters from the grounds. He is about thirty years of age, and good-looking. His white overalls are unbuttoned, showing war ribbons on his waistcoat, flanked by the ribbon of the D.S.O. He has a careless, jaunty air, and evidently takes a decided interest in Susie. He comes in singing softly.*

Surgeon Maxwell :

> Stretched on the couch, Jessie fondled her dress,
> That hid all her beauties just over the knee ;
> And I wondered and said, as I sigh'd, " What a shame,
> That there's no room at all on the couch there for me."

Susie [*to Surgeon Maxwell*]. Twenty-three's at it again.

Surgeon Maxwell. Uh, hopeless case. Half his head in Flanders. May go on like that for another month.

Susie. He keeps the patients awake at night.

Simon. With his " God have mercys on me ", running after every third or fourth tick of the clock.

Harry. 'Tisn't fair to me, 'tisn't fair to me ; I must get my bellyful of sleep if I'm ever going to get well.

Surgeon Maxwell. Oh, the poor devil won't trouble any of you much longer. [*Singing*] :

> Said Jess, with a light in the side of her eyes,
> " A shrewd, mathematical fellow like you,
> With an effort of thought should be able to make
> The couch wide enough for the measure of two."

Susie. Dtch, dtch, Surgeon Maxwell.

Surgeon Maxwell [*singing*] :
> I fixed on a plan, and I carried it through,
> And the eyes of Jess gleam'd as she whisper'd to
> me :
> " The couch, made for one, that was made to hold
> two,
> Has, maybe, been made big enough to hold three ! "
> [*Surgeon Maxwell catches Susie's hand in his. Sylvester
> bursts in from the bathroom, and rushes to his bed,
> colliding with the Surgeon as he passes him.*

Surgeon Maxwell. Hallo, hallo there, what's this ?

Sylvester [*flinging himself into bed, covering himself rapidly
with the clothes, blowing himself warm*]. Pooh, pooh, I
feel as if I was sittin' on the doorstep of pneumonia !
Pooh, oh !

Surgeon Maxwell [*to Sylvester*]. We'll have a look at you
in a moment, Twenty-six, and see what's wrong with
you.
> [*Sylvester subsides down into the bed, and Simon edges
> towards the entrance to grounds, and stands looking into
> the grounds, or watching Surgeon Maxwell examining
> Sylvester.*

Surgeon Maxwell [*to Harry, who is looking intently out into
the grounds*]. Well, how are we to-day, Heegan ?

Harry. I imagine I don't feel quite so dead in myself as
I've felt these last few days back.

Surgeon Maxwell. Oh, well, that's something.

Harry. Sometimes I think I feel a faint, fluttering kind
of a buzz in the tops of my thighs.

Surgeon Maxwell [*touching Harry's thigh*]. Where, here ?

Harry. No ; higher up, doctor ; just where the line is that leaves the one part living and the other part dead.

Surgeon Maxwell. A buzz ?

Harry. A timid, faint, fluttering kind of a buzz.

Surgeon Maxwell. That's good. There might be a lot in that faint, fluttering kind of a buzz.

Harry [*after a pause*]. I'm looking forward to the opera-tion to-morrow.

Surgeon Maxwell. That's the way to take it. While there's life there's hope [*with a grin and a wink at Susie*]. And now we'll have a look at Twenty-six.
　[*Harry, when he hears " while there's life there's hope ", wheels himself madly out left ; half-way out he turns his head and stretches to look out into the grounds, then he goes on.*

Susie. Will the operation to-morrow be successful ?

Surgeon Maxwell. Oh, of course ; very successful.

Susie. Do him any good, d'ye think ?

Surgeon Maxwell. Oh, blast the good it'll do him.
　　　　　　　[*Susie goes over to Sylvester in the bed.*

Susie [*to Sylvester*]. Sit up, Twenty-six, Surgeon Maxwell wants to examine you.

Sylvester [*sitting up with a brave effort but a woeful smile*]. Righto. In the pink !
　[*Surgeon Maxwell comes over, twirling his stethoscope. Simon peeps round the corner of the glass door.*

Susie [*to Surgeon Maxwell*]. What was the cause of the row between the Matron and Nurse Jennings ? [*To Sylvester*] Open your shirt, Twenty-six.

Surgeon Maxwell [*who has fixed the stethoscope in his ears, removing it to speak to Susie*]. Caught doing the tango in the Resident's arms in the Resident's room. Naughty girl, naughty girl. [*To Sylvester*] Say " ninety-nine ".

Sylvester. Ninety-nine.

Susie. Oh, I knew something like that would happen. Daughter of a Dean, too.

Surgeon Maxwell [*to Sylvester*]. Say " ninety-nine ".

Sylvester. Ninety-nine. U-u-uh, it's gettin' very cold here, sitting up !

Surgeon Maxwell [*to Sylvester*]. Again. Don't be frightened ; breathe quietly.

Sylvester. Ninety-nine. Cool as a cucumber, Doctor. Ninety-nine.

Surgeon Maxwell [*to Susie*]. Damn pretty little piece. Not so pretty as you, though.

Sylvester [*to Surgeon Maxwell*]. Yesterday Doctor Joyce, givin' me a run over, said to a couple of medical men that were with him lookin' for tips, that the thing was apparently yieldin' to treatment, and that an operation wouldn't be necessary.

Surgeon Maxwell. Go on ; ninety-nine, ninety-nine.

Sylvester. Ninety-nine, ninety-nine.

Surgeon Maxwell [*to Susie*]. Kicks higher than her head, and you should see her doing the splits.

Sylvester [*to Surgeon Maxwell*]. Any way of gettin' rid of it'll do for me, for I'm not one of them that'll spend a night before an operation in a crowd of prayers.

Susie. Not very useful things to be doing and poor patients awaiting attention.

Surgeon Maxwell [*putting stethoscope into pocket*]. He'll do alright ; quite fit. Great old skin. [*To Sylvester*] You can cover yourself up, now. [*To Susie*] And don't tell me, Nurse Susie, that you've never felt a thrill or left a bedside for a kiss in a corner. [*He tickles her under the arm.*] Kiss in a corner, Nurse !

Susie [*pleased, but coy*]. Please don't, Doctor Maxwell, please.

Surgeon Maxwell [*tickling her again as they go out*]. Kiss in a corner ; ta-ra-ra-ra, kiss in a corner ! 　　　　[*A pause.*

Sylvester [*to Simon*]. Simon, were you listenin' to that conversation ?

Simon. Indeed I was.

Sylvester. We have our hands full, Simon, to keep alive. Think of sinkin' your body to the level of a hand that, ta-ra-ra-ra, would plunge a knife into your middle, haphazard, hurryin' up to run away after a thrill from a kiss in a corner. Did you see me dizzied an' wastin' me time pumpin' ninety-nines out of me, unrecognised, quiverin' with cold an' equivocation !

Simon. Everybody says he's a very clever fellow with the knife.

Sylvester. He'd gouge out your eye, saw off your arm, lift a load of vitals out of your middle, rub his hands, keep down a terrible desire to cheer lookin' at the ruin, an' say, " Twenty-six, when you're a little better, you'll feel a new man ! "

> [*Mrs. Heegan, Mrs. Foran, and Teddy enter from the grounds. Mrs. Foran is leading Teddy, who has a heavy bandage over his eyes, and is dressed in the blue clothes of military hospitals.*

Mrs. Foran [*to Teddy*]. Just a little step here, Ted ; upsh ! That's it ; now we're on the earth again, beside Simon and Sylvester. You'd better sit here.

> [*She puts him sitting on a chair.*

Sylvester [*to Mrs. Heegan, as she kisses him*]. Well, how's the old woman, eh ?

Mrs. Heegan. A little anxious about poor Harry.

Simon. He'll be alright. Tomorrow'll tell a tale.

Susie [*coming in, annoyed*]. Who let you up here at this hour ? Twenty-eight's to have an operation tomorrow, and shouldn't be disturbed.

Mrs. Heegan. Sister Peter Alcantara said we might come up, Nurse.

Mrs. Foran [*loftily*]. Sister Peter Alcantara's authority ought to be good enough, I think.

Mrs. Heegan. Sister Peter Alcantara said a visit might buck him up a bit.

Mrs. Foran. Sister Peter Alcantara knows the responsibility she'd incur by keeping a wife from her husband and a mother from her son.

Susie. Sister Peter Alcantara hasn't got to nurse him.

And remember, nothing is to be said that would make his habit of introspection worse than it is.

Mrs. Foran [*with dignity*]. Thanks for the warnin', Nurse, but them kind of mistakes is unusual with us.

> [*Susie goes out left, as Harry wheels himself rapidly in. Seeing the group, he stops suddenly, and a look of disappointment comes on to his face.*

Mrs. Heegan [*kissing Harry*]. How are you, son?

Mrs. Foran. I brought Teddy, your brother in arms, up to see you, Harry.

Harry [*impatiently*]. Where's Jessie? I thought you were to bring her with you?

Mrs. Heegan. She's comin' after us in a moment.

Harry. Why isn't she here now?

Mrs. Foran. She stopped to have a word in the grounds with someone she knew.

Harry. It was Barney Bagnal, was it? Was it Barney Bagnal?

Teddy. Maybe she wanted to talk to him about gettin' the V.C.

Harry. What V.C.? Who's gettin' the V.C.?

Teddy. Barney. Did he not tell you? [*Mrs. Foran prods his knee.*] What's up?

Harry [*intensely, to Teddy*]. What's he gettin' it for? What's he gettin' the V.C. for?

Teddy. For carryin' you wounded out of the line of fire. [*Mrs. Foran prods his knee.*] What's up?

Harry [*in anguish*]. Christ Almighty, for carryin' me wounded out of the line of fire!

Mrs. Heegan [*rapidly*]. Harry, I wouldn't be thinkin' of anything till we see what the operation'll do to-morrow.

Simon [*rapidly*]. God, if it gave him back the use even of one of his legs.

Mrs. Foran [*rapidly*]. Look at all the places he could toddle to, an' all the things he could do then with the prop of a crutch.

Mrs. Heegan. Even at the worst, he'll never be dependin' on anyone, for he's bound to get the maximum allowance.

Simon. Two quid a week, isn't it?

Sylvester. Yes, a hundred per cent total incapacitation.

Harry. She won't come up if one of you don't go down and bring her up.

Mrs. Heegan. She's bound to come up, for she's got your ukelele.

Harry. Call her up, Simon, call her up — I must see Jessie.

[*Simon goes over to the door leading to the grounds, and looks out.*

Mrs. Foran [*bending over till her face is close to Harry's*]. The drawn look on his face isn't half as bad as when I seen him last.

Mrs. Heegan [*bending and looking into Harry's face*]. Look, the hollows under his eyes is fillin' up, too.

Teddy. I'm afraid he'll have to put Jessie out of his head, for when a man's hit in the spine . . . [*Mrs. Foran prods his knee.*] What's up, woman?

Harry [*impatiently, to Simon*]. Is she coming ? Can you see her anywhere ?

Simon. I see someone like her in the distance, under the trees.

Harry. Call her ; can't you give her a shout, man ?

Simon [*calling*]. Jessie. Is that you, Jessie ! Jessie-e !

Mrs. Heegan [*to Harry*]. What time are you goin' under the operation ?

Harry [*to Simon*]. Call her again, call her again, can't you !

Simon [*calling*]. Jessie ; Jessie-e !

Teddy. Not much of a chance for an injury to the spine, for . . .

Mrs. Foran [*putting her face close to Teddy's*]. Oh, shut up, you !

Harry. Why did you leave her in the grounds ? Why didn't you wait till she came up with you ?

Mrs. Foran [*going over to Simon and calling*]. Jessie, Jessie-e !

Jessie's Voice, in distance. Yehess !

Mrs. Foran [*calling*]. Come up here at once ; we're all waitin' for you !

Jessie's Voice. I'm not going up !

Mrs. Foran [*calling*]. Bring up that ukelele here at once, miss !

Jessie's Voice. Barney 'll bring it up !
[*Harry, who has been listening intently, wheels himself rapidly to where Simon and Mrs. Foran are, pushing through them hurriedly.*

Harry [*calling loudly*]. Jessie ! Jessie ! Jessie-e !

Mrs. Foran. Look at that, now ; she's runnin' away, the young rip !

Harry [*appealingly*]. Jessie, Jessie-e !
 [*Susie enters quickly from left. She goes over to Harry and pulls him back from the door.*

Susie [*indignantly*]. Disgraceful ! Rousing the whole ward with this commotion ! Dear, dear, dear, look at the state of Twenty-eight. Come along, come along, please ; you must all go at once.

Harry. Jessie's coming up for a minute, Nurse.

Susie. No more to come up. We've had enough for one night, and you for a serious operation tomorrow. Come on, all out, please.
 [*Susie conducts Mrs. Heegan, Mrs. Foran, and Teddy out left.*

Mrs. Foran [*going out*]. We're goin', we're goin', thank you. A nice way to treat the flotsum and jetsum of the battlefields !

Susie [*to Harry*]. To bed now, Twenty-eight, please. [*To Simon*] Help me get him to bed, Twenty-seven.
 Susie pushes Harry to his bed, right ; Simon brings portion of a bed-screen which he places around Harry, hiding him from view.

Susie [*turning to speak to Sylvester, who is sitting up in bed, as she arranges screen*]. You're going to have your little operation in the morning, so you'd better go to sleep too.
 [*Sylvester goes pale and a look of dismay and fear crawls over his face.*

Susie. Don't funk it now. They're not going to turn you inside out. It'll be over in ten minutes.

Sylvester [*with a groan*]. When they once get you down your only hope is in the infinite mercy of God !

Simon. If I was you, Sylvester, I wouldn't take this operation too seriously. You know th' oul' song — Let Me· like a Soldier Fall ! If I was you, I'd put it completely out of me mind.

Sylvester [*subsiding on to the pillow — with an agonised look on his face*]. Let me like a soldier fall ! Did anyone ever hear th' equal o' that ! Put it out of me mind completely ! [*He sits up, and glares at Simon.*] Eh, you, look ! If you can't think sensibly, then thry to think without talkin' ! [*He sinks back on the pillow again.*] Let me like a soldier fall. Oh, it's not a fair trial for a sensible man to be stuck down in a world like this !

> [*Sylvester slides down till he lies prone and motionless on the bed. Harry is in bed now. Simon removes the screen, and Susie arranges Harry's quilt for the night.*

Susie [*to Simon*]. Now run and help get the things together for supper. [*Simon goes out left.*] [*Encouragingly to Harry*] After the operation, a stay in the air of the Convalescent may work wonders.

Harry. If I could mingle my breath with the breeze that blows from every sea, and over every land, they wouldn't widen me into anything more than the shrivell'd thing I am.

Susie [*switching off the two hanging lights, so that the red light over the fireplace alone remains*]. Don't be foolish, Twenty-eight. Wheeling yourself about among the beeches and the pines, when the daffodils are hanging out their blossoms, you'll deepen your chance in the courage and renewal of the country.

[*The bell of a Convent in grounds begins to ring for Compline.*

Harry [*with intense bitterness*]. I'll say to the pine, " Give me the grace and beauty of the beech " ; I'll say to the beech, " Give me the strength and stature of the pine ". In a net I'll catch butterflies in bunches ; twist and mangle them between my fingers and fix them wriggling on to mercy's banner. I'll make my chair a Juggernaut, and wheel it over the neck and spine of every daffodil that looks at me, and strew them dead to manifest the mercy of God and the justice of man !

Susie [*shocked*]. Shush, Harry, Harry !

Harry. To hell with you, your country, trees, and things, you jibbering jay !

Susie [*as she is going out*]. Twenty-eight !

Harry [*vehemently*]. To hell with you, your country, trees, and things, you jibbering jay !

[*Susie looks at him, pauses for a few moments, as if to speak, and then goes out.*

[*A pause ; then Barney comes in by door from grounds. An overcoat covers his military hospital uniform of blue. His left arm is in a sling. Under his right arm he carries a ukelele, and in his hand he has a bunch of flowers. Embarrassed, he goes slowly to Harry's bed, drops the flowers at the foot, then he drops the ukelele there.*

Barney [*awkwardly*]. Your ukelele. An' a bunch of flowers from Jessie.   [*Harry remains motionless on the bed.*

Barney. A bunch of flowers from Jessie, and . . . your . . . ukelele.

> [*The Sister of the Ward enters, left, going to the chapel for Compline. She wears a cream habit with a white coif; a large set of Rosary beads hangs from her girdle. She pauses on her way, and a brass Crucifix flashes on her bosom.*

Sister [*to Harry*]. Keeping brave and hopeful, Twenty-eight ?

Harry [*softly*]. Yes, Sister.

Sister. Splendid. And we've got a ukelele too. Can you play it, my child ?

Harry. Yes, Sister.

Sister. Splendid. You must play me something when you're well over the operation. [*To Barney*] Standing guard over your comrade, Twenty-two, eh ?

Barney [*softly and shyly*]. Yes, Sister.

Sister. Grand. Forasmuch as ye do it unto the least of these my brethren, ye do it unto me. Well, God be with you both, my children. [*To Harry*] And Twenty-eight, pray to God, for wonderful He is in His doing toward the children of men.

> [*Calm and dignified she goes out into the grounds.*

Barney [*pausing as he goes out left*]. They're on the bed ; the ukelele, and the bunch of flowers from . . . Jessie.

> [*The Sisters are heard singing in the Convent the hymn of Salve Regina.*

Sisters :

> Salve Regina, mater misericordiae ;
> Vitae dulcedo et spes nostra, salve !

Ad te clamamus, exules filii Hevae ;
Ad te suspiramus, gementes et flentes in hac lacry-
    marum valle.
Eia ergo Advocata nostra,
Illos tuos misericordes oculos ad nos converte,
Et Jesum, benedictum fructum ventris tui—

Harry. God of the miracles, give a poor devil a chance,
give a poor devil a chance !

Sisters :
    Nobis post hoc exsilium ostende,
    O clemens, o pia, o dulcis Virgo Maria !

ACT IV

A room of the dance hall of the Avondale Football Club. At back, left, cutting corners of the back and side walls, is the arched entrance, divided by a slim pillar, to the dance hall. This entrance is hung with crimson and black striped curtains ; whenever these are parted the dancers can be seen swinging or gliding past the entrance if a dance be taking place at the time. Over the entrance is a scroll on which is printed : " Up the Avondales ! " The wall back has a wide, tall window which opens to the garden, in which the shrubs and some sycamore trees can be seen. It is hung with apple-green casement curtains, which are pulled to the side to allow the window to be open as it is at present. Between the entrance to hall and the window is a Roll of Honour containing the names of five members of the Club killed in the war. Underneath the Roll of Honour a wreath of laurel tied with red and black ribbon. To the front left is the fireplace. Between the fireplace and the hall entrance is a door on which is an oval white enamel disc with " Caretaker " painted on it. To the right a long table, covered with a green cloth, on which are numerous bottles of wine and a dozen glasses. On the table, too, is a telephone. A brown carpet covers the floor. Two easy and one ordinary chairs are in the room. Hanging from the ceiling are three lanterns ; the centre one is four times the length of its width, the ones at the side are less than half as long as the centre lantern and hang horizontally ; the lanterns are black, with a broad red stripe running down the centre of the largest and across those hanging at each side, so that, when they are lighted, they suggest an illuminated black cross with an inner one of gleaming red. The hall is vividly decorated with many coloured lanterns, looped with coloured streamers.

When the scene is revealed the curtains are drawn, and the band can be heard playing a fox-trot. Outside in the garden, near the window, Simon and Sylvester can be seen smoking, and Teddy is walking slowly up and down the path. The band is heard playing for a few moments, then the curtains are pulled aside, and Jessie, with Barney holding her hand, comes in and walks rapidly to the table where the wine is standing. They are quickly followed by Harry, who wheels himself a little forward, then stops, watching them. The curtains part again, and Mrs. Heegan is seen watching Harry. Simon and Sylvester, outside, watch those in the room through the window. Barney wears a neat navy-blue suit, with a rather high, stiff collar and black tie. Pinned on the breast of his waistcoat are his war medals, flanked by the Victoria Cross. Harry is also wearing his medals. Jessie has on a very pretty, rather tight-fitting dance frock, with the sleeves falling widely to the elbow, and cut fairly low on her breast. All the dancers, and Harry too, wear coloured, fantastically shaped paper hats.

Jessie [*hot, excited, and uneasy, as with a rapid glance back she sees the curtains parted by Harry*]. Here he comes prowling after us again ! His watching of us is pulling all the enjoyment out of the night. It makes me shiver to feel him wheeling after us.

Barney. We'll watch for a chance to shake him off, an' if he starts again we'll make him take his tangled body somewhere else. [*As Harry moves forward from the curtained entrance.*] Shush, he's comin' near us. [*In a louder tone to Jessie*] Red wine, Jessie, for you, or white wine ?

Harry. Red wine first, Jessie, to the passion and the power and the pain of life, an' then a drink of white wine to the melody that is in them all !

Jessie. I'm so hot.

Harry. I'm so cold ; white wine for the woman warm to make her cold ; red wine for the man that's cold to make him warm !

Jessie. White wine for me.

Harry. For me the red wine till I drink to men puffed up with pride of strength, for even creeping things can praise the Lord !

Barney [*gently to Harry, as he gives a glass of wine to Jessie*]. No more for you now, Harry.

Harry [*mockingly*]. Oh, please, your lusty lordship, just another, an' if I seek a second, smack me well. [*Wheeling his chair viciously against Barney*] Get out, you trimm'd-up clod. There's medals on my breast as well as yours ! [*He fills a glass.*]

Jessie. Let us go back to the dancing, Barney. [*Barney hesitates.*] Please, Barney, let us go back to the dancing !

Harry. To the dancing, for the day cometh when no man can play. And legs were made to dance, to run, to jump, to carry you from one place to another ; but mine can neither walk, nor run, nor jump, nor feel the merry motion of a dance. But stretch me on the floor fair on my belly, and I will turn over on my back, then wriggle back again on to my belly ; and that's more than a dead, dead man can do !

Barney. Jessie wants to dance, an' so we'll go, and leave you here a little.

Harry. Cram pain with pain, and pleasure cram with pleasure. I'm going too. You'd cage me in from seeing you dance, and dance, and dance, with Jessie close to you, and you so close to Jessie. Though you wouldn't think it, yes, I have — I've hammer'd out many a merry measure upon a polish'd floor with a sweet, sweet heifer. [*As Barney and Jessie are moving away he catches hold of Jessie's dress*] Her name ? Oh, any name will do — we'll call her Jessie !

Jessie. Oh, let me go. [*To Barney*] Barney, make him let me go, please.

[*Barney, without a word, removes Harry's hand from Jessie's dress. Jessie and Barney then go out to the dance hall through the curtained entrance. After a while Mrs. Heegan slips away from the entrance into the hall. After a moment's pause Harry follows them into the hall. Simon and Sylvester come in from the garden, leaving Teddy still outside smoking and walking to and fro in the cautious manner of the blind. Simon and Sylvester sit down near the fire and puff in silence for a few moments.*

Sylvester [*earnestly*]. I knew it. I knew it, Simon — strainin', an' strainin' his nerves ; driftin', an' driftin' towards an hallucination !

Simon. Jessie might try to let him down a little more gently, but it would have been better, I think, if Harry hadn't come here tonight.

Sylvester. I concur in that, Simon. What's a decoration to an hospital is an anxiety here.

Simon. To carry life and colour to where there's nothing but the sick and helpless is right ; but to carry the sick and helpless to where there's nothing but life and colour is wrong.   [*The telephone bell rings.*

Sylvester. There's the telephone bell ringing.

Simon. Oh, someone 'll come in and answer it in a second.

Sylvester. To join a little strength to a lot of weakness is what I call sensible ; but to join a little weakness to a lot of strength is what I call a . . .

Simon. A cod.

Sylvester. Exactly.   [*The telephone continues to ring.*

Sylvester. There's that telephone ringin' still.

Simon. Oh, someone 'll come in and answer it in a second.
              [*Teddy has groped his way to French window.*

Teddy. The telephone's tinklin', boys.

Sylvester. Thanks, Teddy.   We hear it, thanks.   [*To Simon*] When he got the invitation from the Committay to come, wearin' his decorations, me an' the old woman tried to persuade him that, seein' his condition, it was better to stop at home, an' let me represent him, but [*with a gesture*] no use !
              [*Teddy resumes his walk to and fro.*

Simon. It was natural he'd want to come, since he was the means of winning the Cup twice before for them, leading up to their keeping the trophy for ever by the win of a year ago.

Sylvester. To bring a boy so helpless as him, whose memory of agility an' strength time hasn't flattened down, to a place wavin' with joy an' dancin', is simply, simply——

Simon. Devastating, I'd say.

Sylvester. Of course it is ! Is that god-damn telephone goin' to keep ringin' all night ?

                        [*Mrs. Foran enters from hall quickly.*

Mrs. Foran. Miss Monican says that one of you is to answer the telephone, an' call her if it's anything important.

Sylvester [*nervously*]. I never handled a telephone in my life.

Simon. I chanced it once and got so hot and quivery that I couldn't hear a word, and didn't know what I was saying myself.

Mrs. Foran. Have a shot at it and see.

                  [*The three of them drift over to the telephone.*

Sylvester. Chance it again, Simon, an' try to keep steady.

                [*As Simon stretches his hand to the receiver.*

Sylvester. Don't rush, don't rush, man, an' make a mess of it. Take it in your stride.

Simon [*pointing to receiver*]. When you lift this down, you're connected, I think.

Sylvester. No use of thinkin' on this job. Don't you turn the handle first ?

Simon [*irritably*]. No, you don't turn no handle, man !

Mrs. Foran. Let Simon do it now ; Simon knows.

        [*Simon tremblingly lifts down the receiver, almost letting it fall.*

Sylvester. Woa, woa, Simon ; careful, careful !

Simon [*speaking in receiver*]. Eh, hallo ! Eh, listen there. Eh, hallo ! listen.

Sylvester. You listen, man, an' give the fellow at the other end a chance to speak.

Simon. If you want me to manipulate the thing, let me manipulate it in tranquillity.

Mrs. Foran [*to Sylvester*]. Oh, don't be puttin' him out, Sylvester.

Simon [*waving them back*]. Don't be crushing in on me ; give me room to manipulate the thing.

> [*Dead silence for some moments.*

Mrs. Foran. Are you hearin' anything from the other end ?

Simon. A kind of a buzzing and a roaring noise.
  [*Sylvester suddenly gives the cord a jerk and pulls the receiver out of Simon's hand.*

[*Angrily*] What the hell are you trying to do, man ? You're after pulling it right out of my mit.

Sylvester [*heatedly*]. There was a knot or a twist an' a tangle in it that was keepin' the sound from travellin'.

Simon. If you want me to work the thing properly, you'll have to keep yourself from interfering. [*Resuming surlily*] Eh, hallo, listen, yes ? Ha ! ha ! ha ! ha ! Yes, yes, yes. No, no, no. Cheerio ! Yes. Eh, hallo, listen, eh. Hallo.

Sylvester. What is it ? What're they sayin' ?

Simon [*hopelessly, taking the receiver from his ear*]. I don't seem to be able to hear a damn sound.

Sylvester. An' Holy God, what are you yessin' and noin' and cheerioin' out of you for then ?

Simon. You couldn't stand here like a fool and say nothing, could you ?

Sylvester. Show it to me, Simon, show it to me — you're not holdin' it at the proper angle.

Mrs. Foran. Give it to Syl, Simon ; it's a delicate contrivance that needs a knack in handlin'.

Sylvester [*as he is taking the receiver from Simon and carefully placing it to his ear*]. You have always to preserve an eqwee-balance between the speakin' mouth and the hearin' ear. [*Speaking into receiver*] Hallo ! Anybody there at the other end of this ? Eh, wha's that ? Yes, yes, I've got you [*taking the receiver from his ear and speaking to Simon and Mrs. Foran*] : Something like wine, or dine, or shine, or something — an' a thing that's hummin'.

Simon. I can see no magnificent meaning jumping out of that !

Mrs. Foran. They couldn't be talkin' about bees, could they ?

Sylvester [*scornfully*]. Bees ! No, they couldn't be talkin' about bees ! That kind of talk, Mrs. Foran, only tends to confuse matters. Bees ! Dtch, dtch, dtch — the stupidity of some persons is . . . terrifyin' !

Simon. Ask them quietly what they want.

Sylvester [*indignantly*]. What the hell's the use of askin' them that, when I can hear something only like a thing that's hummin' ?

Mrs. Foran. It wouldn't be, now, comin', or even bummin' ?

Sylvester. It might even possibly be drummin'. Personally, Mrs. Foran, I think, since you can't help, you might try to keep from hinderin'.

Simon. Put it back, Syl, where it was, an' if it rings again, we'll only have to slip quietly out of this.

Mrs. Foran. Yes, put it back, an' say it never rang.

Sylvester Where was it ? Where do I put it back ?

Simon. On that thing stickin' out there. Nice and gently now.

> [*Sylvester cautiously puts receiver back. They look at the telephone for a few moments, then go back to the fire, one by one. Sylvester stands with his back to it ; Simon sits in a chair, over the back of which Mrs. Foran leans.*

Mrs. Foran. Curious those at the other end of the telephone couldn't make themselves understood.

Simon. Likely they're not accustomed to it, and it's a bit difficult if you're not fully conscious of its manipulation.

Sylvester. Well, let them study an' study it then, or abide by the consequences, for we can't be wastin' time teachin' them.

> [*The curtains at entrance of dance hall are pulled aside, and Teddy, who has disappeared from the garden a little time before, comes in. As he leaves the curtains apart, the dancers can be seen gliding past the entrance in the movements of a tango. Teddy comes down, looks steadily but vacantly towards the group around the fire, then goes over carefully to the table, where he moves his hand about till it touches a bottle, which he takes up in one hand, feeling it questioningly with the other.*

Simon. How goes it, Teddy ?

Teddy [*with a vacant look towards them*]. Sylvester — Simon
— well. What seest thou, Teddy ? Thou seest not
as man seeth. In the garden the trees stand up ; the
green things showeth themselves and fling out flowers
of divers hues. In the sky the sun by day and the moon
and the stars by night — nothing. In the hall the
sound of dancing, the eyes of women, grey and blue
and brown and black, do sparkle and dim and sparkle
again. Their white breasts rise and fall, and rise again.
Slender legs, from red and black, and white and green,
come out, go in again — nothing. Strain as you may,
it stretches from the throne of God to the end of the
hearth of hell.

Simon. What ?

Teddy. The darkness.

Simon [*knowing not what to say*]. Yes, oh yes.

Teddy [*holding up a bottle of wine*]. What colour, Syl ?
It's all the same, but I like the red the best.

Mrs. Foran [*going over to Teddy*]. Just one glass, dear, and
you'll sit down quietly an' take it in sips.
  [*Mrs. Foran fills a glass of wine for Teddy, leads him to a
  chair, puts him sitting down, and gives the glass of wine
  carefully to him. The band in the hall has been playing,
  and through the parted curtains the dancers are seen
  gliding past. Jessie moves by now in the arms of Barney,
  and in a few moments is followed along the side of the
  hall by Harry wheeling himself in his chair and watching
  them. Mrs. Foran and the two men look on and become
  more attentive when among the dancers Susie, in the arms
  of Surgeon Maxwell, Jessie partnered with Barney, and
  Harry move past.*

Sylvester [*as Susie goes by*]. Susie Monican's lookin' game enough to-night for anything.

Simon. Hardly remindful of her one-time fear of God.

Sylvester [*as Jessie goes by followed by Harry*]. There he goes, still followin' them.

Simon. And Jessie's looking as if she was tired of her maidenhood, too.

Mrs. Foran. The thin threads holdin' her dress up sidelin' down over her shoulders, an' her catchin' them up again at the tail end of the second before it was too late.

Simon [*grinning*]. And Barney's hand inching up, inching up to pull them a little lower when they're sliding down.

Mrs. Foran. Astonishin' the way girls are advertisin' their immodesty. Whenever one of them sits down, in my heart I pity the poor men havin' to view the disedifyin' sight of the full length of one leg couched over another.

Teddy [*forgetful*]. A damn nice sight, all the same, I think.

Mrs. Foran [*indignantly*]. One would imagine such a thought would jar a man's mind that had kissed good-bye to the sight of his eyes.

Teddy. Oh, don't be tickin' off every word I say !

Mrs. Foran [*after an astonished pause, whipping the glass out of Teddy's hand*]. Damn the drop more, now, you'll get for the rest of the evenin'.

[*The band suddenly stops playing, and the couples seen just then through the doorway stop dancing and look attentively*

*up the hall.   After a slight pause, Harry in his chair,
pushed by Susie, comes in through the entrance ; his face
is pale and drawn, his breath comes in quick faint gasps,
and his head is leaning sideways on the back of the chair.
Mrs. Heegan is on one side of Harry, and Surgeon
Maxwell, who is in dinner-jacket style of evening dress,
wearing his medals, including the D.S.O., walks on the
other.   Harry is wheeled over near the open window.
Barney and Jessie, standing in the entrance, look on and
listen.*

Maxwell. Here near the window. [*To Mrs. Heegan*]
He'll be all right, Mrs. Heegan, in a second ; a little
faint — too much excitement.   When he recovers a
little, I'd get him home.

Harry [*faintly but doggedly*]. Napoo home, napoo. Not
yet.   I'm all right.   I'll spend a little time longer in
the belly of an hour bulgin' out with merriment.
Carry on.

Maxwell. Better for you to go home, Heegan.

Harry. When they drink to the Club from the Cup —
the Silver Tassie — that I won three times, three
times for them — that first was filled to wet the lips
of Jessie and of me — I'll go, but not yet.   I'm all
right ; my name is yet only a shadow on the Roll of
Honour.

Mrs. Heegan. Come home, Harry ; you're gettin' your
allowance only on the understandin' that you take care
of yourself.

Harry. Get the Cup.   I'll mind it here till you're ready
to send it round to drink to the Avondales — on the
table here beside me.   Bring the Cup ; I'll mind it
here on the table beside me.

Maxwell. Get the Cup for him, someone.

[*Simon goes to the hall and returns with the Cup, which he gives to Harry.*

Harry [*holding the Cup out*]. A first drink again for me, for me alone this time, for the shell that hit me bursts for ever between Jessie and me. [*To Simon*] Go on, man, fill out the wine !

Maxwell [*to Simon*]. A little — just a glass. Won't do him any harm. [*To Harry*] Then you'll have to remain perfectly quiet, Heegan.

Harry. The wine — fill out the wine !

Simon [*to Harry*]. Red wine or white ?

Harry. Red wine, red like the faint remembrance of the fires in France ; red wine like the poppies that spill their petals on the breasts of the dead men. No, white wine, white like the stillness of the millions that have removed their clamours from the crowd of life. No, red wine ; red like the blood that was shed for you and for many for the commission of sin ! [*He drinks the wine.*] Steady, Harry, and lift up thine eyes unto the hills. [*Roughly to those around him*] What are you all gaping at ?

Maxwell. Now, now, Heegan — you must try to keep quiet.

Susie. And when you've rested and feel better, you will sing for us a Negro Spiritual, and point the melody with the ukelele.

Mrs. Heegan. Just as he used to do.

Sylvester. Behind the trenches.

Simon. In the Rest Camps.

Mrs. Foran. Out in France.

Harry. Push your sympathy away from me, for I'll have none of it. [*He wheels his chair quickly towards the dance hall.*] Go on with the dancing and keep the ball a-rolling. [*Calling loudly at the entrance*] Trumpets and drum begin ! [*The band begins to play.*] Dance and dance and dance. [*He listens for a moment.*] Sink into merriment again, and sling your cares to God ! [*He whirls round in the chair to the beat of the tune. Dancers are seen gliding past entrance.*] Dear God, I can't. [*He sinks sideways on his chair.*] I must, must rest. [*He quietly recites :*]

> For a spell here I will stay,
> Then pack up my body and go —
> For mine is a life on the ebb,
> Yours a full life on the flow !

[*Harry goes over to far side of window and looks out into garden. Mrs. Heegan is on his right and Teddy on his left ; Simon and Sylvester a little behind, looking on. Mrs. Foran to the right of Mrs. Heegan. Surgeon Maxwell and Susie. who are a little to the front, watch for a moment, then the Surgeon puts his arm round Susie and the pair glide off into the dance hall.*

[*When Surgeon Maxwell and Susie glide in to the motions of the dance through the entrance into the dance hall, the curtains are pulled together. A few moments' pause. Teddy silently puts his hand on Harry's shoulder, and they both stare into the garden.*

Simon. The air'll do him good.

Sylvester. An' give him breath to sing his song an' play the ukelele.

Mrs. Heegan. Just as he used to do.

Sylvester. Behind the trenches.

Simon. In the Rest Camps.

Mrs. Foran. Out in France.

Harry. I can see, but I cannot dance.

Teddy. I can dance, but I cannot see.

Harry. Would that I had the strength to do the things I see.

Teddy. Would that I could see the things I've strength to do.

Harry. The Lord hath given and the Lord hath taken away.

Teddy. Blessed be the name of the Lord.

Mrs. Foran. I do love the ukelele, especially when it goes tinkle, tinkle, tinkle in the night-time.

Sylvester. Bringin' before you glistenin' bodies of blacks, coilin' themselves an' shufflin' an' prancin' in a great jungle dance ; shakin' assegais an' spears to the rattle, rattle, rattle an' thud, thud, thud of the tom-toms.

Mrs. Foran. There's only one possible musical trimmin' to the air of a Negro Spiritual, an' that's the tinkle, tinkle, tinkle of a ukelele.

Harry, The rising sap in trees I'll never feel.

Teddy. The hues of branch or leaf I'll never see.

Harry. There's something wrong with life when men can walk.

Teddy. There's something wrong with life when men can see.

Harry. I never felt the hand that made me helpless.

Teddy. I never saw the hand that made me blind.

Harry. Life came and took away the half of life.

Teddy. Life took from me the half he left with you.

Harry. The Lord hath given and the Lord hath taken away.

Teddy. Blessed be the name of the Lord.
[*Susie comes quickly in by entrance, goes over to the table and, looking at several bottles of wine, selects one. She is going hurriedly back, when, seeing Harry, she goes over to him.*

Susie [*kindly*]. How are you now, Harry ?

Harry. All right, thank you.

Susie. That's good.
[*Susie is about to hurry away, when Mrs. Foran stops her with a remark.*

Mrs. Foran [*with a meaning gesture*]. He's takin' it cushy till you're ready to hear him singin' his Negro Spiritual, Miss.

Susie. Oh, God, I'd nearly forgotten that. They'll be giving out the balloons at the next dance, and when that fox-trot's over he'll have to come in and sing us the Spiritual.

Mrs. Heegan. Just as he used to do.

Simon. Behind the trenches.

Sylvester. In the Rest Camps.

Mrs. Foran. Out in France.

Susie. As soon as the Balloon Dance is over, Harry, out through the garden and in by the front entrance with you, so that you'll be ready to start as they all sit down. And after the song, we'll drink to the Club from the Silver Tassie.

> [*She hurries back to the hall with the bottle of wine.*

Mrs. Foran. I'm longin' to hear Harry on the ukelele.

Harry. I hope I'll be able to do justice to it.

Mrs. Heegan. Of course you will, Harry.

Harry [*nervously*]. Before a crowd. Forget a word and it's all up with you.

Simon. Try it over now, softly ; the sound couldn't carry as far as the hall.

Sylvester. It'll give you confidence in yourself.

Harry [*to Simon*]. Show us the ukelele, Simon.

> [*Simon gets the ukelele and gives it to Harry.*

Teddy. If I knew the ukelele it might wean me a little way from the darkness.

> [*Harry pulls a few notes, tuning the ukelele, then he softly sings.*

Harry :

> Swing low, sweet chariot, comin' for to carry me home,
>
> Swing low, sweet chariot, comin' for to carry me home.
>
> I looked over Jordan, what did I see, comin' for to carry me home ?
>
> A band of angels comin' after me — comin' for to carry me home.

> [*A voice in the hall is heard shouting through a megaphone.*

Voice. Balloons will be given out now ! Given out now
— the balloons !

Mrs. Foran [*excitedly*]. They're goin' to send up the
balloons ! They're going to let the balloons fly now !

Harry [*singing*] :
Swing low, sweet chariot, comin' for to carry me
home.
Swing low, sweet chariot, comin' for to carry me
home.

Mrs. Foran [*as Harry is singing*]. Miss Monican wants us
all to see the flyin' balloons.
[*She catches Teddy's arm and runs with him into the hall.*

Simon. We must all see the flyin' balloons.

Mrs. Heegan [*running into hall*]. Red balloons and black
balloons.

Simon [*following Mrs. Heegan*]. Green balloons and blue
balloons.

Sylvester [*following Simon*]. Yellow balloons and puce
balloons.
[*All troop into the hall, leaving the curtains apart, and
Harry alone with his ukelele. Through the entrance
various coloured balloons that have been tossed into the
air can be seen, mid sounds of merriment and excitement.*

Harry [*softly and slowly*]. Comin' for to carry me home.
[*He throws the ukelele into an arm-chair, sits still for a
moment, then goes to the table, takes up the silver cup,
and wheels himself into the garden.*
[*After a pause Barney looks in, then enters pulling Jessie by
the hand, letting the curtains fall together again. Then
he goes quickly to window, shuts and bolts it, drawing-to*

*one half of the curtains, goes back to Jessie, catches her
hand again, and tries to draw her towards room on the
left.   During the actions that follow the dance goes
merrily on in the hall.*

Jessie [*holding up a broken shoulder-strap and pulling back
towards the hall*]. Barney, no.   God, I'd be afraid he
might come in on us alone.
    [*Hands part the curtains and throw in coloured streamers
    that encircle Jessie and Barney.*

Barney. Damn them ! . . . He's gone, I tell you, to
sing the song an' play the ukelele.

Jessie [*excited and afraid*]. See, they're watching us.   No,
Barney.   You mustn't.   I'll not go ! [*Barney seizes Jessie
in his arms and forces her towards the door on the left.*] You
wouldn't be good.   I'll not go into that room.

Barney. I will be good, I tell you !   I just want to be
alone with you for a minute.
    [*Barney loosens Jessie's other shoulder-strap, so that her
    dress leaves her shoulders and bosom bare.*

Jessie [*near the door left, as Barney opens it*]. You've loosened
my dress — I knew you weren't going to be good.
[*As she kisses him passionately*] Barney, Barney — you
shouldn't be making me do what I don't want to do !

Barney [*holding her and trying to pull her into room*]. Come on,
Jessie, you needn't be afraid of Barney — we'll just
rest a few minutes from the dancing.
    [*At that part of the window uncurtained Harry is seen
    peering in.   He then wheels his chair back and comes on
    to the centre of the window-frame with a rush, bursting*

*the catch and speeding into the room, coming to a halt,
angry and savage, before Barney and Jessie.*

Harry. So you'd make merry over my helplessness in
front of my face, in front of my face, you pair of
cheats ! You couldn't wait till I'd gone, so that my
eyes wouldn't see the joy I wanted hurrying away from
me over to another ? Hurt her breast pulling your
hand quick out of her bodice, did you ? [*To Jessie*]
Saved you in the nick of time, my lady, did I ? [*To
Barney*] Going to enjoy yourself on the same little
couch where she, before you formed an image in her
eye, acted the part of an amateur wife, and I acted the
part of an amateur husband — the black couch with
the green and crimson butterflies, in the yellow bushes,
where she and me often tired of the things you're
dangling after now !

Jessie. He's a liar, he's a liar, Barney ! He often tried it
on with coaxing first and temper afterwards, but it
always ended in a halt that left him where he started.

Harry. If I had my hands on your white neck I'd leave
marks there that crowds of kisses from your Barney
wouldn't moisten away.

Barney. You half-baked Lazarus, I've put up with you
all the evening, so don't force me now to rough-handle
the bit of life the Jerries left you as a souvenir !

Harry. When I wanted to slip away from life, you
brought me back with your whispered " Think of the
tears of Jess, think of the tears of Jess ", but Jess has
wiped away her tears in the ribbon of your Cross,
and this poor crippled jest gives a flame of joy to the
change ; but when you get her, may you find in her
the pressed down emptiness of a whore !

Barney [*running over and seizing Harry*]. I'll tilt the leaking life out of you, you jealous, peering pimp !

Jessie [*trying to hold Barney back*]. Barney, Barney, don't ! don't !

Harry [*appealingly*]. Barney, Barney ! My heart — you're stopping it !

Jessie [*running to entrance and shouting in*]. Help ! help ! They're killing each other !

> [*In the hall the dance stops. Surgeon Maxwell runs in, followed by Susie, Simon, Sylvester, Mrs. Foran, Mrs. Heegan, and lastly Teddy finding his way over to the window. Dancers gather around entrance and look on.*
> [*Surgeon Maxwell, running over, separates Barney from Harry.*

Maxwell. What's this ? Come, come — we can't have this sort of thing going on.

Mrs. Heegan. He was throttlin' him, throttlin' a poor helpless creature, an' if anything happens, he and that painted slug Jessie Taite 'll be held accountable !

Maxwell. This can't be allowed to go on. You'll have to bring him home. Any more excitement would be dangerous.

Mrs. Heegan. This is what he gets from Jessie Taite for sittin' on the stairs through the yawnin' hours of the night, racin' her off to the play an' the pictures, an' plungin' every penny he could keep from me into presents for the consolidation of the courtship !

Maxwell. Bring the boy home, woman, bring the boy home.

Sylvester [*fiercely to Jessie*]. And money of mine in one of the gewgaws scintillatin' in her hair !

Jessie. What gewgaw ? What gewgaw ?
    [*Coloured streamers are thrown in by those standing at entrance, which fall on and encircle some of the group around Harry.*

Sylvester. The tiarara I gave you two Christmases ago with the yellow berries and the three flutterin' crimson swallows !

Harry [*faintly and bitterly, with a hard little laugh*]. Napoo Barney Bagnal and napoo Jessie Taite. A merry heart throbs coldly in my bosom ; a merry heart in a cold bosom — or is it a cold heart in a merry bosom ? [*He gathers a number of the coloured streamers and winds them round himself and chair.*] Teddy ! [*Harry catches Teddy by the sleeve and winds some more streamers round him.*] Sing a song, man, and show the stuff you're made of !

Maxwell [*catching hold of Mrs. Heegan's arm*]. Bring him home, woman. [*Maxwell catches Sylvester's arm.*] Get him home, man.

Harry. Dear God, this crippled form is still your child. [*To Mrs. Heegan*] Dear mother, this helpless thing is still your son. Harry Heegan, me, who, on the football field, could crash a twelve-stone flyer off his feet. For this dear Club three times I won the Cup, and grieve in reason I was just too weak this year to play again. And now, before I go, I give you all the Cup, the Silver Tassie, to have and to hold for ever, evermore. [*From his chair he takes the Cup with the two sides hammered close together, and holds it out to them]* Mangled and bruised as I am bruised and mangled. Hammered free from all its comely shape. Look, there is Jessie writ, and here is Harry, the one name safely separated from the other. *[He flings it on the floor.]* Treat it kindly. With care it may be opened out, for Barney there to drink to Jess, and Jessie there to drink to Barney.

Teddy. Come, Harry, home to where the air is soft. No longer can you stand upon a hill-top ; these empty eyes of mine can never see from one. Our best is all behind us — what's in front we'll face like men, dear comrade of the blood-fight and the battle-front !

Harry. What's in front we'll face like men ! *[Harry goes out by the window, Sylvester pushing the chair, Teddy's hand on Harry's shoulder, Mrs. Heegan slowly following. Those left in the room watch them going out through the garden, turning to the right till they are all out of sight. As he goes out of window]* The Lord hath given and man hath taken away !

Teddy [heard from the garden]. Blessed be the name of the Lord !
    [The band in the hall begin to play again. Those in hall begin to dance.

Maxwell. Come on, all, we've wasted too much time already.

Susie [to Jessie, who is sitting quietly in a chair]. Come on, Jessie — get your partner ; *[roguishly]* you can have a quiet time with Barney later on.

Jessie. Poor Harry !

Susie. Oh nonsense ! If you'd passed as many through your hands as I, you'd hardly notice one. [*To Jessie*] Jessie, Teddy Foran and Harry Heegan have gone to live their own way in another world. Neither I nor you can lift them out of it. No longer can they do the things we do. We can't give sight to the blind or make the lame walk. We would if we could. It is the misfortune of war. As long as wars are waged, we shall be vexed by woe ; strong legs shall be made useless and bright eyes made dark. But we, who have come through the fire unharmed, must go on living. [*Pulling Jessie from the chair*] Come along, and take your part in life ! [*To Barney*] Come along, Barney, and take your partner into the dance !

    [*Barney comes over, puts his arm round Jessie, and they dance into the hall. Susie and Surgeon Maxwell dance together. As they dance the Waltz " Over the Waves," some remain behind drinking. Two of these sing the song to the same tune as the dance.*

Maxwell :

        Swing into the dance,
        Take joy when it comes, ere it go ;
        For the full flavour of life
        Is either a kiss or a blow.
        He to whom joy is a foe,
        Let him wrap himself up in his woe ;
        For he is a life on the ebb,
        We a full life on the flow !

    [*All in the hall dance away with streamers and balloons flying. Simon and Mrs. Foran sit down and watch the fun through the entrance. Mrs. Foran lights a cigarette and smokes. A pause as they look on.*

Mrs. Foran. It's a terrible pity Harry was too weak to stay an' sing his song, for there's nothing I love more than the ukelele's tinkle, tinkle in the night-time.

CURTAIN

SONGS AND CHANTS IN
THE SILVER TASSIE

1st CHANT.

Intonation

I sees the mis-sus paryd-ing a - long Wal-ham Green, Through the jewels

Mediation

an' silks on the cos-ters' carts, Em - mie a - pull-ing her skirt

Ending

an' mut-ter-ing, "A bal-loon, a bal-loon, I wants a bal - loon",

The mis-sus . . . an' your fa-ther fight-ing: You'll wait . . . that's wot I wants to know!

Tabs 'll . . . for-ty-eight bat-ta-lion, The Yel-low . . . leg up on the path to glo-ry;

Now with . . . Ar-my of the Marne, An' all the time . . . two men looking after business.

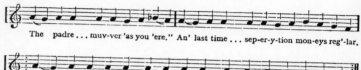

The padre ... muv-ver 'as you 'ere." An' last time ... sep-er-y-tion mon-eys reg'-lar.

But wy - 'r we 'ere, wy - 'r we 'ere—that's wot I wants to know?

2nd CHANT.

A Brass-hat ... world an' the Es - tam - i - nay's daugh-ter,

In a py-jam-a'd ... an Es-tam-i-na-y cock, An' I was pinch'd ...

with a pint of peas. And the hens ... a place of des - o - la-tion!

3rd CHANT.

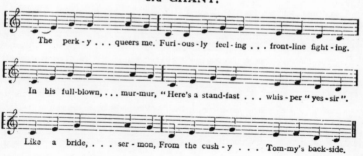

The perk - y ... queers me. Furi - ous-ly feel-ing ... front-line fight-ing.

In his full-blown, ... mur-mur, "Here's a stand-fast ... whis-per "yes - sir".

Like a bride, ... ser - mon, From the cush - y ... Tom-my's back-side.

4th CHANT.

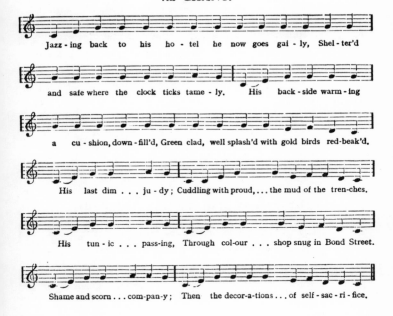

Jazz - ing back to his ho - tel he now goes gai - ly, Shel - ter'd

and safe where the clock ticks tame - ly.   His   back - side warm - ing

a   cu - shion, down - fill'd, Green clad, well splash'd with gold birds red-beak'd.

His   last dim . . . ju - dy ; Cuddling with proud, . . . the mud of the tren-ches.

His   tun - ic . . . pass-ing, Through col-our . . . shop snug in Bond Street.

Shame and scorn . . . com-pan-y ;   Then   the decor-a-tions . . . of self - sac - ri - fice.

5th CHANT.

A   warn-ing . . . give,   To the front . . . do, to   God.

God, un-chang-ing, . . . night sky   To mask . . . His self-slay-ing chil-dren.

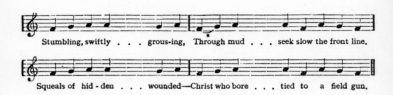

Stumbling, swiftly . . . grous-ing, Through mud . . . seek slow the front line.

Squeals of hid-den . . . wounded—Christ who bore . . . tied to a field gun.

THE ENEMY HAS BROKEN THROUGH.

The en-em-y has brok-en through, brok-en through, brok-en through! Ev-ery

man born of wo-man to the guns, to the guns. To the

guns, to the guns, to the guns! Those at prayer, all in bed and the

swillers drinking deeply in the pubs. To the guns, to the guns. All the

bat-men, ev-ery cook, ev-ery bitch's son that hides A whiff of

cour-age in his veins, Shelter'd vig-our in his bod-y, That can

run, or can walk, ev - en crawl— . . . Dig him

out, dig him out, shove him on— . . . To the guns!

SONG TO THE GUN.

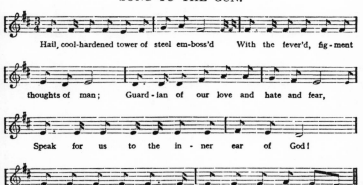

Hail, cool-hardened tower of steel em-boss'd With the fever'd, fig-ment

thoughts of man; Guard - ian of our love and hate and fear,

Speak for us to the in - ner ear of God!

We be - lieve in God and we be - lieve in thee.

WOULD GOD, I SMOK'D.

Would God, I smok'd and walk'd and watch'd - - The dance of a
Would God, I smok'd and lift - ed car - goes From the lad - en
To hang here ev - en a lit - tle lon - ger, Loung - ing
If you creep to rest in a clos'd-up cof - fin, A tail of
Each spar - row, hop - ping, ir - re - sponsible, Is in - den - tur'd

gol - den Brim - stone but - ter - fly, - - To the
shoul - ders of Lon - don's riv - er - way; - - The
through fear - swell'd, anx - ious moments; The
com - rades see - ing you safe home; - - Or a
in God's migh - ty mem - o - ry; - - And we,

sau - cy pipe of a green - finch rest - ing In a
holi - day'd, roar - ing out courage and move-ment To the
hin - der - parts of The god of bat - tles Shading our
ker - nel lost in a shell ex - plod - ing— It's all,
more than they all, shall not be lost In the for-

drowsy, brambled lane in Cumber - land. In Cumber - land.
mus - cled ma-chines of Tottenham Hotspur. Of Tottenham Hotspur,
war - tir'd eyes from his flam - ing face. From his flaming face.
sure, on - ly in a life - time. A life - time.
get - ful - ness of the Lord of Hosts. Of the Lord of Hosts.

SURGEON'S SONG.

Stret - ched on the couch, Jess - ie fon - dled her dress, That

hid all her beaut - ies just o - ver the knee; And I won-dered and said, as I

sigh'd, "What a shame, that there's no room at all on the couch there for me."

STRETCHER-BEARERS' SONG.

Oh, bear it gent - ly, car - ry it soft - ly—A bull-et or a shell said

stop, stop, stop. It's had its day, and it's left the play, Since it

gam - boll'd ov - er the top, top, top. It's had its day and it's

left the play, Since it gam - boll'd o - - ver the top.

WITHIN THE GATES

STAGE VERSION

IF possible, the Curtain intervening between the opening of the play and the scenes following, should be one showing the Park Gates, stiff and formal, dignified and insolent. The bars should shine with the silver gleam of aluminium paint, and cross or diagonal bars should be a deep and sombre black. All space between the bars should be dark — but not too dark — green. The gates proper are flanked by generous panels of a vivid yellow, representing the piers, lower than the bars, and topped by copings of orange-coloured panels. This curtain, when it is pulled back, represents the opening of the gates; and, when it falls back into its place, represents the closing of the gates : or, the outline of the gates may be suggested on the curtain.

The above idea of a front curtain was derived from Eugene O'Neill's suggestion of a front curtain for his great play, *Mourning Becomes Electra*.

CHARACTERS IN THE PLAY

THE DREAMER
OLDER CHAIR ATTENDANT
YOUNGER CHAIR ATTENDANT
THE BISHOP
THE BISHOP'S SISTER
THE ATHEIST
THE POLICEWOMAN
1ST NURSEMAID
2ND NURSEMAID
A GUARDSMAN
A GARDENER
1ST EVANGELIST
2ND EVANGELIST
THE YOUNG WOMAN
A YOUNG SALVATION ARMY OFFICER
THE OLD WOMAN
A MAN WEARING A BOWLER HAT
THE MAN WITH THE STICK (*afterwards, an umbrella*)
MAN WEARING A TRILBY HAT
MAN WEARING A STRAW ONE (*afterwards, a cap*)
A CROWD OF THE DOWN-AND-OUT

A Chorus of Young Men and Maidens

Scene I

Within a Park.
On a Spring Morning.

Scene II

Within a Park.
On a Summer Noon.

Scene III

Within a Park.
On an Autumn Evening.

Scene IV

Within a Park.
On a Winter's Night.

SCENE I

Spring. Morning.

Within a park on a Spring morning.

A clear, light-blue sky, against which is shown, in places, the interlaced dark-brown branches of trees, dotted with green, yellow, and red buds.

The green sward in front slopes up towards the back, but in no way high enough to prevent a view of the spaciousness of the park behind. In the centre of the slope are a few wide steps leading to the top, where, a little to one side, stands a War Memorial in the form of a steel-helmeted soldier, the head bent on the breast, skeleton-like hands leaning on the butt-end of a rifle. Bushes allow the figure to be seen only from the waist up. The body and arms of the figure are shaped in a sharply defined way; the hat a wide circle; and the features are cut in long, sharp, and angular lines. The figure stands out grey against the blue sky and the green shrubs, and seems to be shrinking back from the growing interests brought into being by new life and her thrusting activities.

The rise of the slope is sprinkled with large, formalized figures of daffodils.

At the foot of the slope are paths branching to the right and to the left, that on the left flowing into a wider one encircling the Park lake, from which can be occasionally heard the cries of the water-fowl swimming on the water or preening themselves on the banks.

Birds are heard singing in a subdued but busy way, as they search for food or build their nests.

Formally shaped chairs are here and there, and one or two stiff and dignified-looking benches are near the foot of the slope.

They are painted so as to mingle with the colours of the scene, and are hardly noticeable. The scheme of colour is a delicate green and light blue, patterned by the yellow daffodils and the bare, bud-dotted branches of the trees.

As the gates are opening, the Dreamer enters, and passes through them into the Park. He is gazing with an intensely dreaming expression at a paper which he holds in his left hand. His right hand, holding a short pencil, moves in a gentle, dreamy way, beating time, as he murmurs the opening bars of " Our Mother the Earth is a Maiden Again ". He crosses out as the Chorus enters, singing, followed by various people, who move about at the back, up, down, and about the paths, without jostle or confusion.

A Chorus of Young Boys and Girls, representing trees and flowers, enter, singing.

First, a girl whose skirt represents a white crocus, veined with blue ; next, a boy in black on whose breast is a stylised pattern of a beech tree leaf ; then a girl whose skirt represents a blue cornflower ; next, a boy on whose breast is a formally shaped oak leaf ; then a girl whose skirt represents a daffodil ; next, a boy on whose breast is the pattern of a maple leaf.

The Chorus remain in front, while the crowd move about as they listen, or when they join in the singing.

Chorus [*singing*] :

> Our mother, the earth, is a maiden again, young, fair, and a maiden again.
> Our mother, the earth, is a maiden again, she's young, fair, and a maiden again.
> Her thoughts are a dance as she seeks out her Bridegroom, the Sun, through the lovely confusion of singing of birds, and of blossom and bud.
> She feels the touch of his hand on her hair, on her cheeks ; in the budding of trees,

She feels the kiss of his love on her mouth, on her
breast, as she dances along,

Crowd [*joining in*] :
Through the lovely confusion of singing of birds, and
of blossom and bud.
Her thoughts are a dance as she seeks out her Bride-
groom, the Sun, through the lovely confusion of
singing of birds, and of blossom and bud.

Chorus :
She hears the fiercely sung song of the birds, busy
building new homes in the hedge ;
She hears a challenge to life and to death as she
dances along,

Crowd [*joining in*] :
Through the lovely confusion of singing of birds, and
of blossom and bud.
Her thoughts are a dance as she seeks out her Bride-
groom, the Sun, through the lovely confusion of
singing of birds, and of blossom and bud.

Chorus and Crowd :
Our mother, the earth, is a maiden again, young,
fair, and a maiden again.

[*While the last line is being sung, the Crowd and the
Chorus go out by different ways, leaving only the two
Chair Attendants dusting the chairs and arranging them.
One is young and thin and the other is old and stocky,
and both are in the last lap of physical decay. One has a
stiff right leg, and the other has a stiff left one. They
are dressed in long, khaki-coloured cotton coats, and wear
peaked caps.*

Older One. 'Ow's the poor old leg, todye, 'Erbert ?

Young One. Oh Gord ! 'Ow's yours ?

Older One. Aw — sime wye, with honours ! I seen thet poet chap atryin' to cadge a chire again ; sits dahn on one till 'ee sees me comin' in the distance.

Young One [*not listening — pensively*]. Wot'll we do when we file to be able to walk ! 'En this singin' gets me dahn. 'Eartless for a crahwd to sing when a man's in misery.

Older One [*testily*]. Don't let us think of them things ! It's our destiny. But I 'ates that poet chap ; I 'ates 'im ! 'Ate 'is liveliness. Fair cheek 'ee 'as. A bum — that's wot 'ee 'is. Wouldn't do a dye's work for Gord Almighty. I'd say it to 'is fice, I would.

Young One. Look aht ! 'Ere 'ee is.
[*The Dreamer comes down the grass slope, crosses over, and sits down on a bench. He watches the Two Attendants. He is a young man, lithely built, though a little thin and pale now from a hard time ; but he carries himself buoyantly. His features are rugged ; his eyes bright, sometimes flashing in an imaginative mood, but usually quiet and dreamy-looking. His head is covered with a soft black, broad-brimmed hat, and he is wearing a tightly-belted trench mackintosh. Outside the trench coat, around his neck, is a light, vivid orange scarf.*

Dreamer [*suddenly*]. Here, you two derelict worshippers of fine raiment — when are you going to die ?

Older One [*angrily*]. Mind your own business, see ! We 'as more right to life than you 'as. We work — you don't - eh, Godfrey ?

Young One. My oath, we 'as !

Dreamer. No one has a right to life who doesn't fight to make it greater. I've watched you fawning on the bishop and on every good coat that sits down on a chair.

Young One. You mind your own business !

[*The Young Woman comes down the slope and crosses the sward to go out to the left. She has a preoccupied and rather anxious look on her face, and appears to be searching for someone.*

[*She is very pretty, and her figure would make most young men immediately forget the seventh commandment. Her face is a little pale, but this paleness is hidden by a cautious and clever make-up. She has an intelligent look, which is becoming a little worn by contact with the selfishness and meanness of the few clients that have patronised her ; for these, though unable to resist the desire to have her, hate her subconsciously before they go with her, and consciously detest her when their desires have been satisfied. She has read a little, but not enough ; she has thought a little, but not enough ; she is deficient in self-assurance, and is too generous and sensitive to be a clever whore, and her heart is not in the business.*

[*Convent tales of punishments reserved for the particular sins tangled round sex expression have left in her mind lusty images of hellfire. She is dressed in a black tailored suit, topped by a scarlet hat. On the hat is an ornament, in black, of a crescent ; and the hip of her dress is decorated with a scarlet one. The Dreamer sees her, rises, and is about to follow her. She stops and faces him.*

Young Woman. I am troubled ; I am anxious ; please don't follow me.

Dreamer. I shall follow after loveliness all the days of my life.

Young Woman. Not just now, please ; I do not want you. [*She turns to go ; he follows slowly. She turns, to say hysterically*] Go away, please !
  [*She goes out. He returns, crestfallen, to his seat on the bench. The Attendants snigger.*

Older One. The likes of 'er ain't for the likes of 'im.

Young One [*to the Dreamer*]. A fine choke-off, wha' ?
  [*Dreamer rises, catches each by the coat-collar, and shakes them.*

Dreamer [*roughly*]. Ye lost ones ! Will ye starve and droop and die without a dream ? Even the lame and the halt can hunt out a shrine ! Will ye mock at the better ones who refuse to die like sheep ?

Attendants [*together*]. Eh, there, leggo ! Someone call a perliceman !
  [*The Atheist comes in from a path above, sees the angry scene, and hurries down to stop it.*

Atheist [*catching the Dreamer by the arm*]. Now then, friend, now then ; let withered life die in its own sour way, without pushing it to a sudden and unprovided end !

Dreamer [*pushing the Attendants from him — one to the right, the other to the left*]. Away, and cower in your corner, till life hoodooes you out of the misery you both love ! Away, the pair of you, who make a nightmare of the dream of God !
  [*The Attendants slink off, one to the right, the other to the left. The Dreamer and the Atheist sit on the bench together.*

Atheist [*warningly*]. Take care, friend : you'd pay as high a penalty for hurting hopelessness as you would for a life of promise or one of proved production.

Dreamer. I know ; I lost my temper. Never mind that now. I've seen her ; she passed by here just before you came.

Atheist [*rising*]. Passed by 'ere ? I'm off in the opposite direction.

Dreamer [*stopping him*]. No fear of meeting her ; she won't come back. I tried to keep her, but she wouldn't stay a second.

Atheist. Oh, lay off the young lass, Dreamer. Let 'er go 'er own wye — up the hill of life or dahn it.

Dreamer. She's too lonely to be left alone, Ned ; and too pretty ; intelligent, too, as you say.

Atheist [*impatiently*]. I know all that ! She 'as a fine mind, if she'd only use it the right way. But it's forever darting forward, back ; to the left today, to the right tomorrow — no 'uman being could stand it. I'm glad I'm only her step-da.

Dreamer. Who is, and where is, her real daddy ?

Atheist. Stoodent of theology, the story goes : fell in love with a pretty housemaid, and she responded. When the mother knew what was abaht to happen, she knocked at the college gate, but was driven off. When a few years old, the kid was shoved into a church institoo-tion, where the nuns, being what she was — a child of sin —, paid her special attention ; an' the terrors an' dangers of hell became the child's chief enjoyment !

Dreamer. Good God ! [*Earnestly*] Ned, we must never ease off the fight for a life that is free from fear !

Atheist. Never, Dreamer, never. Then the mother married an Irish dragoon, a brave, decent man,

C.P.—II   I

Dreamer, home from the front on leave ; had a star-lit time with the warrior for a week ; then the dragoon disappeared in one of those vanishing advances from the front line an' the widow settles dahn on 'er pension.

Dreamer. Then she fastened on to you, eh ?

Atheist. To tell the truth, it was I fastened on to 'er. Even when I met 'er, she was still the kind of woman would make a man long for something to 'appen — you know, Dreamer ?

Dreamer. Ay, I know — too damned well !

Atheist. Then I delivered the child from the church in-stitootion, sayin' I was the father. I did my best for 'er, takin' awye a supernatural 'eaven from over 'er 'ead, an' an unnatural 'ell from under 'er feet ; but she never quite escaped. D'ye know, one time, the lass near knew the whole of Pine's *Age of Reason* off by 'eart !

Dreamer. And did you bring her into touch with song ?

Atheist. Song ? Oh, I had no time for song !

Dreamer. You led her from one darkness into another, man. [*He rises and walks about — angrily*] Will none of you ever guess that man can study man, or worship God, in dance and song and story ! [*Appealingly*] Ah, Ned, if you could but see her with the eyes of youth, you would not let her live so lonely.

Atheist. I helped her all I could. Out of the earnings of a first-class carpenter, I gave 'er a good education, an' taught 'er a lot myself ; but it was all no good — she refused to think as I did. The 'ome's broken up, now, and I'm not eager to try to get it together agine.

Dreamer. How broken up ?

Atheist. You see, when the maid came close to woman-hood, the mother turned religious, an' begun to 'ate the kid, sayin' that while the kid was there, 'er sin was ever in front of 'er fice. Then she took to drink an' violence.

Dreamer. A sweet home for a girl coming also to woman-hood !

Atheist. After a long time of patient endoorance, one day the girl ups an', withaht a word, goes ; an' a month after, I goes too ; so 'ere she is, her whole life a desire for a bright time of it ; an' 'ere I am, a speaker rending the strands of superstition's web thet keeps poor men from movin'.

Dreamer. Give the lovely lass one more chance, speaker ; live the last years of your life with loveliness.

Atheist. Not damn likely ; the longer I'm by myself, the more I likes it.
    [*While they have been speaking the last few words, the Man with the Stick has appeared on the slope above.*

Man with Stick [*calling down to Atheist*]. 'Ave you got to-night's speech ready, Ned ?

Atheist [*taking note-book from a pocket*]. Not yet, Bill.

Man with Stick. Get a move on : we 'as to bounce the idea of a Gord from men's minds, so make it strong.
    [*The Two Chair Attendants limp in, carrying a chair between them. They set it down, stand panting for a while, then the Older One begins to give it a dust, the Man with the Stick watching them contemptuously, and dubiously shaking his grey head.*

Man with Stick [*going close to Older Attendant*]. 'Ere, 'ave you an inquirin' mind, friend ?

Older One. Eh ?　Wot ?

Man with Stick. I asks if you 'as an inquirin' mind. [*He taps the chair with the stick.*] Wot is this ?　A chair. Does thet tell you all abaht it ?　No.　Wot's it myde of ?　Wood.　Nah, if it was myde of cork it would be lighter ; but if it was myde of lead it would be 'eavier — see ?

Older One. Ay ?

Man with Stick. Ay ?　Not ay, but wye ?

Older One. Wye ?　Wot wye ?

Man with Stick [*impatiently*]. Wot wye !　Listen, man. [*Hitting the chair with stick.*] Wood ; 'ard.　Nah wye's the chair 'ard ?　Is it doo to density, or is it not ?

Older One. I don't ask no questions of chairs.

Young One. We 'as to attend to our werk, see ?

Man with Stick [*woe in his voice*]. No brrine !
　　[*The two Nursemaids, the Under One pushing the fine pram, appear behind Man with the Stick.*

Younger Nursemaid [*imperiously*]. Gangway there !
　　[*The pram strikes his heels, and he jumps aside, his mouth opening for an angry exclamation ; but when he sees the splendid pram, he closes it without saying a word.　The Upper Nursemaid picks out a chair farthest from the others.　The Chair Attendants run over bearing a chair between them for the Under Maid, and the Older One dusts both the chairs vigorously.*

Older One [*after dusting*]. Now, miss.　Nice day, miss.

Upper Nursemaid [*shortly*]. Very nice.

Older One. To cart such a byeby abaht's responsible thing, I'd say, miss.

Upper Nursemaid [*stiffly*]. I suppose so. I don't feel it. [*She sees his dirty hand is resting on the pram.*] Take that dirty paw off the pram at once ! This is a countess's baby !

Older One [*pulling his hand away as if the pram was red-hot*]. Oh, excuse me, miss. I forgot for the minute !

Upper Nursemaid [*loftily*]. Go away ; we're season tickets ; go away !
   [*The Attendant slinks off from the pram as the Bishop, followed by his Sister, appears coming down the slope from behind the Memorial. The Policewoman strolls in from the path on the left.*

Atheist [*mockingly — over to the Nursemaids*]. Must be careful of a countess's byeby !

Upper Nursemaid [*with great dignity*]. A countess's byeby's a considerytion. I'd like you all to know.
   [*The Bishop and his Sister come down among the crowd. The Bishop is a heavily built man of sixty or so. His head, his feet, and hands are large ; his voice, once deep and sonorous, has become a little husky. The pretentious briskness of his movements are an attempt to hide from others the fact that he is beginning to fail. He is anxious to show to all he meets that he is an up-to-the-present-minute clergyman, and that those who wear the stole are, on the whole, a lusty, natural, broad-minded, cheery crowd. He is in a black cassock, wears a purple stock round his neck, and his head is covered with a purple biretta or a scarlet one. A black ribbon is round his neck, and from the ends of this, which meet on his chest,*

hangs a large red cross, on which is a white figure of the Saviour.

[*His Sister is a few years younger, grey-haired, stiff, and formal. She has more common sense than her brother, but, while there is a suggestion of good-nature about the Bishop, there is no suggestion whatever of softness about the form or manner of his Sister. Her dress is of grey stuff, stiff like steel.*

Bishop [*breezily*]. Hello, boys ; good morning, Constable. [*To Nursemaids*] Hello, girls !

Attendants [*together*]. 'Ello, your reverence.

Policewoman [*with a dignified salute*]. Morning, sir.

Bishop [*buoyantly*]. Glorious nip of crispness in the air of a Spring morning, isn't there ?

Policewoman. Exhilarating, I'd say.

Older One. Gits a man goin'.

Younger One [*lilting*]. Yes, let me like a soldier fall, dideray diderum dideree.

Bishop. Flowers appear on the earth ; the time of singing of birds is come, and the voice of the turtle is heard in the land — God speaking of Spring, friends !

Policewoman. Quate, sir.

Young One. 'Its it off nacely, sir.

Dreamer [*to the Bishop*]. Not God, but a poet speaking of Spring, sir. Render to God the things that are God's and to the poet the things that are his.

Bishop [*to the Dreamer — smilingly*]. God is in all, and God is all things, sir.

Atheist [*combatively*]. Would the reverend en' learned

gentleman tell us poor people 'oo is Gord, wot 'e is, en' where 'e is located ?

Policewoman [*to the Atheist, stiffly*]. You keep your almighty arguments for your meetings.

Older One [*viciously*]. 'Ear, 'ear !

Bishop [*to Policewoman — graciously*]. Never mind, Constable ; there are always those who never will give thanks to God for life.

Dreamer. Always, when there are those who have no life for which to thank Him.

> [*Two prowling Evangelists come shuffling in. Each has a frame strapped to his body from which rise two upright pieces between which is a poster, looking like a square banner over their heads. On the first one, in red, is the phrase Once to Die, and on the second, in black, Then the Judgment.*
>
> *The First Evangelist has a lemon-shaped head, staring, stupid-looking eyes, shrunken cheeks, surly lines round a wide mouth, and ears that stick out from the side of his head.*
>
> *The Second has a big head, coarse face, heavy, hanging lips, and a small snubby nose. As he chants, he continually blinks his eyes. Both are shabbily dressed, and look, for all the world, like sullen, long-forgotten clowns. They shuffle in among the disputants, each pointing to the warning posters over their heads.*

1st Evangelist. Once to Die.

2nd Evangelist. After that The Judgment.

1st Evangelist [*chanting*] :
  Is it well with thy soul ?
  Is it well, is it well with thy soul ?

2nd Evangelist [*chanting*] :
    It is well with my soul.
    It is well, it is well with my soul.

    [*They chant themselves out, looking back to gather the others
    into the warning they give.*

Atheist [*mockingly — to the Bishop*]. Two more Richmonds
    in the field !

Young One [*encouraging the Bishop*]. Never you mind 'im or
    them, sir ; — go on torking abaht the Spring en' the
    birds !   [*The birds sing merrily.*

Bishop [*joyously*]. Listen !   The busy birds warbling a
    sylvan sonata.   Facing out life with a song !   No
    shaking of the head here in denial of God's goodness
    and glory.   Sursum corda — lift up your hearts !

Dreamer. We lift them up unto the birds.

Older One [*gushingly*]. The birds bring a man 'ope.   Even
    with the doo 'eavy on the grass, a feller begins to feel
    spry en' elevated when they stert their chirruping.

Policewoman. Not a daht abaht it.

Bishop's Sister. Gilbert, come and look at the swans.

Bishop [*with conviction — to the Policewoman*]. Do you know,
    Constable, that, to an observing mind, it seems to be
    conclusive that the most beautiful part of God's crea-
    tion — apart from man, of course —

Policewoman. Quate — setting man en' woman aside for
    a moment.

Bishop. Quite.   The most beautiful part of God's mani-
    fold creation is, undoubtedly, the birds !

[*The Bishop lifts his head and looks up at the sky ; then the Policewoman does the same, and, lastly, the two Chair Attendants lift their heads and crane their necks in an upward look.*

Bishop. Brave little birds.

Policewoman. Beautiful little birds.

Attendants [*together*]. Beautiful, innocent little birds.

Man with Stick [*suddenly leaning forward — imperatively*]. 'Ere, 'ow do birds resist the lawrs of gravitation ? Come, quick — the lot of you — think !
> [*They all lower their heads again, together.*

Young One [*enthusiastically*]. Never you mind 'im, sir. Wot you says reminds man that Gord watches even over the fall of the sparrer !

Atheist [*mockingly*]. Ay, an' the fall of the 'awk on the sparrer to tear it to pieces !

Older One [*hotly*]. You shut your rotten mouth, will you ! Warnt to 'ear yourself torkin', torkin', do you ? Try to look at things in perspective, carn't you ? Wot's you or me in the general scheme of things, eh ? Speck o' dust, blide o' grass, a nought, a nothing. Wish Jimmy Douglas of the *Daily Express* was 'ere to 'ear you. 'Ee's the man would stun you both with truth ! [*To his fellow Attendant*] Wot d'ye sye, Godfrey ?

Young One. 'Ee's a man as knows 'oo's 'oo en' wot's wot.

Older One. You bet 'ee does. 'Ow on a 'olidye, sitting by the sea, under the stars, wot 'ee sawr en' wot 'ee 'eard. 'Ow 'ee marvelled at the star dust 'ee could see en' the star dust 'ee couldn't see ; en' 'ow 'ee was filled with terror en' fear as 'ee 'eard the clock of eternity ticking !

Dreamer. It won't be long, old man, till you hear the clock of eternity ticking !

Older One [*stormily*]. Wot if it won't ? It ain't the end, is it ?

Dreamer [*rising from the bench — fervently*]. Kill off the withered mind, the violently-stupid, O Lord, who having nothing to give, have nothing to get !

Bishop's Sister [*pulling Bishop's cassock*]. Gilbert, do come to watch the swans !

Older One [*catching hold of Dreamer's sleeve — violently*]. Thinkin' thet life doesn't keep agoing on when it ends ! I yells it aht, I yells it aht — death's only the gytewye to a fuller en' a nobler life !

Dreamer [*angrily shaking off the Attendant's hold*]. Take that dead hand off me ! There are some here equal in value to a countess's baby. [*He shoves the Attendant roughly from him so that he lurches back against the pram.*] Be off, and die, and keep a holy distance from the quick and the lively !

Young One [*bawling to the Older One*]. 'Erbert, eh, mind the countess's byeby !

Atheist [*mockingly — to the Nursemaid*]. Lady, lady, this is no place for a countess's byeby !

Policewoman [*going to the Nursemaid*]. 'Ee's right ; better conduct it to a calmer locality.

[*The two Nursemaids rise hurriedly, cross over the sward, preceded by the Policewoman, and disappear with the pram behind the trees to the left.*

Bishop's Sister [*plucking at his cassock*]. You see, Gilbert ! A bishop should be in the midst of the incense, in the sanctuary, safe away from the sour touch of common humanity.

Bishop [*jovially*]. Nonsense, dear ! I lose no dignity in getting close to the common people. Get them to talk with us ; laugh and joke with us ; and then we can expect them to pray with us.

Atheist [*over to the Bishop*]. Prayer ? For what ? To whom ?
  Old memories, faiths infirm and dead,
  Ye fools ; for which among you deems
  His prayer can alter green to red,
  Or stones to bread ?

Bishop's Sister [*pulling the Bishop away*]. You but mould mockery from the profane thoughts of others. Come and watch the swans. Remember what happened to you in your student days !
  [*The Bishop, at the last phrase, stiffens, his face clenches, and he goes off with his Sister without another word.*

Atheist [*as the Bishop is pulled out*]. He 'as a better charnce with the swans than 'ee 'as with us !

Man with Stick [*calling from top of slope*]. 'Ere, are you comin' to look up wot it says in *The Origin of the Idea of a God* ?

Atheist [*rising to go*]. Must be off, Dreamer. Will you come a bit of the way ?

Dreamer. No ; I've got a song shaping in my mind, and I must think it out : Song of the Down-and-Out.

Atheist [*indifferently*]. Oh, hymn for the unemployed ?

Dreamer. No, no ; not the unemployed. They remain

men in their misfortune. I keen those who whine through today and dread tomorrow ; who would for ever furl the flag of life ; who fear any idea common thought hasn't had time to bless ; those who have a sigh for a song and a sad sigh for a drumbeat.

Atheist. A fair crowd, Dreamer. Well, so-long for the present.

Dreamer. See you at the old place, and we'll have coffee and a sandwich ?

Atheist. I'll be there.

[*He goes off with the Man with the Stick. The Dreamer takes out a notebook, and writes in it. The Gardener appears behind, trimming the shrubs with a pair of shears. The Dreamer then strolls up to watch him, the two Chair Attendants put some chairs in order.*

Older One [*attempting brightness*]. I listened to the wireless last night, Godfrey.

Young One. 'Eard anything worthwhile ?

Older One. Part of Pageant of England. Wunnerful ! Mide ne feel prahd to be en' Englishman !

Young One. Wot was it abaht ?

Older One. The guys as was once kings en stytesmen wot mide us all wot we is. Mide me thrill, it did, to 'ear the sahnd of Drike's drum !

Young One. 'Oo's drum ?

Older One. Drike's. The bloke wot beat the Spanish Armyda, en' drove them back to Spine. A ghost-drum is alwyes 'eard beatin' whenever England's in dineger.

Young One [*scornfully*]. Superstition !

    [*In the distance are heard faint sounds of the sombre music of the Down-and-Out chant, saddened with the slow beat of a muffled drum. The Attendants stand stiff, a look of fright on their faces.*

Attendants [*together*]. The drum-beat of the Down-and-Out !

Older One [*to his companion*]. Wot'r you stiffenin' for ?

Young One [*tensely*]. I warn't stiffenin'. [*A pause.*] Wot'r you styrin' at ?

Older One [*tensely*]. I warnt styrin'. Didja hear anything ?

Younger One [*tensely*]. No, nothing ; did you ?

Older One. Nothing.

    [*They go slowly by each other, one to the left, the other to the right, and go out — a deeper limp coming into each lame leg, keeping time to the distant chant and drumbeat.*

    [*The Dreamer is watching the Gardener working, handling the blossoms.*

Dreamer. Happy man to be handling the purple, blue, and yellow of the blossoms.

Gardener. Let them live and let them die, for I'm not thinking of blossoms at all.

Dreamer. What are you thinking of then ?

Gardener. Of a dance I take a sweet little lass to, when the sun goes in and the stars come out.

Dreamer. I envy you the handling of a flower by day and of a girl by night.

Gardener. When the dance ends, I go to her little flat, her very own flat, where [*he lilts*] She'll be the honey-suckle, I'll be the bee !

Dreamer. I hope a bee that never leaves a sting behind.

Gardener. You should see her — a beauty ! Thinks I'll marry her ; I'm too young to marry yet. Mad to have a kid — matrimony's signature tune ; but not for me, though. An odd lass. A little too serious. Says she wants a chance sometimes to sit and wonder.

Dreamer [*musingly*]. I hear a song in what you've said.

Gardener [*surprised*]. A song ? In what ?

Dreamer. In the flowers, heaven, and the girl.

Gardener. You do, do you ? Funny !
> [*The Gardener goes on arranging the flowers, while the Dreamer slowly goes off till he is hidden behind the shrubs. After a pause, the Gardener begins to sing.*

A fig for th' blossoms th' biggest vase can hold,
The flow'rs that face the world shy, the ones that face it bold.
Men may praise them and worship them as something fine and rare,
Lounging through their gorgeous perfumes so deftly hidden there.
But I'll never wonder though some in glee disclose
The white of whitest lily, the red of reddest rose ;
For I'll fold in my arms a girl as bright as she is gay,
And tonight the primrose path of love will be a wonder way !
> [*Couples, linking arms, enter from different points, mix and cross by each other, parade about, keeping time with the tune as they join in the singing. The Gardener moves out of sight. The Young Woman is seen moving hurriedly*

*among the couples, taking no heed of the singing, weaving
a way through the couples without spoiling the ordered
movements, but she doesn't keep in time with the lilt. She
looks anxious, and appears to be searching for someone.
She disappears while the song is being sung.*

The Crowd of Couples [*singing*] :

When Adam first corner'd Eve, he stood bewildered
there,
For he saw beauty shining through a mist of golden
hair ;
But Eve quickly coaxed him on, and show'd him
woman's way,
And so the lover and his lass are king and queen
today !

So here's to the lasses who bow in beauty's fane,
Who kiss in costly parlour or kiss in country lane ;
Let man bend his back to work or bend down his
knee to pray,
Still the primrose path of love will ever be a wonder
way !

[*When the couples go, the only ones left are the Guardsman
and the Nursemaid, and the Man with the Stick. The
Nursemaid and the Guardsman, who has his arm round
her, go to a bench. He sits down, and as the Nursemaid
proceeds to do the same, he catches her, and sweeps her on
to his knee. The Man with the Stick, who has been at the
butt of the slope shaking his head contemptuously at the
singing, now comes down to where the couple is seated,
and swings his stick in disdain.*

Man with Stick [*scornfully — swinging the stick*]. Nonsense !
A lot of it is all nonsense, nonsense !

Guardsman. Lot of wot ?

Man with Stick. Babble abaht life ! Life, man, life ! Before we can get sense into it, we've gotta know its meaning : wot it is, where it came from, where it goes.

Guardsman. Where wot goes ?

Man with Stick. Life, man, life !

Nursemaid [*indignantly*]. You push off. We want to be left alone. We've important things to talk abaht, so push off, please !

Man with Stick [*taken aback*]. Oh ? If you ain't eager to learn the truth, I'll push off — [*he sees the Two Evangelists approaching, displaying their placards*] now ! [*Muttering as he goes*] Bumptious, brazen ignorance !
  [*The Two Evangelists prowl forward, looking left and right for sinners. They spy the Guardsman and the Nursemaid, and shuffle over slowly to them.*

1st Evangelist [*to the Couple*]. Remember, brother and sister, it's a terrible thing when it comes.

Guardsman. Wot is ? When wot comes ?

1st Evangelist. Death, brother, Death !

2nd Evangelist. An' after death The Judgment !

1st Evangelist. Oh, be converted before it is too late.

2nd Evangelist. Before it is too, too late, too late.

1st Evangelist. It may be upon you today, in an hour, in a moment.

Guardsman. Wot mye ?

1st Evangelist. Death, brother, death !

Nursemaid [*indignantly*]. We want to be left alone.

We've important business to talk about an' do, so push off, please.

1st Evangelist. Left alone ! Devil's desire that, sister. You won't be left alone in hell.

Guardsman [*rising angrily, and pushing them away*]. Here, git ! We wants privacy, so git !

Nursemaid [*rising from bench as he is about to sit down again, having got rid of the Evangelists*]. Let's sit dahn on th' grass, 'Arry — it's more comfortable.

Guardsman. So it is.
[*They recline on the slope. He puts his arms round her, kisses her, and is about to kiss again, when the Police-woman appears opposite, and stares reprovingly at them. She goes over to them.*

Policewoman. You can't do the like of that 'ere. Control yourselves. It doesn't allow such conduct in a public place.

Guardsman [*embarrassed, but trying to be defiant*]. Wot dorsen't ?

Policewoman [*sharply*]. Th' lawr, young man, the lawr !
[*The Couple rise, and go off embarrassed, followed by the Policewoman. As they go off, the Young Woman and the Atheist appear at the top of the slope, and come down it.*

Guardsman [*to the Nursemaid, as they go off*]. As I was asayein', th' orderly officer says to me, Private Odgerson, says 'ee, seein' as you're a man of intelligence, says 'ee, en' th' best shot in the battalion, 'ee says, we warnt your edvice, 'ee says, in a kinda fix we're in —
[*They disappear.*

Young Woman [*indicating a bench to the Atheist*]. I'll sit down on a seat, Dad, for a minute. My legs are giving way under me. Let me sit down a second.

Atheist [*irritably — as they sit down*]. You shouldn't have rushed after me the way you did. En' 'urry up — I've gotta read up some things in *The Origin of the Idea of a God*.

Young Woman [*between breaths*]. I was afraid, if I didn't run, I'd lose sight of you, and I wanted to see you.

Atheist [*as he helps the Young Woman to sit down*]. Damn stupid to rush yourself into a heart attack.

Young Woman [*frightened*]. There's a shadow passing over my eyes again ! [*Grasping the Atheist's arm*] Dad, I'm afraid I'm far from well.

Atheist [*soothingly*]. Just a little flutter from over-exertion, that's all. All our hearts jump at times.

Young Woman [*vehemently*]. I tell you it's deeper than that, an' I'll croak suddenly, sooner or later. The other night I had a man with me, an' when I was half stripped it came on me as he was coming over to paw me. In a mist I saw the fright in his eyes, saw him huddling his clothes on an' hurrying away. Then I fell down. In a faint I fell down, till the morning came an' brought up the woman below to find me still in a faint where I fell down.

Atheist. Excitement, over-excitement.

Young Woman [*hysterically*]. If I have to die, I'll die game ; I'll die dancing !

Atheist. Hush ! Not so loud — we're in a park.

Young Woman [*persuasively catching hold of his arm*]. I want you to help me, Dad; I'll go mad if I have to live alone any longer.

Atheist [*firmly*]. No, no; no more of that. Live your own life. I'm not your father, so cut out the daddy business.

Young Woman [*moving closer to him*]. You crept into a father's place when you took me away from the nuns who were moulding my life round the sin of my mother. You made me call you Dad when you saved me from their crosses, their crowns, and their canes, and lifted my hands up in salute to the sun and the moon and the stars. [*She puts an arm around him.*] You'll give me one more chance, won't you? You will, you will!

Atheist [*restlessly*]. I did that twice before, and, as soon as you felt well, you hurried off, leaving me with rooms I didn't want and furniture I couldn't sell.

Young Woman [*leaning wearily against his shoulder*]. I can't live alone any longer, Dad. When I lie down in bed and stretch out in search of sleep, the darkness reddens into a glow from the fire that can never be quenched.

Atheist [*impatiently*]. Oh, the old, false, foolish fear again!

Young Woman. Green-eyed, barrel-bellied men glare and grin at me; huge-headed, yellow-eyed women beckon to me out of the glow from the fire that can never be quenched. Black-feathered owls, with eyes like great white moons, peck at me as they fly through the glow from the fire that can never be quenched. Save me, Dad, oh, save me!

Atheist [*scornful and angry*]. The hell en' red-fire for ever talk of the nuns ! They frame the world en' fill life with it, till we eat, sleep, work, en' play for ever in the smoke of hell !

Young Woman [*humbly*]. It will be only for awhile, Dad, for I'm going to marry the Gardener. He's not much, but, at least, he is safety, and, maybe, peace too.

Atheist [*impatiently*]. For Gord's sike, put 'im aht of your little 'ead, girl ! 'Ee 'as as much intention of marryin' you as I have.

Young Woman. We're to go to a dance tonight, and afterwards we'll settle everything.

Atheist [*positively*]. I'm tellin' you all 'ee wants is a good en' warm time free o' cost.

    [*A handsome young Salvation Army Officer enters from the right above, crosses slope, and comes down towards a seat some distance away from the Young Woman and the Atheist. He is trying to read a book as he walks along. He is wearing a yellow mackintosh, which is open, showing the red jersey of a Staff Officer. The Officer glances at the Young Woman as he passes, and she returns the look. He sits down on a seat and steals a furtive look at the Young Woman. He meets her eyes and lowers his glance to the ground. He again glances at her, at her face, and then at her legs.*

Young Woman [*turning her thoughts away from the Officer, and pressing close to the Atheist, as she puts an arm coaxingly round his neck*]. You'll do what I ask you, this once, Dad, only this once, won't you ?

Atheist [*firmly removing her arm from around his neck*]. No, never again. Swing along on your own sweet way, and leave your dad out of it.

Young Woman [*tensely*]. You won't ? You won't, Dad ?

Atheist [*in a tone of finality*]. No, I won't !
> [*There is a pause, during which the Young Woman, with tightened lips and a sullen look in her eyes, stares in front of her.*

Young Woman [*suddenly thrusting her face close to the Atheist's*]. I believe in God, see ! And that in the beginning He created heaven and earth.

Atheist [*moving his face away from the Young Woman's*]. I see, I see.

Young Woman [*following the face of the Atheist with her own, while the Salvation Army Officer listens intently to what she is saying*]. And in the resurrection of the dead, when they that have done good shall go into life everlasting, and they that have done evil into everlasting fire !
> [*The Atheist rises from the bench without a word, and goes up the centre path to the slope, and passes out.*

Young Woman [*rising, follows him part of the way, and speaks loudly after him*]. And I believe that God's near them who need His help, and helps them who ask His help — see !

S.A. Officer [*softly and prayerfully*]. God be praised !
> [*The Young Woman returns to the bench, sinks down on it, and begins to cry softly and resentfully. The Salvation Army Officer after a moment's hesitation comes over, looking with a shy interest at the pretty legs displayed by a disarranged skirt, and then slowly sits down beside her.*

S.A. Officer [*earnestly*]. No need to cry, sister, for no one trusts to God in vain.

Young Woman [*resentfully*]. Oh, go away ; I'm miserable,

for he that's gone is the only real friend I have in the
world.

S.A. Officer. God is your only friend.

Young Woman. I've not called upon Him for years, and
He will not hasten to hear me now.

S.A. Officer [*putting his hand gently on her knee*]. God would
empty heaven of His angels rather than let the humblest
penitent perish.

Young Woman [*in low tones*]. If I ask for help, will He hear?

S.A. Officer. He will hear.

Young Woman. And hearing, will He listen?

S.A. Officer. Hearing, He will listen.

Young Woman [*grasping his arm appealingly*]. And listening,
will He grant what the sinner asks, to save the sinner
from a life of sin?

S.A. Officer [*fervently, as he caresses her knee*]. God is able to
save to the uttermost all them that come to Him.

Young Woman [*earnestly, after a few moments' thought*]. I'll
pray and pray and pray till all that's done's annulled,
and all that is to do is blessed by God's agreement.

S.A. Officer [*fervently and softly*]. God be praised, sister!

Young Woman [*becoming conscious that he is caressing her knee*].
Oh, God, don't do that, please! You'll make a ladder,
and silk stockings aren't easy to get.
  [*She pushes his hand away, pulls down her skirt, and looks
  at him questioningly. He stands up, embarrassed, and
  fidgets with his cap.*

S.A. Officer [*nervously*] I must go on, now, to our meeting,

Will you come? [*She is silent.*] No? Some other time, then. I should like to keep in touch with you. Very much indeed. Sister, you are not very far from God. Goodbye.

Young Woman [*in a tired voice, void of interest*]. Goodbye.

[*He turns up the centre path, looks back for a moment at the Young Woman, then crosses the slope, and goes out. She leans her arm on the arm of the bench, and shades her eyes wearily with her hand. After a few moments have passed, the Gardener enters carrying a tall, slender May-pole, painted black. On the top of the pole is a hoop from which hang long green, blue, and rich yellow ribbons. He fixes it in the centre of the sward. The Young Woman, with a long sigh, raises her head, sees the Gardener. She runs over to him, and flings her arms around his neck.*

Gardener [*astonished*]. What has brought you here? Aren't you working?

Young Woman. No, I've given it up.

Gardener. Why?

Young Woman. You know well enough, you know well enough. How often have I told you that the swine of a manager brings good-looking girls, one at a time, to a silent storeroom to sort chemises, and then sends his slimy paw flickering around under their skirts. When he made a clutch at me, I came away.

Gardener [*peevishly*]. Oh, you should have fenced him off as every girl does with a man like that. What are you going to do if you can't get another job?

Young Woman [*coaxingly*]. That's why I wanted to speak

to you. You'll have to live with me ; I'm frightened,
I'm frightened to live alone any longer.

Gardener [*suspiciously*]. Live with you — how live with
you ?

Young Woman [*with calm confidence*]. Marry me, Ned. You
want me or you do not want me. I'm not going to be
just a dance number for you any longer. Do you want
me or do you not ?

Gardener [*nervously*]. Look here, Jannice, I'm busy getting
ready for some damned fools to practise folk-dancing.
They're trying to make England merry again. So I've
no time to talk to you now, dear.

Young Woman [*impetuously*]. Do you want me or do you not
want me ?

Gardener [*coaxingly*]. Of course, I want you, but we can
talk about this tonight.

Young Woman. No, now ; what we say now will last our
lives out. There will only be our two selves — for
awhile ; we needn't have a kid till we can afford one.
[*Appealingly*] You will, you will, Ned ; this means
everything to me, everything.

    [*At the beginning of the Young Woman's appeal, the Man
      with the Stick appears on the slope above, and halts to
      listen.*

Gardener. A kid ! Oh, be sensible, woman, for God's
sake ! We can't talk of these things here.

Young Woman [*vehemently*]. Oh, be a man, Ned, be a man,
and, if you want a thing, take a risk to get it ! I want
something for what I mean to give. Answer me — is
it yes or no !

Gardener [*roughly removing her arms*]. Buzz off, I tell you. I'll see you tonight.

Young Woman. Answer the question : yes or no, yes or no, yes or no !

Gardener [*with a shout*]. No !
  [*The Young Woman looks at him silently for a few moments, then turns away, and goes out, her face tense, but her lips quivering. The Gardener returns his attention to the Maypole.*

Man with Stick [*from top of slope*]. You've lost something, friend, you've lost a lot. If I was young as you, I'd ha' carried 'er 'ome !

Gardener [*resentfully*]. Mind your own affairs. I've got my werk to do.

Man with Stick [*extending the stick towards the Maypole*]. 'Ere, d'ye know what that there pole is a symbol of — what it represents ?

Gardener [*surlily*]. No, en' don't want to know.

Man with Stick. You oughter then ; knowledge is power, my friend. It represents life, new life about to be born ; fertility ; th' urge wot was in the young lass you hunted away.

Gardener [*mockingly*]. You don't say !

Man with Stick. Ay ; en' Pharaoh 'ad one, en' on May Day used to pull it up with golden cords, en' orl the people darnced rahnd it.

Gardener. 'Ow d'ye know ? You weren't there.

Man with Stick. Scholars were, man. Ask any scholar, en' 'ee'll tell you the sime.

Gardener [*stepping back to view the Maypole*]. I'm not con-
cerned with what Pharaoh did or didn't do.

> [*A group of lively Boys and Girls run in, and catch in their
> hands the ribbons hanging from the Maypole. They are
> dressed in fancy folk-dress. They dance round the pole,
> keeping time to the first part of the folk-tune " Haste to
> the Wedding ". Then they suddenly stop as the Young
> Woman enters from the direction by which she left,
> closely followed by the Policewoman. The Young Woman
> is sobbing softly. The Gardener and the Man with the
> Stick stare at them. They cross over.*

Policewoman [*complacently*]. I caught you in the act that
time, my lyedy.

Young Woman [*sobbing*]. It was he spoke to me, miss ; on
my word of honour, it was he spoke to me first.

Policewoman. On your word of honour ! Tell that to the
magistrite when you're in front of 'im. If I'm eny
kind of a guesser, you'll not solicit eny more young 'en
innocent men for a month to come.

> [*The two of them pass out. The Gardener and the Man
> with the Stick stare after them. The Folk-Dancers begin
> again, and dance through the second part of the tune,
> " Haste to the Wedding "*

THE GATES CLOSE

Scene II

Summer noon. The same as the preceding one on a noonday in summer. The colours now are mainly golden glows, tinged with a gentle red. The green on the sward still lingers, but it, too, is tinted with a golden yellow. Instead of daffodils, big-faced hollyhocks, yellow, white, and red, peep out at life from the shrubbery. The Memorial, touched by the sun, now resembles a giant clad in gleaming steel.

The Dreamer enters as the gates open, and passes through them into the Park. He has a thoughtful look on his face, and is gazing at a piece of manuscript in his hand. His right hand moves gently as he beats time with the song that is being sung. People are moving about, all gay with a sensuous enjoyment of the loveliness of the day. They are singing at the top of their bent. The Dreamer passes through them, and goes out.

People [*singing*] :

    Ye who are haggard and giddy with care, busy counting your profit and losses,

    Showing the might of your name unto God in the gay-coloured page of a cheque book ;

    Storing the best of your life in a drawer of your desk at the office :

    Bellow goodbye to the buggerin' lot 'n come out

    To bow down the head 'n bend down the knee to the bee, the bird, 'n the blossom,

    Bann'ring the breast of the earth with a wonderful beauty !

> Ye who are twisting a prayer from your thoughts in
>   the dimness and gloom of the churches,
> Lighting your candle-petitions away to chalk-
>   coloured virgins and martyrs,
> Racking your life for the hope of a cosy corner in
>   heaven :

All Crowd Together :
> Bellow, etc.

Some of the Crowd :
> Ye who in senates, 'n Parliaments, talk, talk on
>   through the day 'n the night-time,
> Talk, and still talk, and still talk, and talk on through
>   the hundreds of centuries passing,
> Till the wide ear of the wide world is deafen'd with
>   wisdom !

> Bellow, etc.

> [*When the song has ended, the Atheist, the Man wearing the
> Trilby Hat, and the Man with the Stick are seen argu-
> ing together. On a bench towards the back sit the
> two Nursemaids, between them the pram enfolding the
> countess's baby. The Bishop is on a seat nearer the front.
> He has been reading a book, but this is now lying open
> on his knee, and he is bending forward to hear the better
> what is being said by the disputants. The two Chair
> Attendants are lying, half asleep, at the foot of the slope.*

Man wearing Trilby. An 'eathen song ! Say wot you
like, you'll find every man at 'eart is religious.

Atheist. Look, brother, no question can be solved by a
generalization. All men are not religious no more'n
all men are liars. The more a man uses 'is mind, the
less 'ee uses Gord.

Man wearing Trilby. If we was to set aside Deity, we'd let loose all manner of evil among ourselves — everyone knows that. There'd be no authority nowhere.

Bishop [*speaking over to them*]. Our friend is right : there must be the few who rule and the many whose duty it is to obey, or there would be an end to order.

Atheist [*to the Bishop*]. It 'as been the few rebels life gave us, the ones who forget to obey, that have rushed the world ahead ! You think of Copernicus, Galileo, en' Darwin — rebels against the thought en' dooty of the time. [*He points an accusing finger at the Bishop.*] There isn't a single rebel in your calendar of saints !

Bishop. Nonsense, friend.

Man with Stick [*with a long-drawn, impatient sigh*]. Aw, wot's the use of arguin' with 'im !

Atheist [*to Bishop*]. 'Ere, d'ye believe that the ten commandments constitoot a competent rule of life en' conduct ?

Bishop [*smiling indulgently*]. I'd venture to say they do, sir.

Man wearing Trilby. I'd sye so, too.

Nursemaid [*joining in*]. Of course they does.

Atheist [*mockingly*]. Christian countries don't seem to think so, then, for even England, dooring the last thirty years, 'as myde over two thousand lawrs, covering sixteen thousand pages of cep imperial octavo, a tidy addition to the lawr of loving your neighbour as yourself, sir.

Man with Stick [*gleefully*]. En' they ain't finished mikeing them yet !

Man wearing Trilby. Where's your authority for thet ?

Man with Stick. [*angrily*].   Where's your authority for wot you sye ?

Man wearing Trilby [*firmly*].   The Bible, sir ;   the 'Oly Book, every word inspired, every verse infallible.

Attendants [*together*].   'Ear, 'ear !

Nursemaid [*with calm conviction*].   Even from time immemorial, the Bible 'as myde truth pline to all people.

Man with Stick [*taking a few steps to go in disgust, and returning to thrust his face close to that of the Man wearing the Trilby*].   Aw, come on, Jenner ;   I'm off — no brrains ! [*He taps his stick heatedly on the ground, and makes to go ;   he hesitates for a moment, then returns and comes close to Man wearing Trilby.*]   'Ere, d'ye believe the Bible where it syes the whyle swallowed Jonah ?

Man wearing Trilby.   'Course I does.

Man with Stick.   You does !

Nursemaid.   En' wye wouldn't 'ee ?

Man wearing Trilby [*tapping Man with Stick on the chest*].   If the Bible said Jonah swallowed the whyle, I'd believe it ;   but I'm not asked to believe anything so absurd.

Man with Stick [*catching the Atheist's arm, and drawing him away*].   Aw, come on, man !   We're just wastin' our knowledge 'ere.   [*They go off.*

Attendants [*as they are going — together*].   Booh !

Bishop [*raising a hand to silence the boobing*].   Friends, let our misguided brothers go in peace.   [*To Man wearing Trilby*] I shouldn't harp too much on the whale story, friend ;   it's but an allegory, you know.

Man wearing Trilby [*indignantly*]. Is that all you know about it ! The Bible says the whyle swallowed Jonah, son of Amittae. It's a plyne fact, en' you should be ashymed to derny it. [*He crosses to go out ; halts ; and turns to glare at the Bishop.*] Tyke warnin' you at wot 'appened to Jonah, son of Amittae, for you're worse'n 'ee was !   [*He goes out.*

Nursemaid [*consolingly — to Bishop*]. Never mind 'im, sir ; 'ee don't know wot 'ee's asaying of.

Older One. Ignorance torkin'.

Young One. Just ignorance.

Bishop [*cheerfully*]. Never mind ! [*He goes over to the Nursemaids.*] Aha, here we have the fair countess's baby. No guile here. The world hasn't been long enough yet with the young lamb. [*To Upper Nursemaid*] And where's your boy-friend — that gallant guardsman I've seen you with so often ?

Nursemaid [*after a moment's hesitation*]. We ain't on speaking terms, sir ; he misbehaved himself by takin' walks with another girl.
   [*The head and half the body of the Guardsman has appeared above the bushes at top of the slope. He stares down at the Nursemaid, dodging down whenever he thinks anyone might see him.*

Bishop. Oh ? Maybe he is sorry.

Under Nursemaid [*to Bishop*]. 'Ee is, sir. It's agettin' 'im dahn. [*To Upper Nursemaid*] I'd try to forgive 'im, Greeta, even if 'ee was to blime. You never knows wot a quarrel 'll lead to — mye mean a parting for ever !

Bishop. In this life, we have to forgive many things.

Under Nursemaid. Besides, 'ee asserted thet it was 'is sister.

Upper Nursemaid [*indignantly*]. 'Is sister ! I seen them in the bushes when 'ee was atuckin' 'er into 'im. No ; I'm determined to be adamant. I don't allow for deception. When 'ee knew how to respect me, 'ee 'ad me ; when 'ee doesn't, 'ee 'asn't ; en' I'm determined to be adamant !

Under Nursemaid [*catching a glimpse of the soldier's head as it pops up and down — excitedly*]. 'Ee's behind the 'edge awatching us, Greeta ! Oh, 'is fice 'as altered, worn en' unhappy like — Greeta, 'ave a 'eart : 'ee is suffering !

Bishop. Do be kind to him, dear.

Under Nursemaid. I feel for 'im when I see the sorrowful look in 'is eyes. You are 'ard, Greeta.

Upper Nursemaid [*rising and tidying the pram, preparatory to moving away*]. A little suffering'll do 'im good. No, Reeta ; unless 'ee writes en' apologizes humbly ; unless 'ee writes en' explines ; unless 'ee writes en' asks me to forgive 'im, 'ee'll never 'ave a chance of being with yours truly agine !

[*She goes off, pushing the pram, stiff and dignified, never glancing at where the head of the Guardsman is gaping over the bushes. She is followed by the other Nursemaid, shaking her head, and sending a sympathetic glance to the soldier. When they have gone, the Guardsman comes down the slope to follow ; but the Bishop halts him by catching his arm in a friendly way.*

Bishop [*sympathetically*]. Friend, a little kindly advice to you : write a humble letter of apology to your sweetheart. Then there'll be harmony, and everything in the garden'll look lovely. [*Smilingly*] Your conduct calls for an apology, you know.

Guardsman [*coldly*]. Ow, does it ? [*Angrily*] En' wot the 'ell is it to you wether it does or not ? Powkin' your big nose into other people's business. You keep off my affyres, see !

   [*He goes angrily off after the Nurses, leaving the good Bishop embarrassed.*

Older One [*with almost tearful sympathy*]. Wot a shime, sir ! You see wot 'appens when religion's lost. Upsets the mind. There ought to be some lawr to mike people respect religion.

Young One. We goes to church reglar, don't we, 'Erbert ? We was brought up thet wye, wasn't we, 'Erbert ? Respectful like.

Bishop [*feelingly*]. I know ; I guessed it from the first.

Older One [*slyly*]. Where's the lyedy as is always with you, sir ?

Bishop [*slyly, too*]. I gave her — what do you call it ? — I gave her the slip, today. My sister, you know ; she's too cautious ; afraid I'll come to harm by being familiar with the common people.

Older One. Harm ! Ahar har ! [*He chuckles at the idea.*] Harm !

Young One. Nice thing to see a clergyman merry an' bright, an' ready to tork to 'umble men, like us — isn't it, 'Erbert ?

Older One. I cencur with thet.

Bishop [*gaily*]. Oh, the Church isn't altogether so solemn an institution as many people seem to think — she can laugh, sing, and skip — at a suitable time, at a suitable time.

Older One. I always said the clergy was 'uman — didn't I, Godfrey ?

Young One. Often en' often.

Older One [*confidently*]. We've a friend 'ere — d'ye know thet, Godfrey ?

Young One. The gentleman's got a kind 'eart, I'd sye.

Older One. You've only got to look at 'is fine fice to see thet. [*Affectionately linking his arm in that of the Bishop's, an act which makes the Bishop stiffen a little in doubt.*] At the moment, sir, the pire of us is in a bad wye, a bad wye ; we 'ave lost our jobs, en' don't know wot to do. A pahnd or two, now, would 'elp a lot — wouldn't it, Godfrey ?

Young One. I'd sye so.

Bishop [*growing stiffer, and withdrawing his arm from the contact of the Older Attendant's*]. No, no, please. My sister deals with all matters of help to the needy. Apply to her. If she approves, she'll assist you. One must be careful in the dispensation of charity.

Older One [*peevishly*]. Aw, your sister wouldn't be no good to us ! She wouldn't listen right. She'd warnt to know the why en' wherefore of everything.

Bishop [*firmly*]. And rightly so, friend. The giving away of money is a great responsibility. She'd be very angry if I did what you ask.

Older One, She'd never know, sir.   Me nor Godfrey would never sye a word — would we, Godfrey ?

Young One. We'd keep it dark, orlright.

Bishop [*decisively*]. No no ;   a rule is a rule, so let us change the subject.   [*A silent pause.*

Older One [*bitterly*]. Chynge the subject !   En' why did you coax innercent people into queuein' up behind the idea of the clergy bein' 'uman ?   [*Hotly*] Whaja warnt to force your company on them as didn't warnt it !

Young One. I knew it all along.   The clergy alwyes fail when they're asked a pline question.

Older One [*indignantly*]. 'Op en' skip en' jump !   Here's one as 'opes they'll 'op outa this place !   [*The Bishop sits down on a bench, takes out his book, and begins to read again.*]   Ow, we're goin' to read, are we ?   Well, if I was asittin' on a bench, en' got a 'int to go, I'd push off — wouldn't you, Godfrey ?

Young One. Quick !

Bishop [*with quiet determination*]. I choose this place in which to rest, and I shall go when I think it dignified to do so.   [*He resumes his reading.*

Older One [*recklessly and loudly — to the Young One*]. Know wot I'd like to do, Godfrey, honest ?   Gambol a gime with en 'eifer in front of a clergyman, strite, I would !   Show 'im a little of the gaiety of life, strite, I would !

Young One. Don't know as it would shock them, 'Erbert — I bet they 'as their 'ectic moments on the sly !

Older One. You bet they 'as ! Wot do they do in their palaces when the lamps is lighted en' the blinds is drawn ? We eats, they eats ; we drinks, they drinks ; we sleeps, they sleeps ; but wot do they do in their palaces when the lamps is lighted en' the blinds is drawn ?

> [*The Young Woman enters, and, after a glance at the Bishop, sits down on a bench directly opposite him. She takes out mirror and puff from her handbag, and gives her face a few deft touches.*

Young One [*giving a few stiff steps of a dance — echoing the Older Attendant*]. Ay, wot do they do in their palaces when the lamps is lighted en' the blinds is drawn !

Older One [*poking him in the side to draw his attention to the Young Woman*]. Look, Godfrey, oh, look ! Wot a peach ! 'Ow would you like to tuck 'er up at night, Godfrey ?

> [*Lines of ugly joy swarm over their faces at the delightful thought, while they stare brazenly at the Young Woman. Suddenly, in the near distance, is heard the roll of a muffled drum, and the mournful chant of the Down-and-Out. The scene seems to grow dark and the air chilly. The two Attendants stiffen, and lines of fright chase away the lines of joy from their faces. The Young Woman, frightened too, turns pale, half rises from her seat, and stares into the distance.*

Down-and-Out [*chanting in the near distance*] :
Life has pass'd us by to the loud roll of her drum,
With her waving flags of green and yellow held high,
All starr'd with the golden, flaming names of her
  most mighty children. [*The chant fades away.*

[*The two Attendants slink out, bent-backed and silent, one to the right, the other to the left, as the chant fades away. The Young Woman, shivering, sinks slowly down on to the seat again. There is a pause. She is very attractive, sitting there in her tailor-made coat and her bright hat. Her slim legs looking slimmer in their elegant silk stockings are for all to see from the knees down. The Bishop suddenly sighs, closes the book he has been reading, puts it in his pocket, and, turning a little round, sees the Young Woman. He looks at her pretty face, thoughtfully bent towards the ground, at her neatly dressed body, and, finally, his eyes linger a little over the slim legs visible from the knees down. An old interest seems to stir in him as he looks at her. Ashamed, he turns his head away for a few moments. He looks at her again, first at her face, then at her body, and then, more consciously, at her legs. He turns his gaze away again and moves uneasily in his seat, lets his head sink forward till his chin rests on his breast. He lifts his head and looks at her ; she turns at the same time, and they stare at each other for a moment ; then the Bishop's head sinks down on his breast again.*

[*Suddenly the Young Woman rises swiftly, as if she had come to a sudden resolution, hurries to where the Bishop is, sits down on the bench beside him, and, catching his arm, speaks to him imploringly.*

Young Woman [*appealingly*]. I want you to help me. You are near to God, but I am out of reach.

Bishop [*frightened*]. Oh, my child, I'm afraid I can help only those whom I know.

Young Woman. Listen to me, listen to me, first. My heart is bad, and doctors say that death may seize me at any moment, and take me out of life. There's a young man who loves me, and is going to marry me, but I want you to come with me to see him, and make him marry me at once.

Bishop [*bewildered*]. But I know nothing about you or about him.

Young Woman. You will, please, you must ; you are a man after God's own heart — you'll help a young girl whose one chance is help at once.

Bishop [*frightened to be seen talking to the girl — looking round him nervously*]. Why do you run to the priest for help only when you begin to feel the terrible consequences of your shame ?

Young Woman [*irritated at the Bishop's thought*]. Oh, I'm not going to have a kid, man, if that's what you mean. Nothing like that for me yet, thank you ! It's because I'd love to have one that I came to you ; — to save me from falling into the condition that could never give me one.

Bishop. But you can't discuss such things with a man and a perfect stranger, girl.

Young Woman. You're neither a man nor a stranger : you are a priest of the most high God.

Bishop [*frightened and petulant*]. Oh, be sensible, girl ! Go and talk these things with your father and mother.

Young Woman [*bitterly*]. I never knew my father, and my mother drinks, and hates me.

Bishop [*reprovingly*]. You mustn't talk like that about

your mother. Whatever she may be, she should be
sacred to you.

Young Woman [*impatiently*]. Sacred to me ! A mother
can be sacred only when she makes herself sacred to her
children ; — can't you understand that, man ?

Bishop [*coldly*]. I have no help to offer you, and I must
ask you to go away, please.

Young Woman [*impulsively sitting down beside him*]. Do
listen to me, please do, Lord Bishop. I've seen you
laughing and talking with common people, and it gave
me heart to speak to you.

Bishop [*in his best manner ; putting his hand on her knee and
patting it*]. Go and live with your mother, and show
her you realise what a mother really is. Work steadily,
cultivate thrifty habits, and in a few years' time you'll
be able to face marriage far more brightly and firmly
than you could possibly face it now.

Young Woman [*trembling and agitated, pushing his hand from
her knee*]. Oh, piping out of you the same old rot that
I've heard a thousand times — mother, work, and
thrift ! [*Indignantly*] If you knew what a rip she was,
I wonder if you'd like to live with her ? I wonder, if
you were a girl, and good-looking, would you bray
about the happiness of work ? [*Raising her voice a little*]
Do you know why I had to fly out of the two last jobs
I was in, had to — d'ye hear — had to fly out of them ?

Bishop [*taking a book from his pocket and beginning to read —
coldly*]. I do not want to know the reason.

Young Woman [*vehemently*]. Because I wouldn't let the
manager see how I looked with nothing on. Oh, you

hide behind your book when facts frighten you. There's many an old graven image has made a girl dance out of her job and chance the streets, sooner than strip herself for his benefit, with nine hours a day and three pounds a week added on to the pleasure.

Bishop [*from behind his book*]. You mustn't annoy me in this way. Please leave me in peace.

Young Woman [*vehemently*]. It's the truth. Can't you put your book down for a second and listen? [*She pushes the book aside.*] Come with me to the shop, and I'll bring you face to face with the man!

Bishop [*beginning to read again*]. Be good enough to go away, please.

Young Woman [*imploringly*]. Please listen to me! Are you afraid to find a lie in what you think to be the truth, or the truth in what you think to be a lie? Come and tell the manager you're my friend, and make him give me back the job I have had to leave. Oh, do, do, please!
    [*The Bishop still remains behind the shelter of his book.*

Young Woman [*after a pause*]. Won't you help me?

Bishop [*in cold and final tones*]. No.

Young Woman [*with quiet bitterness*]. I suppose you'd have helped me had I let you go on handling my knee.

Bishop [*in cold and tense voice*]. If you don't go away at once, I'll have you handed over to the police for annoying me!
    [*The Young Woman sits silent and shocked for a few moments, looking fixedly at the Bishop.*

Young Woman [*mockingly*]. Oh, hand me over to a policeman, would you ? I see. Easy way of getting over a
difficulty by handing it over to a policeman. [*She stands
up*]. Get back, get back, please ; gangway, gangway,
there — policemen making a gangway for Jesus Christ !
[*The Bishop stiffens himself behind his book. With intense
scorn and bitterness*] You and your goodness are of no use
to God ! If Christ came again, He'd have to call, not
the sinners, but the righteous to repentance. Go out
into the sun, and pick the yellow primroses ! Take
your elegant and perfumed soul out of the stress, the
stain, the horrid cries, the noisy laugh of life ; and go
out into the sun to pick the yellow primroses ! When
you go to where your God is throned, tell the gaping
saints you never soiled a hand in Jesu's service. Tell
them a pretty little lass, well on her way to hell, once
tempted you to help her ; but you saved yourself by
the calm and cunning of a holy mind, an' went out
into the sun to pick the yellow primroses, leaving her,
sin-soddened, in the strain, the stain, the horrid cries,
an' the noisy laugh of life. Tell them you were ever
calm before the agony in other faces, an', an' the tip of
your finger never touched a brow beaded with a bloody
sweat !

> [*The horrified Bishop suddenly closes his book, and rises from
> his seat to go away, but the Young Woman with a
> vigorous push from her hand, sends him sitting down in
> the seat again.*

Young Woman [*passionately, thrusting her face close to the
Bishop's*]. A tired Christ would be afraid to lean on your
arm. Your Christ wears a bowler hat, carries a cane,
twiddles his lavender gloves, an' sends out gilt-edged
cards of thanks to callers. Out with you, you old

shivering sham, an' go away into the sun to pick the yellow primroses !

[*As the Young Woman is speaking her last few sentences the Old Woman enters. She is pale and haggard, and vicious lines harden the look of her mouth. Her hair is white, but her black eyes are still undimmed by age. Her thin body is still upright, showing that in her youth she was slim and vigorous, and her face still shelters traces of what were once very good looks. Her boots, though polished, are old and broken, and everything about her, though old and patched and shabby, is clean and neat. Constant, quiet drinking has made her a little incoherent in her thoughts. In one hand she carries a small wreath of red poppies and laurel leaves, which has a bunch of violets where the wreath is tied together by a bow of black ribbon. She had heard the voice of the Young Woman, and comes down to where the girl is speaking, gripping her roughly by the arm as the Young Woman is about to go away from the Bishop.*]

Old Woman [*to the Young Woman*]. Putting yourself again on the market for men, are you ? Piling up money, and not a penny nor the thought of a penny for your lonely and suffering mother. [*As the Young Woman tries to free herself*] No use your trying to get away. [*She drops the wreath on the ground, and holds the girl tighter.*] I have you and I hold you till I get a little to help me on in life for a day or two !

Young Woman [*doggedly*]. I haven't any money ; and, even if I had, I wouldn't part with a penny to you, for all you want it for is drink !

Old Woman [*furiously*]. Drink ! Hear that now ! Is it any wonder God has given her a heart that may go phut any minute ! [*Over to the Bishop*] Hear what she says, you ? That I want the money for drink !

Young Woman [*with a frightened laugh*]. Let me go, will you ? If my heart does go phut, I'll go game, see ! Pass out dancing — see ?
　　[*The Old Woman claws at the girl's hat, pulls it off, and flings in on the ground.*

Old Woman [*wildly*]. Want the money for drink, do I ? I'll tear every stitch on you into ribbons !

Young Woman [*appealing*]. Please, please, Mother, don't ruin the few little decent things I have to wear !
　　[*The Bishop gets up from his seat, goes over to the struggling Women, and tries to separate them.*

Bishop [*trying to restore peace*]. For shame, for shame ! Mother and daughter, — for shame, for shame !
　　[*As soon as she hears the Bishop's voice the Old Woman releases her hold on the girl, and stares at the Bishop. The Young Woman, excited and exhausted, sinks into a seat a little distance away. The Bishop returns the Old Woman's look for a moment, and then rather hastily returns to his seat and resumes the reading of his book. The Old Woman's eyes follow the Bishop and, after a moment's hesitation, she comes up close to him.*

Old Woman [*looking fixedly at the Bishop — murmuringly*]. Your voice has a strange echo in it. Behind that wizened face is hidden a look of the first young man who conquered me on a Sunday night, after the ora pro nobis people had pulled down their blinds and were slinking into sleep. There under a yellow moon, among the shadows by a grove of birch trees, on a bed of flattened bluebells, one of the prettiest fillies that ever wore a skirt was jockeyed into sin, and out of the rapture and the risk came this girl who dares to fancy men more than she does her own mother. [*Suddenly*] Is your name Gilbert ?

Bishop [*over the top of his book — looking very uneasy*]. Go away, you wretched and forgotten creature. My name is not Gilbert !

Old Woman [*still staring at him — murmuring*]. I'm not much to look at now ; but the man who first got the better of me's a big jack-a-dandy in the church, for I saw him once in a holy procession, helping to sing a canticle, a purple cape hanging from his shoulders. [*Suddenly pushing the Bishop's book aside*] Eh, you, is your name Gilbert ?

Bishop [*roughly*]. Get away, get away, woman. My name is not Gilbert. Get away, get away, I tell you !
   [*The Old Woman goes over to the Young Woman, limping, sitting on a seat. The Bishop leans forward with his elbows on his knees and his head in his hands.*

Old Woman [*to the Young Woman — whiningly*]. Why don't you try to be decent to your poor mother ? She won't trouble you for long. I feel a few more months will see the end of me.

Young Woman [*savagely*]. I'd dance and sing if I thought you'd die in an hour !

Old Woman [*wildly*]. You'd dance and sing if I died in an hour ? Hear that, now ? Dance and sing ? How can God listen to such a saying and not strike you dead ? [*Over to the Bishop*] Didja hear what she said ? — dance and sing if I died in an hour ? Come over and bruise her hopes with a grim curse from God.

Bishop [*his hands covering his face*]. Oh, hush, hush, woman ; hush and go home.

Old Woman [*wrathful at the Bishop's indifference*]. Hush, hush, and go home you ! Hear what she said to me, said to her mother ? Dance if I died in an hour, and you take her part. You ought to be driven helter-skelter out of everything holy. Hush you, and go home, with your ora pro pugeree mugeree rigmarolum ! [*Turning violently on the Young Woman*] In league with you, is he ? [*She seizes hold of the Young Woman and shakes her violently.*] Dance if I was dead today, or died tomorrow, would you ?

Young Woman [*terrified*]. Mother, mind ; don't — I didn't mean anything !

Old Woman [*shaking her more violently still*]. I think of nothing but drink, do I not ?

Young Woman [*hysterically*]. My heart, my heart — you'll be the death of me !

> [*The Dreamer appears on the slope above and looks on at those below.*

Old Woman [*fiercely flinging her back so that the girl falls on her knees*]. I'll teach you a little of the duty a daughter owes to her mother !

> [*She raises a hand to strike the girl, but the Dreamer, who has come close, seizes her, and prevents her arm from falling. The Bishop rises, makes a step forward to interfere, but stops in hesitation.*

Dreamer [*gently shaking the Old Woman*]. Now then, now then — what's this ?

> [*The Young Woman pulls herself on to a seat. She is panting for breath. She reclines down on the bench, closing her eyes, while trying to regain her breath.*

Young Woman [*her eyes closed — between breaths*]. Get her away ; send her away, for God's sake !

Dreamer [*firmly conducting the Old Woman out*]. Go away ; go home, old woman, better go home. Let the old pray by the fire, and leave a way for the young to live.

Old Woman [*murmuringly, as she goes out*]. No pity in the young ; only waiting for time to hustle us off. [*She brushes with her hand the laurel wreath she has picked up from the ground.*] The bad present, and the good absent ; the shame living, and the pride buried ; gone from my grasp and my sight in the flame and smoke of the war. Oh, Jesus, is there no rest to be found anywhere !

   [*The Old Woman goes out, and the Dreamer returning to the Young Woman, sees the Bishop beckoning to him. He goes to him.*]

Bishop [*anxiously*]. Do you think she'll be all right ?

Dreamer. Yes ; she'll be herself again in a few minutes.

Bishop [*handing the Dreamer three pound notes*]. Steal over and slip these in her handbag. Don't mention me. I've no real interest in her, you understand ? Still I pity her in a way. I must go now. It's all the money I have with me. I'll return this way again, later on. [*He turns to go, wheels, and grasps the Dreamer's arm tight.*] Please don't be anyway cruel to her. She is — God's child.

Dreamer. I'll watch her till she has recovered.

Bishop. Thanks.

[*The Bishop goes up the slope. The Dreamer steals over to
where the Young Woman is reclining on the bench. He
takes up her handbag ; sees the Bishop's back is turned ;
slips one of the notes into his pocket, and the other two into
the handbag. When the Bishop reaches the top of the
slope, he turns back to look at the Young Woman. The
Dreamer waves a hand reassuringly, and the Bishop goes
out. The Dreamer goes to the Young Woman, and sits
down beside her.*

Dreamer [*to the Young Woman*]. Feeling a little better
now ?

Young Woman [*still panting a little*]. Bit better now. It's
my heart — goes curious now when anything happens.
Please sit down beside me for a minute or two.

Dreamer. For a year and a day, if you like.
[*He sits beside her and takes her hand in his and strokes it.*

Young Woman [*bitterly*]. I'll go off in one of these attacks
yet. Nice thing to have for a mother, isn't she ? I
love the dear silver that shines in her hair ! Feeling
better, now, anyhow. [*Slyly*] Well, how do you like
the hand ?

Dreamer. Lovely — like a blue-veined, pink-tipp'd lily.

Young Woman [*taking her hand away*]. Well, let it go for a
minute, till I straighten myself up a little.
[*She arranges her hat, smoothes the folds of her skirt, gives a
few touches to her blouse, and sits down again.*

Young Woman. I'm a little more presentable now.

Dreamer [*moving a hand semi-circularly over her breasts*].
There's a wrinkle or two in your blouse still.

Young Woman [*taking his hand away*]. Now, now ! Dad's spoken about you. Not the real Dad, — never saw my real father ; don't even know who or what he was. Hard lines, isn't it ?

Dreamer. It doesn't matter very much now, dear.

Young Woman. My second Dad — the Atheist, you know — calls you a poet. How do you live ?

Dreamer. Oh, I sell an odd article, or, maybe, a song or a story, and so manage to live an austere life. But oughtn't you to go home and have a rest ? I'll see you safe there.

Young Woman [*slyly*]. Tuck me up, and sing me to sleep with one of your songs ?

Dreamer [*earnestly*]. I'd love to ! [*He rises and catches her by an arm.*] Come ! Don't let this rosy chance be pulled to bits by prudence. Come, sweet lass, and let's transmute vague years of life into a glowing hour of love !

Young Woman [*pulling her arm free, and speaking somewhat sharply*]. Not so quick, please ! Men are always ready to rush a pretty woman into love, looking for joy, and behold, trouble. Supposing I go and give, what do I get ?

Dreamer. I'll pay your merry kindness with a song.

Young Woman [*a little scornfully*]. A song ! A puff of scented air ! You're out on the hunt for bargains, young man. Go with a priest for a prayer and with a poet for a song ! It's a poor offer, young sir.

Dreamer [*sitting beside her. Earnestly — close to the Young Woman's face*]. Young lady, many great queens and many grand ladies have joyfully snared themselves in the golden meshes of a poet's song !

Young Woman [*laughingly*]. Well, I'm neither a great queen nor a grand lady ; I'm not even a clergyman's daughter.

Dreamer. To me you're a great lady and a grand queen, and it was for you I wrote the song.

Young Woman [*a little recklessly*]. Well, let's see if your little song can snare the hapless heart of a pretty little maiden.

Dreamer. Wait till we get to your flat, so that I can kiss you between the verses.

Young Woman. Oh, you're travelling quick along your own little road, young singer. Sing it now or sing it never.

Dreamer [*resignedly*]. Oh, all right, then. We'll call it by your name — what is it ?

Young Woman. Just Jannice.

Dreamer. What a pretty name ! Well, we'll call the song just *Jannice*. [*He gives a shy little cough and sings. He is standing now, with one foot on the seat of the bench*] :
    Her legs are as pliant and slim
    As fresh, golden branches of willow ;
    I see lustre of love on each limb,
    Looking down from the heights of a pillow !
    Looking down from the heights of a pillow !

Tossed by a soft breeze in the spring,
The blooms of an apple tree billow ;
And her breasts are as lovely to me,
Looking down from the heights of a pillow,
Looking down from the heights of a pillow !

Gay, white apple-blossoms her breast,
Her legs golden branches of willow ;
I'd enjoy for a year and a day,
Looking down from the heights of a pillow,
Looking down from the heights of a pillow !

Dreamer [*after a pause — expectantly*]. Well ?

Young Woman [*not satisfied, but pleased withal on account of the praise that is in it*]. A pretty song, young singer, but its grace and meaning are hardly a fit for me. I cannot live, or even hope, on the sweet sound of a song. Have you nothing else to offer ?

Dreamer [*reluctantly*]. I could give you a pound.

Young Woman. A pound ! A small gift of gold for a grand lady or a great queen ! Have you nothing more ?

Dreamer [*rather wearily*]. A few shillings for a meal today and a meal tomorrow.

Young Woman [*laying a hand almost affectionately on his arm. He covers her hand with his*]. Keep the little you have for yourself, young singer, for your life seems uncertain as my own.
  [*The Bishop has strolled in, and now sits on the bench opposite, apparently reading his book, but really watching the Young Woman. She gives him a hasty, scornful glance.*

Dreamer [*tightening his grip on her hand*]. Well, at least, let me walk across the park with you.

Young Woman [*releasing her hand, and rising*] No, no ; I don't want you. Why do you keep insisting that I need you with me ?

Dreamer. I am thinking, not of your need, but of my own, Jannice.
[*The young Salvation Army Officer enters, and comes down the slope slowly. He keeps looking at the Young Woman.*

Young Woman [*to Dreamer*]. That is selfish. Your way, young singer, though bright with song, is dim with danger. At the end of the way, I might find myself even lower than I am. There is no peace with you. [*She indicates the Salvation Army Officer.*] Here is a real friend who offers peace as a child might offer a friend a new-blown daisy.

Dreamer. His voice is not the voice of peace, but of fear.
[*The Young Woman goes to meet the young Salvation Army Officer.*

Young Woman [*gayly*] :
Good morrow, good morrow, young sir ;
Let's sanction this bold, sunny weather,
By lying aside in the shade,
And cooling warm feelings together !

S.A. Officer [*seriously*]. God's blessing on you, sister, though your thoughtless manner is fashioned to the woe of the world.

Young Woman [*putting her arms round the neck of the Salvation Army Officer — recklessly*]. Oh, come out of the gloom for a moment, dear ! Come into the sun, and kiss me with the kisses of thy mouth !

S.A. Officer [*gently removing the arms of the Young Woman*]. Our ways are not your ways, sister ; we have been led to turn our eyes aside from the gaudy beckoning of the world's vanities.

Young Woman [*a little abashed*]. Sometimes it is very hard to choose. If I lodge where you do, can your people be my people, and your God my God ?

S.A. Officer [*eagerly*]. Ah, if you only will it, sister, it is so ! Out of self, into Christ, into glory ! It is as simple as that, sister.

Bishop [*over to the Salvation Army Officer — sharply*]. The saints didn't find it quite so simple, my young friend.

S.A. Officer [*to Young Woman*]. Never heed him, sister. He would hide God's countenance with a cloud of ritual. Come with me : the yoke is easy ; the burden light.

Young Woman. To peace ?

S.A. Officer. To peace that is perfect, and peace everlasting.

Young Woman. I will go a little way to hear more of the peace that seems so far away. [*She takes the arm of the Salvation Army Officer, and bows mockingly to the Bishop*] Goodbye, old man, who, saving yourself, had no time to save others.

> [*The Bishop does not reply, but sits sadly on the bench looking down towards the ground. The Dreamer sits sadly on the bench opposite, watching the Young Woman go with the Salvation Army Officer. The air of " Jannice " is heard softly, either on flute or fiddle. The Salvation Army Officer and the Young Woman go slowly up the*

slope. When they reach the top, and are about to go off, the Young Woman turns and looks down towards the Dreamer.

Young Woman [*down to the Dreamer*]. I have not quite forgotten your sweet song, young singer !

[*The two go out.*

THE GATES CLOSE

Scene III

The same part of the Park on an Autumn evening. The sky now is a deep rich crimson, faintly touched at the horizon with golden yellow; while the upper part has a plainly-visible and sweeping border of purple and mauve. The leaves of the trees are red and yellow, the trunks a rich bronze. Now and again, one of them flutters to the ground. At the back, against the slope, are a number of tall, gaunt sunflowers, something like those shown to us by Van Gogh. The figure of the Soldier now shows a deep black against the crimson hue of the sky. Chairs having coloured cloth seats and backs, are here and there.

The Two Attendants, looking more haggard and decayed than ever, are lying, apparently asleep, on the slope.

Before the gates open, a band, somewhere in the Park, is heard playing " Land of Hope and Glory ". The music is quite clear and definite, but when the Park is in view the music becomes fainter, as if it was being played at some distance away. The music ceases when the Young Woman and the Dreamer appear.

Older One [*suddenly rousing up and leaning on his elbow to listen*]. " Land of 'Ope en' Glory " ! There's not much of the glory left, en' none of the 'ope. [*He nudges his sleeping companion.*] Eh, Godfrey, 'ear wot they're playin' ? [*Younger Attendant grunts sleepily.*] " Land of 'Ope en' Glory " ! Wot d'ye think of that ?

Young One [*in a sleepy mutter*]. Aw, wot they plays don't concern us.

Older One [*somewhat sharply*]. 'Course it concerns us! Why aren't we part of the 'ope en' the glory? There's that Dreamer, the Atheist, the Man with the Stick, and that gay-dressed young 'eifer goin' abaht good en' proper, denyin' of Gord en' all as is His; en' 'ere we are, two God-fearin', upright men, en' wot's the misery for? [*The Young Attendant takes no notice, so he pokes him.*] Two God-fearin' men, Godfrey, I syes.

Young One [*drowsily*]. Yeh; two God-fearin' young men, ri' enough. I wanna go asleep.

Older One [*bending over and giving him a shake — impatiently*]. Not tykin' no interest in public affaires helps us dahn. Is there a Gord or ain't there? [*His head falls on his breast for a few moments, and he falls back a little in sleepiness, but jerks himself upright again.*] Wot I said before, I syes again: There'll be nothing left if we lift th' pahnd off th' gold stannard. [*He shakes the Younger Attendant again.*] I 'olds we're ruined if we go off th' gold stannard! [*He sinks slowly down on the slope, weary, and full of sleep.*]   [*A pause.*

Young One [*suddenly sitting up*]. En' I syes no! Give the British pahnd a charnce in the world's market. While we keep on sterling, we lose our gold in masses. I olds we're ruined, if we don't go off the stannard.

                             [*He sinks down.*

Older One [*sleepily*]. I 'olds we're ruined if we does!
    [*They both apparently sink into sleep as the Young Woman and the Dreamer appear above, and come down the slope, passing the sleeping figures by. She is pale, but her eyes are asparkle, though she has the Dreamer by the arm, and leans a little on him.*

Young Woman [*as she is coming down*]. I shouldn't have taken the wine, Dreamer. It has made me unsteady, inclining me to see the world fairer than I should.

Dreamer. It was good wine, then. You see clearly, for wine is the mirror of the heart.

Young Woman. I feel uneasy, feeling so much joy.

Dreamer [setting her on a seat]. Wait for me here, Jannice. I must cash the cheque I got this morning. I won't be from you over half an hour.

Young Woman. I wish you wouldn't go, dear Dreamer. Alone, I feel afraid of myself. [A little roguishly] Supposing when you are gone, Salvation's Officer comes and I go with him ?

Dreamer. I'm not afraid of him : there's no peace or joy for you where he is. To him, peace may bring joy ; to such as you, only joy can give you peace.

Young Woman. Still, stay here, Dreamer. I've two pounds I found suddenly in my bag this morning.

Dreamer. Keep them. I'll go. The music of the band will keep you company till I come again. A kiss !
   [He kisses her, and goes, waving back from the top of the slope, while she reclines a little sleepily on the seat, as the Man wearing the Trilby comes hurriedly in, followed as quickly by the Man with the Stick ; he is followed a little more slowly by the Atheist, a Man wearing a Bowler Hat, and a Man wearing a Straw Hat — commonly called " a boater ". They come together, and form an arguing group. Each, excepting the Atheist, carries a big newspaper under an arm.

Man with Stick [calling to Man wearing Trilby]. Eh, stand your ground ! If we wants knorledge, we must ask questions.

Man wearing Trilby [*halting, and letting the rest come up to him*]. Let there be an end of mockery, then.

Man wearing Bowler. Yes ; let's conduct the debate with decorum.

Man with Stick. I wasn't mockin' enyone — I was only mockin' Genesis.

Man wearing Trilby. Well, Genesis is part of me, en' I'm part of Genesis.

Man with Stick [*looking at the sky, and giving a long, impatient sigh*]. Uuh !

Atheist [*gently to Man wearing Trilby*]. You see, friend, your arguments for existence of a Gord can't be the cause of belief, for the reason that the belief was there before them ; and this belief was born into the mind of primitive man by ignorance and fear.

Man wearing Straw Hat. So you say !

Atheist [*turning to him*]. And so say the most eminent anthropologists we have. [*To Man wearing Trilby*] You, my friend, are arguing for the arguments usually set forth to prove the belief, and not for the belief itself which existed before the arguments — see ?

Man with Stick. 'Ee don't warnt to see !

Man wearing Trilby. All I syes is use your eyes, use your ears, use your brine, en' wot's the explyenation of all the wunnerful things we sees en' 'ears arahnd us — on the earth en' above us in the sky — en' I syes Gord myde them orl !

Man with Stick [*impatiently*]. Ah, wot we warnt to know, man, is who myde Gord !

Man wearing Straw Hat [*pushing in truculently*]. 'Ee always existed ! In the beginning all things was myde by 'im, en' withaht 'im was not enything myde wot was myde !

Man with Stick [*with another look at the sky*]. Aw, aw — we're back to Genesis again !

Atheist [*quietly and firmly*]. There never was a beginning, friend. Nothing 'as been myde, en' everything's been evolved out of matter, energy, en' force ; forms chynging, but substance remineing the syme.

Man with Stick [*tapping the ground affimatively*]. 'Course they 'as.

Man wearing Trilby [*hesitant*]. Yes ; in a way, yes ; but even Einstein syes —

Man with Stick [*interrupting fiercely*]. Aw, we're not responsible for wot Einstein syes !

Atheist [*deprecatingly — to Man with Stick*]. Patience, brother.

Man wearing Trilby. Wot first created this matter en' this energy en' this force you speak abaht ? If it was always, 'ow was it always, en' where was it always ? We gets nowhere when we syes thet wot's to come comes aht of wot is, en' wot is, is aht of wot was : it only mystifies a man ; so I syes in the beginning, before enything wot is was, was Gord, en' it was 'e manipulated energy en' force to mike us wot we are.

Young Woman [*who has been listening abstractedly for some time — running a little unsteadily over to them, and pushing her way into the group*]. And aren't you fellows a fine example of what we are ! [*To Atheist*] No beginning ? As it was in the beginning, is now, and ever shall be ; world without end. Amen. See ?

Man with Stick [*indignantly*]. You mustn't interrupt, young woman ! Your mind isn't able to comprehend wot we're torking abaht.

Young Woman. And yours is ? Why, the wisdom each of you has, taken together, would fit on a spoon. [*She pushes them about a little wildly.*] Oh, go away, you little chirrupers, and leave the Park to peace. Let a quiet place enjoy the quietness it gives.

Atheist [*moving off*]. The discussion's ended, gentlemen, for the present. Go and read your papers.

[*He goes off.*

[*The four men, Man with Stick, Man wearing Trilby, Man wearing Bowler, and Man wearing Straw Hat, sit down on the seats having coloured cloth seats and backs. The seats are so placed that if a line was drawn to each of them, the lines would make an X. They take the papers from under their arms, spread them out, and begin to read. Each of the newspapers on the page facing outwards has one large word only. One has Murder, another Rape, another Suicide, on the fourth Divorce. The Young Woman returns, still a little unsteady, to the bench. As the men read, the Band is heard softly playing " London Bridge is Falling Down ". As the tune is played for the second time, the Man wearing the Straw Hat sings the words half to himself.*

Man wearing Straw Hat [*singing*] :
    London Bridge is falling down, falling down, falling down,
    London Bridge is falling down, my fair lady.

Man wearing Bowler [*with complacent dignity — singing*] :
    Build it up with gold and silver, gold and silver, gold and silver,
    Build it up with gold and silver, my fair lady.

Young Woman [*singing with distinct note of denial*] :
   Gold and silver will not do, will not do, will not do,
   Gold and silver will not do, my fair lady.

Man wearing Straw Hat [*singing a little sadly*] :
   Gold and silver's grown a god, grown a god, grown
      a god,
   Gold and silver's grown a god, my fair lady.

Young Woman [*standing up, stamping her foot, and singing
fiercely*] :
   Let it fall to pieces then, pieces then, pieces then,
   Let it fall to pieces then, my fair lady !

Older One [*rising from the slope to lean on his elbow — in a
protesting, whining snarl*]. Wot's yous warnt to make
such a row when two poor men is tryin' to sleep awye
the worries of the world !
               [*The Older Attendant sinks down to sleep again.*

Young Woman [*mockingly — after watching the Readers for a
few moments*]. Let every sound be hushed, for the
oblate fathers are busy reading the gospel for the day.
Furnishing their minds with holy thoughts, and
storing wisdom there.   Let us pray !   Oh, Lucifer,
Lucifer, who has caused all newspapers to be written
for our learning — stars of the morning and stars of
the evening — grant we may so read them that we
may always find a punch in them, hot stuff in them,
and sound tips in them ; so that, outwardly in our
bodies and inwardly in our souls, we may get closer
and closer to thee !   [*Indignantly*] Why the hell don't
you all say Amen !

Man wearing Trilby [*to Young Woman*]. Hush, woman : we
want quietness when our minds are busy.

Young Woman [*rising and moving about among the Readers recklessly*]. I've had a few drinks, but what about it ! A short life and a merry one ! My heart's due to stop beating any minute now, but what about it ! [*She contemplates the Readers.*] Devoted, body and soul, to the love of learning. Listen : Jannice is going to die dancing. [*Vehemently*] Are all you damn perishers deaf and dumb ?

Man wearing Bowler [*with irritation*]. Oh, go away ; we want to read in peace.

Young Woman [*singing softly, but a little drunkenly*] :
　　　Stirr'd by a soft breeze in the Spring,
　　　The blooms of an apple tree billow ;
　　　And her breast is as fragrant to me,
　　　Looking down from the height of a pillow,
　　　Looking down from the height of a pillow !
　　[*She coughs, becomes a little breathless, and presses a hand to her side.*
I'm a sick woman. [*She bends her head down on her breast.*] Death has touched me, and is telling me to be ready ; take your things off, and come with me. [*Defiantly*] I'll not give in, I'll not hold back. And when I go, should God's angels beckon me up or push me down, I'll go game. [*Horrified*] Jesu, Son of Mary, what'm I saying ? I'll fold all the things done in this life round me like a mantle, and wait for judgment.
　　[*She sinks down on a seat, and stares thoughtfully in front of her.*

Man with Stick [*reading from behind the paper marked Murder*]. The condemned man, who is to be hanged for cutting a woman into bits, ate a hearty breakfast, spent an edifying time with the chaplain, smoked a cigarette while being pinioned, and walked with a goose-step to the gallows.

Rest of the Readers [*in chorus*]. Walked with a goose-step to the gallows.

Man with Straw Hat [*reading from behind the paper marked Suicide*]. The dead man left a letter saying, I have ruined thousands and have made many mad ; I have shaken hands with Dukes and Duchesses ; before I put the pistol-point to my ear and scatter my brains, I kiss the pictures of my little darlings ; knowing that, while all men condemn, all men will understand.

Rest of the Readers [*in chorus*]. All men will understand.

Young Woman [*getting up from the bench with a half-hysterical laugh*]. Never say die till you're dead ! [*She looks at the Readers.*] Rape, murder, and suicide ! A bit of a change from the life of the saints. [*Loudly to the Readers*] What will you fellows do when you die, and have to leave it all behind you !

The Readers [*in chorus*]. Go away, young woman — we want quietness.

Man wearing Bowler [*reading from behind the paper marked Divorce*]. The housemaid said she climbed the ivy, got to the verandah, looked in through the window, saw the co-respondent in bed, the respondent in her camisole trotting towards the bed ; then came darkness, and she would leave the judge and jury to guess the rest.

Rest of the Readers [*in chorus*]. Leave the learned judge and jury to guess the rest.
        [*While the last phrase is being chorused by the Readers, the*

Bishop appears on the slope above, looking down anxiously at the Young Woman.

Bishop [*from the slope above*]. Jannice !

Young Woman [*up to the Bishop*]. Are you following me still ? [*Angrily*] Go away, go away and leave me in peace ! Let me run my race in my own way. Don't be mousing after me.

Bishop [*pleadingly*]. I want to help you, Jannice ; let me help you !

Young Woman [*loudly*]. Go away, I tell you ; I want no God's grenadier running after me. [*In a half-scream*] Go away ! [*The Bishop goes back to the Memorial, and the Young Woman again contemplates the Readers.*] What are you all seeking ? You look like a silent gang of monkeys searching for fleas !

The Readers [*in chorus*]. Go away ; we want to read our papers in peace !

Young Woman [*softly and thoughtfully*]. Most important thing, too, is peace ; most important. Peace most pure and peace most perfect, due to the children of the Prince of Peace. [*Recklessly*] But what have I to do with peace ! When I come to the temple of peace, the veil of the temple turns to steel ! Is there no-one far enough from the way of the world to take an interval of rest, and have a look at me ? [*The tune of " The Danube Waltz" has been heard for a few moments before, played softly by the Band. She begins to dance to the tune, in and out among the Readers*] Now, you deaf and dumb perishers, have a look at a lovely pair of legs, if you're not blind as well ! [*She lifts her skirts as she dances, and makes her movements keep time with the tune.*

The Readers look over the tops of their papers and watch her.]
All interested now ? Well, what do you think of
them — saucy, eh ? [*Slapping her left leg*] This one's
lovely. [*Slapping the right one*] This divine ! [*She stops
breathless, and scans them scornfully. The music slowly
fades away. Breathless and scornful*] You bunch of high-
minded .toads, don't look at me long, for there's only
venom for a woman in the things ye think of her. The
dear joy of a sin ye turn to a sting and a bruising. [*She
half sinks on a seat.*] Oh, my heart, my heart's restless
again ! [*She speaks in a lower tone to the Readers.*] In your
looking after a woman there is no kindliness ; before
ye no image of loveliness, neither can ye hear the sound
of a song as ye follow her, for your desire's but a
venomous heat and a shame and a bruising !

[*She sinks down, pale, breathless, and frightened, on the
seat. The Readers return to their reading ; and take no
more notice of her.*

Man wearing Bowler [*reading from behind his paper*]. The
great cricketer, unbuckling his pads, said, You may
take it from me that out there somewhere is a supreme,
infinitely wise mind, which we call God, behind everything. God won't let the English people dahn. He'll
keep our wicket up, and the bat of faith will drive
the bad ball of unbelief far away over the boundary of
England !

Man with Stick [*with scornful disgust*]. Wot the 'ell does a
cricketer know abaht them abstruse things !

Young Woman [*who has been moving uneasily on the bench*]. I
can't breathe, I can't breathe ! [*She pulls the neck of her
bodice open.*] It's on me again, but I'll go game, I'll go
game. Eyes front up or down ! [*The Bishop begins to*

*come down slowly towards the Young Woman. In a panic of
fear*] Dance, sing, and strip for the fun of the thing —
that's all they want from a woman ! A sigh, a sob of
pain, a thought higher than their own from a woman,
and they're all hurrying home. [*Turning towards the
Readers*] God damn you, will none of you stir to help
when you see a Christian in danger ! [*She calls out in a
semi-scream*] Dreamer, Dreamer — where's the Dreamer !
   [*She sinks down half fainting on the bench. The Bishop
   comes quickly to her, now, and chafes her hands. The
   Readers have risen from their seats, have folded up their
   newspapers, and now come to where the Young Woman
   and the Bishop are, forming a semi-circle around them.*

Bishop [*gently and fervently*]. Jannice, my little Jannice,
   I've come to help you ; everything will be all right
   soon. [*Addressing the Readers*] Don't gather round,
   friends. Leave the girl to me. I'll watch over her.
   [*As they don't stir — sharply*] Leave us alone, I say, and
   don't stand there, staring like apes ! [*All but the Man
   with the Stick go silently and slowly out. To Man with the
   Stick*] Didn't you hear me tell you to go away, man ?

Man with Stick [*indignantly*]. 'Oo are you to sye come en'
   'e cometh, en' go en' 'e goeth ? Wot she warnts is a
   doctor, en' not a pryer !

Bishop [*in a burst of fury — using some of the strength of his
   younger days, and pushing him out roughly*]. Oh, go to
   hell !
   [*He returns to the Young Woman as she recovers slightly,
   looking up at him without any confidence in her look.*

Bishop [*returning a little to formal speech, but softly, and with
   feeling*]. You are ill, my child ; and you are lonely.
   You have forgotten God for a few moments, but He

sends you His help in time of trouble ; and, through me, unworthy messenger, a share of His sympathy and love.

[*He sits down beside her. She recovers a little, sits up, and stretches out a hand to him, which he takes in his own, and strokes gently.*

Young Woman [*with a sigh of relief*]. I'm glad you came. I was very lonely. My heart's beating a bit steadier now, thank God.

Bishop [*gently patting her hand*]. That's good, now ; that's good.

Young Woman [*regaining confidence*]. A lot steadier now. I think it's more fear than anything else. I've had a hard time of it ; and I get into a panic whenever my heart gives a double-time beat. I feel nearly normal again.

Bishop [*encouragingly*]. That's good. Keep calm for a little while and you'll soon be all right.

Young Woman. I'm waiting for the Dreamer. He'll be here shortly, and then I'll be safe again.

Bishop [*still stroking her hand — a little coldly*]. My child, I shouldn't think too much of the Dreamer, or make a friend of him. The things he writes give scandal, and tend to undermine morality and overthrow tradition. He is a bad influence, my child.

Young Woman [*taking her hand out of the Bishop's — firmly*]. I won't hear a word said against the Dreamer. He was the only one from whom I got courage and help. The Atheist, when he acted as my dad, was kind, too, in his own self-interested way. [*She looks innocently into the Bishop's face.*] I never saw my real father. Mother often said he had a high place in your church ; but he never had the courage to come and claim his child.

Bishop [*coldly*]. From what I saw of her, your mother isn't to be trusted.

Young Woman [*emphatically*]. Well, the Dreamer is. He is as poor as I am, but he gaily shares with me his money and his joy. So, you see, he is more important to me than the God you praise.

Bishop [*shocked*]. You mustn't say such things, my child ! I am here to help you, showing how kind and gentle God can be to — er — a straying lamb seeking in devious ways to find a way back to the waiting flock.

Young Woman [*fretfully*]. Oh, the flock doesn't care a damn whether I'm in or out, man. The flock ! So long as they get their four meals a day, with a gay hour after, and a cosy fire in the Winter, they'll never stretch a neck to see where a ram or a ewe has wandered.

Bishop [*soothingly*]. Well, never mind, now, and don't let your thoughts irritate you into any excitement, child. What you need most, now, is rest, and a chance to live a sober and a quiet life.

Young Woman [*more irritably than ever*]. And follow the commandments of God — always trying to crimp people into piety. You cross, crown, and anchor boys expect the very linnets to sing hymns in their spare time. The Salvation Army Officer, too, has the same gloomy glimpse of life. Miserere, miserere, all the way to heaven !

Bishop. Hush. Forget everything but your own help-lessness ; and don't get excited.

Young Woman [*vehemently*]. I have to get a little farther away from the devil before I try to get a little nearer to God. I've a long way to travel yet before the white and holy candles are lit, and the golden incense scattered.

Bishop. My child, the sinner is always nearer to God than the sinner dares to think.

Young Woman [*a little hysterically*]. Amen, and let us get to business. Make me safe and make me happy, and I'll give sweet thanks to God. Why've you been following me about for days ? I sought you once, and you sent me empty away. Why do you want to help me now ? [*Indicating sleeping Attendants*] Why don't you try to help those poor sleeping devils there ?

Bishop [*a little impatiently*]. Oh, it would be waste of time to think of them.

Young Woman. They're still God's children, aren't they ?

Bishop [*more impatiently*]. We'll see about them another time. You seem to be an interesting case — young and intelligent. You don't seem to be an ordinary — eh — what shall I say ?

Young Woman [*bitterly*]. Oh, a whore ! You may as well say it as think it. [*The Bishop is shocked at the girl's bluntness. He stiffens, and stays silent. Looking intently at the Bishop's face*] What was it made you light on me, I wonder ? There are hundreds of girls, some of them better, some of them worse, than me, and it's curious that I should be the lucky dip. [*The Bishop remains silent.*] Well, go on ; open up the overture, and play us something nice.

Bishop [*trying to control his impatience*]. My child, your present way of life is an evil one. I wish to give you a chance to turn aside from it ; so please try to be decently attentive, and listen seriously to what I am about to say.

Young Woman [*with a half-suppressed giggle*]. Wine's beginning to take effect again. I had a wild time all this week with the Dreamer. He got an advance on a book that's to be published soon, and he's gone for another advance now. [*She prods the Bishop's breast.*] If he comes back before our treaty's signed, I'm off, and you won't see me again till what he gets is gone : so go ahead, and strike a light, and let us see the way we're walking.

Bishop [*with gloomy indignation*]. I can't listen any longer to these frivolous remarks. You have no pity for yourself. You have gone too far away for any helping hand to reach. I will leave you alone. [*He rises from the bench to go.*] I have done my best. I will leave you alone.

Young Woman [*catching his cassock — pleadingly*]. No, no ; don't go away. I will listen ; I will listen quietly ; I promise. Be kind, and help me. I do want to try to do what is lawful and right. In God's name, be kind, dear Bishop.

Bishop [*rather sternly*]. Listen, child, then, and be serious. When trying to help you, I must be careful of what others may think.

Young Woman. Why have you to be careful ? Can't you yourself pray, or push yourself out of the fear of what may be said about you ? What does it matter how many say a man's a sinner if God thinks him a saint ?

Bishop [*very annoyed*]. I can't waste time going into those questions now. You said you were going to be serious. Well, then, one more flippant word and I leave you, never to turn a thought to you again.

Young Woman [*earnestly*]. I will be serious ; I promise. I fix my face, and am serious. I'll do anything you ask me to do.

[*She pulls gently at his cassock, and he slowly resumes his seat on the bench beside her.*

Bishop [*with some embarrassment*]. I'm about to say something now which, I fear, will sound very unpleasant to you, perhaps even harsh and ungenerous ; something that will bite deeply into all that you may think to be a pleasure. [*He puts a hand gently and appealingly on her shoulder.*] God alone knows, my dear daughter, how deep is my desire to save you !

Young Woman [*with calm and innocent confidence*]. Oh, with your power and position, you should be able to push me into a job that wouldn't make the change such a sad one.

Bishop [*taking his hand from her shoulder, and speaking harshly*]. I wouldn't think of getting you a place till, after a year or two of trial, I felt certain you had learned how to behave yourself.   [*A pause and a tense silence.*

Young Woman [*with a stifled sob of humiliation*]. I see. [*A pause.*] How am I to live through the two years ?

Bishop [*forcing himself to speak harshly*]. I've arranged that a pious Sisterhood should receive you into their Hostel, where the Reverend Mother will care for you, watch over you, and help you to live with becoming circumspection. In return, when you begin to feel at home, you can make yourself useful to the good Sisters.

Young Woman [*with tightened lips*]. I see.

> [*The Policewoman enters, crosses in front of the Young Woman and the Bishop, and looks fixedly and wonderingly at the pair of them. The Young Woman looks down at her feet and the Bishop stares in front of him.*]

Policewoman [*speaking towards the Bishop*]. Nice die, m'lud.

Bishop. I beg your pardon?

Policewoman. Said it was a nice die, m'lud.

Bishop [*stammeringly*]. Oh yes, quite; lovely day, beautiful day; yes, indeed, a very beautiful day. [*The Policewoman, watching them as long as possible, goes slowly out. Appealingly*] Why do you keep silent? Take your chance, take your last chance; for God's sake take your last chance. [*The Young Woman sits silent.*] Do you hear me? The offer I have made is a good offer. In it is peace, and a fair hope of better things to come. Go on, girl, speak; make up your mind, make up your mind.

Young Woman [*rising with hysterical laughter that rouses the sleeping Attendants, who lean on their elbows, watching*]. Wine's beginning to take effect again. Your old mind must be worn out thinking of such a wonderful plan. He lifted me up and set me down in the midst of a holy sisterhood. Refugium peccatorum, but not for me, thank you kindly. [*She bows mockingly to the Bishop.*] Chained fast to prayer and firm to fasting! [*She puts her face near the Bishop's.*] Not for me, thank you kindly!

Bishop [*with intense feeling*]. What will you do when your good looks go, and you lose the means to earn your bread?

Young Woman [*with a snarling look on her face as she thrusts it close to the Bishop's*]. Die, I dare say, while you heap up hopes in the books of a bank, and carry your faith about in a coffin !

> [*She hurriedly opens her handbag, takes out two notes, and holds them close to the Bishop's nose. The Two Attendants are now alert, and are watching intently.*

Young Woman [*viciously*]. See, old purple buttons — the last two between all I need and me ! [*She rolls each into the shape of a crumpled ball, and calls to the Attendants.*] Eh, you there — up, and see what God has sent you ! [*She flings a crumpled note to each of them. They open them, smoothe them out, and put them joyously into their pockets. To the Bishop — recklessly*] I fling my wealth away ! [*She points a finger at the Bishop's nose.*] Faith in God, old purple buttons, faith in God ! Be merry, man, for a minute, for you'll be a long time dead ! [*The Bishop, full of sorrow and disappointment, mixed with shame, bends forward on the seat, and rests his head in his hands. The Young Woman dances round with mock stateliness as she sings words to the tune of "Little Brown Jug". The Two Chair Attendants, as far as their game legs will allow, imitate her in a reckless manner, beating out time, one with his good right leg, and the other with his good left one. Singing and dancing round with mock stateliness*] :

> Sing and dance, dance and sing,
> Brief life should be a joyous thing ;
> The minds that are to troubles wed
> Are fit to host but with the dead !
> Ha ha ha, you and me, till we both have ceased to be,
> Sling out woe, hug joy instead,
> For we will be a long time dead !

Chair Attendants [*joining vigorously in*] :
> Sling aht woe, 'ug joy instead,
> For we will be a long time dead !

Young Woman [*singing*] :
>   Life is born and has its day,
>   Sings a song, then slinks away ;
>   Speaks a word — the word is said,
>   Then hurries off to join the dead !
>   Ha ha ha, you and me, till we both have ceased to be,
>   Sling out woe, hug joy instead,
>   For we will be a long time dead !

Attendants [*joining in*] :
>   Sling aht woe, 'ug joy instead,
>   For we will be a long time dead !

> [*During the singing of the second verse of the song the Atheist has made his appearance on the top of the slope, and stands there watching what is going on below. As the Young Woman is ending the latter verse of the song, the drum-beat and chant of the Down-and-Out is heard in the near distance, coming nearer and nearer. The Chair Attendants hear it, stiffen with fear, and end the chorus weakly. Then the Young Woman recognises it, and stands stiff, frightened, while she listens intently. Together.*] The drum-beat and chant of the Down-and-Out !

> *The scene grows dark and chilly, and even the Bishop shivers, though the Atheist seems not to notice the change. The sky seems to turn a cold grey, and against it, the Down-and-Out pass by. They are all grey, vague figures of young and old men and women, hopelessness graven on every grey face. They go by in a rather slow shuffling march, chanting their miserere to the monotonous tap, tap of the drum-beat. They go behind the Atheist, but he stands there, indifferent to march or chant. The Attendants sink down to their knees, one on the right of the grass sward, the other to the left of it.*

Down-and-Outs [*chanting*] :

We challenge life no more, no more, with our dead faith, and our dead hope ;

We carry furl'd the fainting flag of a dead hope and a dead faith.

Day sings no song, neither is there room for rest beside night in her sleeping ;

We've but a sigh for a song, and a deep sigh for a drum-beat.

Oh where shall we go when the day calls ?

Oh where shall we sleep when the night falls ?

We've but a sigh for a song, and a deep sigh for a drum-beat !

[*The Down-and-Out pass out, their song fading out in the repetition of the line, " We've but a sigh for a song, and a deep sigh for a drum-beat ".*

Bishop [*pointing towards where the Down-and-Out have gone*]. There go God's own aristocracy, the poor in spirit ! Their slogan, Welcome be the Will of God ; their life of meek obedience and resignation in that state of poverty unto which it has pleased God to call them, a testimony that God's in His heaven, all's well with the world. [*To the Attendants*] Join them, my sons. [*To Young Woman*] Join them, my daughter, in the spirit of penitence and prayer !

Atheist [*from the slope above*]. Jannice, stand firm, and remember that you are the bride of the Dreamer. Tell him that the world shall be, not what his God wills, but what fighting man can make it. Tell him you have given life a dance and the Dreamer has given life a song !

Bishop [*coming close to the Young Woman, who is leaning for help on the back of a bench*]. They came close, my child, they came close. They will get you some day, if you do not let me save you now.

Young Woman [*with a quivering lip*]. No !

Attendants [*together*]. Save us, sir ; save us !
        [*The Bishop takes no notice of them.*

Bishop [*bending over the Young Woman*]. The day is fair, my daughter, the day is fair ; but what of the night, when youth has faded, and the shadows fall, and the heart is lonely ?

Young Woman [*tonelessly, but defiantly*]. When youth has gone, when night has fallen, and when the heart is lonely, I will stand and stare steady at a God who has filled the wealthy with good things and has sent the poor empty away.

Bishop [*sorrowfully*]. Don't say such things, child. Come with me, I beg of you to come with me.

Young Woman [*with tight lips*]. No.
 [*The Bishop looks sadly at her for a moment, then turns and goes slowly up the slope.*
 [*The Young Salvation Army Officer followed by other members of the Army, all in uniform, peaked caps and red jerseys, come in, and group themselves in a half-circle, near the centre, to the left of the grass sward. One of them has a trombone, another a cornet, and a third, a big drum. Beside them is raised the red and blue and yellow banner of the sect. A small, box-like stand is placed on the grass, so that a speaker may be raised a little above the crowd. Around them gather various people, among them the Man wearing a Bowler Hat, the Man wearing a Straw Hat, the Man wearing a Trilby,*

*the Nursemaid with her Guardsman, the Attendants,
and the Man with the Stick, who stands off, nearer to the
Atheist, as if for protection. The Young Salvation Army
Officer stands out to watch the Bishop going slowly up
the slope. When he reaches the top, he turns, and speaks
pleadingly down to the Young Woman.*

Bishop [*making a quiet sign of the cross*]. My poor child, I ask
you, in the Name of God — come !

Young Woman [*firmly, though her lips quiver a little*]. No !
[*The Bishop looks sadly at her for a moment, and then turns,
goes by the Atheist, and passes out. The Young Woman
reclines weakly back on the bench, silent and desolate-
looking. The scene brightens and the birds sing once
more. The Young Salvation Army Officer goes over close
to the Young Woman.*

S.A. Officer [*to Young Woman*]. The ritualist has left you
in your need, but the evangelist is here to comfort and
help you — if you will. Dear sister, set your foot, by
faith, on the path that leads to the land that is fairer
than day ; where the Father waits to prepare you a
dwelling-place — a house not made with hands, eternal
in the heavens.
[*She is silent, and stirs not. He quietly signals to the
musicians, and they softly play the tune, " There were
Ninety and Nine ", the rest of the Army and some of the
crowd singing the words.*

Crowd :
There were ninety and nine that safely lay
In the shelter of the fold,
But one was out on the hills away,
Far off from the gates of gold,

Away on the mountains wild and bare,
Away from the tender Shepherd's care ;
Away from the tender Shepherd's care.

S.A. *Officer* [*to Young Woman*]. You, sister. But the Lord
was anxious, and would not be satisfied with His ninety
and nine who were safe. So He set out to find His lost
sheep — you, dear sister, you !

[*He again quietly signals the musicians, who play the air
again, while the rest sing the words.*

Crowd :

But none of the ransomed ever knew
How deep were the waters crossed,
Nor how dark was the night that the Lord pass'd
through,
Ere He found His sheep that was lost.
Out in the desert He heard its cry —
Sick and helpless and ready to die ;
Sick and helpless and ready to die.

[*The Young Woman is visibly affected. She rises from
the bench, and half turns towards where the Salvation
Army members are grouped. The Young Salvation Army
Officer, seeing this, lays a hand gently on her shoulder.*

S.A. *Officer* [*with uplifted eyes — prayerfully*]. There is a
young sinner with us now who needs the pardon Christ
can give. Let her come to the foot of the cross. She
must struggle down to the cross before she can climb
up to the crown. Brothers and sisters, let us pray that
she may turn from her sin, and be saved ! [*As he is
speaking the Dreamer appears on the top of the slope above, gets
in front of the Atheist, and stands to look at what is happening.*]
Save this wandering lamb, O God, and bring her
safely home !

Salvationists [*in chorus*]. Save her, great and most merciful Redeemer !

S.A. Officer. That the trumpets of the angels may have a new note in their sounding !

Salvationists [*in chorus*]. Save her, great and most merciful Redeemer !

S.A. Officer. That the crown of thorns on the head of the crucified one may shine as the sun in the season of summer !

Salvationists [*in chorus*]. Save her, great and most merciful Redeemer !

S.A. Officer. That the nails in His hands and His feet may gleam like the moon at the full in the season of harvest !

Young Woman [*in a frightened voice*]. Ah, save me from the fire that is never quenched, and give me peace !

Dreamer [*from the slope above*]. Jannice, Jannice, the Dreamer calls !

  [*The air of " Jannice " is faintly heard, as if from a distance. The Young Woman stands listening, and the look of fright fades from her face.*

S.A. Officer [*up to the Dreamer*]. Go your wild way, young man ; for our sister has shut herself away from the pride and vanity of your thoughtless life.

Dreamer [*to S.A. Officer*]. The rose that once has opened can never close again. [*To the Young Woman*] Jannice, here is peace ; peace unharmed by the fire of life. I have that will give another month of gay and crowded life ; of wine and laughter ; joy in our going out and our coming in ; and the dear pain from the golden flame of love. Jannice, the Dreamer calls !

[*The tune of " Jannice " is heard much more clearly now. The Young Woman has retreated away from the Salvationist group ; now the Young Salvation Army Officer holds out his arms to her, but she backs away from him and half turns towards the Dreamer.*

S.A. Officer [*sadly*]. Let us all pray silently and together against the power trying to draw our young sister from the offer of redemption.

[*The Attendants fall on their knees, and with outspread fingers cover their faces. The Men Salvationists remove their caps and bend their heads in an attitude of prayer. The Women Salvationists do the same, but do not remove their bonnets. The Young Salvation Army Officer takes off his cap, and covers his face with one hand. The tune of " Jannice " is heard clearly.*

Dreamer [*taking a step down the slope*]. Jannice, the Dreamer calls you to the deep kiss and clutch of love ; to sing our song with the song that is sung by a thousand stars of the evening !

[*The Young Woman moves slowly away from the praying group, gradually quickens her movement, till finally she runs to be clasped in the arms of the Dreamer ; while the Atheist looks down on the Salvationists with a slight twist of mockery disarranging his lips.*

[*The Young Salvation Army Officer glances up, and sees that the Young Woman is about to go with the Dreamer. He bends his head on his breast — a picture of disappointment, and, maybe, of vanity cheated of its due. The Musicians, replacing their caps on their heads, play the tune of " Ninety and Nine " very softly, and the rest sing the words as softly, too, for the tune of " Jannice " has faded away as the Young Woman goes into the arms of the Dreamer, as the Dreamer and the Young Woman pass out on their way together.*

Oh, sad is the fate of the lamb who strays
Far off from her Shepherd's care,
Leaving fair fields where the sunlight plays
For the gloom of the mountains bare ;
Oh, sad is the Shepherd seeking his sheep,
To find that his lov'd one is nowhere there ;
To find that his lov'd one is nowhere there !

THE GATES CLOSE

Scene IV

A Winter's night in the Park. The colour of the sky is a deep black, brightening from the centre to the horizon to a rich violet, deepening to a full purple hue. To the right, where the purple sky begins to sink into the darkness, is a group of stars; one red, the other golden, and a third, silver. The trees are quite bare of leaves, and their branches form a pattern against the purple parts of the sky.

Light from an electric lamp behind the War Memorial shines on the head and shoulders of the figure, making them glow like burnished aluminium; and the bent head appears to be looking down at the life going on below it.

A Group of Men are standing to the right, looking as if they were directly under the stars. They are the Man wearing a Trilby, the Man wearing a Bowler Hat, the Man who wore a Straw One, but now is wearing a Tweed Cap, the Man with the Stick, and some others. They are all wearing topcoats or mackintoshes, and their collars are pulled up as high as they can go around their throats. The Man with the Stick now carries an Umbrella. As the scene is opening, the latter part of the bugle-call, The Last Post, *is heard sounding in the far distance.*

Man wearing Cap [*to the Others*]. Wot's that, now?

Man wearing Bowler. Sounds like *The Last Post*.

Man wearing Trilby. It is *The Last Post*.

Man wearing Cap. Wunner where's it from?

Man wearing Trilby. From the barracks up Kensington way. You can 'ear any sound pline on a still, clear night like this one.

Man wearing Bowler. Creepy sound, 'asn't it ? Alwyes mikes me think of grives when I 'ears it.

Man with Umbrella. En' wot if it does ? A grive's as common as a crydle, man, en' we've no caurse to be afride of either.

Man wearing Cap. It's easy to talk, but a grive's a grive ; en' with winter 'ere, en' the Park nearly desolyte, the sahnd of *The Last Post* 'as en eerie effect on me.

Man wearing Trilby [suddenly]. 'Ere 'e is agine ! Like 'Amlet's ghost. Wot interest 'as 'e in the girl, I wunner ?

Man with Umbrella. Up to no good, I bet. No bishop ever is. Keep back in the gloom so as 'e won't see.

> [*They retire a little.*
> [*The Bishop comes down the slope, looking from right to left, then stopping to look behind him. His face is grey, and a deep look of worry lines it. He is followed by his Sister, who looks stern and appears to be annoyed.*

Bishop's Sister [with suppressed anger]. Gilbert, for goodness' sake, have sense. Why do you trouble yourself like this for a trollop ?

Bishop [angrily]. Don't call her by that name ; I won't have it, I won't have it !

Bishop's Sister. You're a fool, Gilbert ! She never was your child ; and even if she ever had a claim, she ceased to be your child when we put her into the Institution.

Bishop. Even if she ceased to be my child, she, nevertheless, remains a child of God ; she still has her claim to the kingdom of heaven. I must not forget that now ; I must never forget that again !

Bishop's Sister. If you go on like this much longer, Gilbert, you'll find yourself becoming ridiculous to respectable and important opinion.

Bishop [*vehemently*]. That has been my besetting sin all along — fear of the respectable opinion of others. I renounce it now ! She herself has said, What does it matter how many think a man to be a sinner if God believes him to be a saint. That's what she said — to my very face.

Bishop's Sister. Just like the impudent and semi - blas - phemous thing such as she would say !

Bishop [*impatiently*]. Don't waste time talking, woman. [*Catching her arm*] Look at that figure out there in the shadows. [*He points with his finger.*] Can you see ? Is it she ?

Bishop's Sister [*freeing her arm*]. I refuse to look ! What has happened to you, Gilbert, after all these years of forgetfulness ? Why do you suddenly so concern your-self with such a trivial thing.

Bishop. A human soul is not a trivial thing.

Bishop's Sister. Some souls are, and well you know it, and she is one of them. I tell you this fancy solicitude of yours is just a sentimental fear of something done years ago in a foolish moment. I tell you, such a soul is a trivial thing to be a torment to you.

Bishop [*sadly*]. Not hers, but our souls, I'm afraid, are the trivial things in the sight of God, and in the minds of brave men. [*Fiercely*] But mine's going to be trivial no longer ! I go to seek her, and don't follow me.

Bishop's Sister [*doggedly*]. I will follow you ! You're not sensible enough to be left alone.

Bishop [*angrily*]. Go home, woman. Being too sensible has been my curse all along. By trying to save my honoured soul, I am losing it. Go home, woman, and let me find a way to my girl and my God !

[*He hurries away among the trees to the left, and, after a moment's hesitation, his Sister follows him. The Man with the Umbrella comes out from the group, and peers after them. The others, too, come out of the gloom and join the Man with the Umbrella in staring towards the direction in which the Bishop and his Sister have gone. As they stare, the Guardsman and the Nursemaid, arm-in-arm, enter from the opposite direction, and, seeing the men staring, are interested, so they join the group of peerers.*

Man with Umbrella [*pointing with his umbrella*]. There they go, one after the other — foller my leader like. Thet sister of 'is'll 'ave to keep a close eye on 'er brother. At 'is age too, runnin' after a girl as might 'ave been 'is daughter !

Guardsman [*wonderingly*]. 'Oo ?

Man wearing Trilby. Now, now ; the gentleman 'as no evil aims in 'is afollowing 'er. I 'eard 'im sye 'e warnted to save 'is soul en' 'ers.

Guardsman [*wonderingly*]. 'Oo's soul, wot soul ?

Man with Umbrella [*contemptuously*]. Soul ! There ain't no soul. Wot you 'ave in your mind is mind ; the mind wot conquers time, spice, en' material conditions.

Man wearing Trilby. En' when did mind begin, en' 'oo myde it ?

Man with Umbrella. Nothing begins, man ; things like

mind simply appear, sudden like ; when, 'ow, or where, we don't know.

Guardsman [*impatiently*]. But what was it arunning after the girl ?

Man with Umbrella. That clergyman fella 'oo's been runnin' rahnd tryin' to mike free with ordinary people.

Guardsman [*indignantly*]. 'Im, is it ? Th' bloke wot tried to interfere once with me en' my girl. Why didn't some of you tell 'im orf ?

Nursemaid [*chucking his arm*]. Aw, come on, Harry.

Guardsman [*impatiently to Nursemaid*]. Wyte a minute, carn't you ! [*To the group*] Wot prevented you from atellin' 'im orf ? I'd ha' done it. Our company sergeant-major's a fire terror, 'e is. Gives you a feelin' 'e 'ites everyone, 'e does, en' wishes you was dead. But whenever 'e gets me on the rawr, I tells 'im orf, I do, s'elp me !

Man with Umbrella [*with amused scorn*]. You does, does you ?

Guardsman [*getting warm to his subject*]. T'other dye, Guardsman Odgerson, 'e syes, wot's th' meanin' of your bed not bein' properly folded ? Git your poor mind movin' 'e roars, fer Gord's syke, en' sye wye your bed's not properly folded, 'e syes.

Nursemaid. 'E's en' ign'rant barstid, 'e is ; we all knows 'im.

Guardsman [*mimicking how he did it*]. I gits 'old of a byenet en' chises 'im rahnd the barrack square till I was caught up by the picket !

Man wearing Trilby. A serious thing to do in the Awmy.

Guardsman. When I was on the carpet before the Myjor,

'e did look fierce. Serious breach of discipline, 'e
syes. But, 'e syes, considering the provocytion, 'e
syes, admonished, 'e syes, I think will meet the cyse.
Agoin' aht, 'e syes to me, private, served 'im right,
Guardsman Odgerson ; pity you didn't give 'im a
jeb, 'e syes — I know th' bugger !

Nursemaid. A real torf, the myjor, 'e is ; a proper torf.
Come on, Harry.

Guardsman. Wyte a minute, carn't you.

Man wearing Trilby. Well, I won't wyte no longer for
the Atheist to come en' amuse us with his relativity
ideas. I knew 'e wouldn't fyce us aht, for everyone
knows spice is one thing en' time is another.

Man with Umbrella. It's not 'im's afryde to come ; it's
you're afryde to stye. Spice-time gives a noo meanin'
to th' universe. Spice is relative to time, en' time is
relative to spice — there's nothin' easier to understand.

Man wearing Trilby [dubiously]. Yes, quite ; I gets thet,
but—

Man with Umbrella [interrupting impatiently]. Wyte, 'old on
a second. Don't question me, yet. Listen carefully ;
let your mind foller wot I sye, en' you'll get th' idear.

Guardsman. Listen cautiously to wot th' gentleman's
asyein' — 'e knows wot 'e's torking abaht.

Nursemaid [tugging at the Guardsman's sleeve]. Aw, c'm on,
Harry ; you knows I 'as to be back by ten.
                    [*The Guardsman takes no notice.*

Man with Umbrella [pompously]. Now try to remember
that all th' old idears of the cosmos — Greek for all

things th' 'uman mind knows of — are buried with Copernicus, Kepler, Newton, en' all that crew.

Guardsman [*emphatically*]. 'Course they is, en' deep too.

Man with Umbrella. Now we all know that the clock created time, en' the measuring-rod created spice, so that there is really neither spice nor time ; but there is such a thing as spice-time. See ? Get that ?

Man wearing Trilby [*with confidence*]. Quite ; that much is perfectly clear.

Man with Umbrella. Right. Now, suppose that one night, when we all slept, th' universe we knows sank down to the size of a football, en' all the clocks began to move a thousand times quicker, — no, slower — it wouldn't mike the slightest difference to us, for we wouldn't realize that any difference 'ad tyken plice, though each of us would live a thousand times longer, en' man couldn't be seen, even under a microscope.

Guardsman [*jocularly*]. Could a woman be seen under a microscope ?

Man wearing Cap [*to Guardsman*]. Levity's outa plice, friend, when men are trying to think out th' truth of things.

Guardsman. But 'ow could th' world sink dahn to th' size of a football ? Doesn't seem a sife thing to me.

Man with Umbrella [*with cold dignity*]. I said *if* it did, friend.

Guardsman [*trying to find a way out*]. Yes ; but if a man couldn't be seen under a microscope, wot abaht 'is kids ?

Man with Umbrella. I simply styted a hypothenuse, friend.

Man wearing Cap [*to Guardsman*]. It's only en hypothenuse, you understand ? [*To Man with Umbrella*] But it's en impossible one, I think. D'ye mean that under your hypothenuse, en hour of the clock would stretch aht into ten years of time ?

Man with Umbrella. Exactly that in spice-time ; en 'undred years if you like.

Man wearing Cap. Wot ? Then in your spice-time, a man doin' eight hours would be workin' for eight 'undred years !

Guardsman [*to Man with Umbrella*]. You're barmy, man ! Wot abaht th' bloke doin' penal servitude fer life ? When is 'e agoin' to get aht ? You're barmy, man !

Nursemaid [*to Guardsman — chucking his arm*]. Are you comin', Harry ? If you don't 'urry, I'll 'ave to go, en' you'll 'ave to go withaht even a firewell squeeze.

Man with Umbrella [*annoyed — to Guardsman*]. Look, friend, if I was you, I'd go with the girl ; for it's pline your mind 'asn't been educyted yet to grasp the complicyted functions of wot we know as spice-time problems.

Guardsman [*with heat*]. 'Oo 'asn't a mind ? 'Oo're you to sye I 'asn't a mind ? I 'asn't a mind as would warnt to tern th' world into a football. It's a punch on the jawr you warnts for thinkin' people warnts the world to be a football. Wye's there different thoughts in every mind, en' different rules in every country ? Becorse people like you 'as th' world turned upside dahn ! Wot do I mean when I syes th' world is upside dahn ? Why, I means th' whole world is upside dahn, en' ennyone as 'as a mind'll unnerstend me !

Man with Umbrella [*to Guardsman*]. Wite a minute, wite a minute — you've got it all wrong.

Nursemaid [*anxiously — pulling Guardsman's arm*]. Come awye, do ! They'll get you with their tork right on the carpet, in front of the colonel ; so mind yourself, for I warn you, en' everyone knows as 'ow it ain't never allowed by the War Office to tork politics — soldiers is above them things.

Guardsman [*freeing himself — stormily*]. I won't let no blighter sye as 'ow I ain't got no eddicytion to tork of things ! [*To Group*] Where would you muckers be if it warnt for us swaddies, eh ? Poor swaddies rovin' the world, pickin' up fevers, to keep you sife at 'ome, en' 'appy. 'Oo is it does it, I asks ? [*He strikes his chest.*] We blighters, us blokes !

Man with Trilby. Tike it easy, soldier ; tike it easy.

Guardsman [*more stormily still*]. 'Oo was it, en' 'oo is it is holdin' dahn Africar en' Indiar, en' teachin' 'em 'ow to behive theirselves proper, eh ? [*He strikes his breast.*] We blighters, us poor blokes !

Nursemaid [*butting in hotly*]. Yes, en' we done a thing or two for the Chinks of China, too !

Guardsman. Too true, we did !

Nursemaid [*dragging the Guardsman away*]. Come on, come aht — we're wastin' our time torkin' to these silly old cacklers !

Guardsman [*as he is being pulled out*]. If it warn't my dooty to see my gal 'ome sife, I'd mike you muckers do a right-about-wheel en' quick march off the field ; I would, en' proper, too, blimey ; if I was to spend a month in clink for it, s'help me, I would !

                    [*He and the Nursemaid pass out of view.*

Man with Umbrella. There's en example, a fine example of militarism for us !

Man wearing Bowler [*deprecatingly*]. He wasn't altogether to blime. It was en unfortunate hypothenuse to set before ignorent minds ; en', to me, wholly ahtside respect to things unknowable, which should be left with 'Im 'oo mide things comprehensible en' incomprehensible. Introducin' the universe as a football was a regrettable en' might become a dingerous conception, even as a mere hypothenuse, as you might sye.

[*While the Man wearing the Bowler Hat has been speaking, the Old Woman comes in slowly and wearily, and now and again gives an unsteady step, as if she had a little drink taken. She plods along till she is beside the Group of Men. She stops and looks rather vacantly at them. She carries a laurel wreath tied with red ribbon.*

Old Woman [*tonelessly*]. Anyone here see a young girl pass ? My daughter ; a poor one ; yes, indeed, regardless of her poor mother. A scarlet crescent on the hip of a black dress ; a black one on the side of a scarlet hat. My dearest daughter. A good mother I've been ; some say too good ; but she doesn't care, never thinks of me. [*To the Group*] Did she pass you by ?

Man wearing Bowler. I shouldn't worry, ma'am ; she'll soon be in good hands — the Bishop is seeking for her.

Old Woman [*cocking an ear*]. The Bishop ? That villain ! He took her part against me — against her own mother. What does he want with her ?

Man wearing Bowler. Don't know, ma'am ; he seemed to be anxious to find her.

Old Woman [*musingly*]. My first husband is now a man

like him. Somewhere he stands before an altar
jewelled with candlelight, wearing a crimson cassock
and a golden cope. And a mean heart is hiding under
them. He left me alone. Somewhere he's powerful
and pompous ; in some place or other he's brightly
hidden away where I can't reach. [*She sighs.*] Everything golden is going into the bellies of the worms.

Man wearing Cap. Maybe the Bishop could help you,
ma'am.

Old Woman. Him ? He'd help no one. God can, though.
I never have to raise my voice, for God can hear a
whisper better than a thunderclap. Yet a little while,
and He'll level down to nothing the stir that still
remains around us ; for everything golden is going
into the bellies of the worms.

Man wearing Trilby. If I was you, ma'am, I'd go home
and have a rest.

Old Woman. There can be no rest nor work nor play
where there is no life, and the golden infancy of
England's life is tarnishing now in the bellies of the
worms. But God can save us, maybe, even at this
late hour.

Man with Umbrella [*mockingly*]. Gord's a poor prop for
enny one to lean on, ma'am.

Old Woman [*awake and lively at once*]. Who said that about
God ? [*To Man with Umbrella — fiercely*] You did, you,
you worm ! Is it any wonder we're all as we are, and
I'm as I am ? Provoking God to hide His goodness and
His mercy. Go away you — [*She raises an arm as if to
strike him. He stretches out the hand holding the umbrella to
guard himself, and she, with an unexpected jerk, snatches it
from him and flings it from her.*] Ah, you'd strike an old

woman, would you ; and with a weapon, too ? [*With bitterness*] And to think that all our hero soldiers died that such as you might live ! [*She catches sight of the wreath she is carrying.*] May this little token ease the anger of the dead. [*She wanders over till she is facing the base of the War Memorial. She remains silent before it for a few moments, with head bent ; then speaks tonelessly and sadly.*] A few more moments of time, and Spring'll be dancing among us again ; dancing in gold and purple pavilions of laburnum an' lilac ; the birds'll be busy at building small worlds of their own in the safe an' snug breast of the hedges ; the girls will go rambling round, each big with the thought of the life in the loins of the young men ; but those who are gone shall sink into stillness, deep under the stillness that shelters the dead !

Man wearing Trilby [*removing his hat*]. May they all rest in peace !

Man wearing Bowler [*removing his hat*]. Amen !
[*The Old Woman lifts the wreath she is carrying, high above her head, much in the same way a priest elevates the Host. Man with Umbrella has picked it up.*

Old Woman [*lifting her head till she faces the Memorial Figure*]. O soldier in bronze, cold guard of remembrance for those who rode out on swift horses to battle, and fell, I lay at thy feet this circle of green and ribbon of red as a signal of shame unto those who've forgotten the dead. [*She bends down and lays the wreath at the foot of the Memorial. Then she sings softly and quietly, without moving, the following verse. Singing :*
When souls are lin'd out on th' cold Judgment Day,
To stand shaking and sad in sin's wild disarray ;

When pardon is lost, and all hopes lie in ruin,
May God give a thought to an Irish Dragoon !

Voices [*singing*] :
May God give a thought to an Irish Dragoon !

Old Woman [*singing*] :
Who fought on hills high and who fought in lands
low,
Till a blustering bullet came swift from a foe,
And left me alone, though I'll follow full soon
The path blaz'd to death by an Irish Dragoon !

Voices [*singing*] :
The path blaz'd to death by her Irish Dragoon !

[*She turns down and slowly comes towards the Group of
Men, singing as she goes.*

Old Woman [*singing*] :
Though God makes the brightest of mornings look
sad,
Though He's taken from me all the joys I once had ;
Though He deny all, let Him grant me one boon,
To sleep when I die with my Irish Dragoon !

Voices [*singing*] :
To sleep when she dies with her Irish Dragoon !

[*As she crosses while singing the last line, the Bishop,
followed by his Sister, comes in from the opposite side, his
face full of anxiety and dejection.   He and the Old
Woman meet when they reach the Group of Men.*

Old Woman [*lifting her head, and seeing the Bishop*]. Ah,
his reverence, the Bishop !   Looking for my daughter,
too.   And what may you want with her, your reverence ?

Bishop's Sister [*getting in front of the Bishop — to Old Woman*].
Get away, woman! He isn't looking for your
daughter. She would be the last person he would wish
to meet!

Old Woman. Aha, are you another of the night-strollers
seeking lightsome contacts in the gloomier parts of the
Park?

Bishop's Sister [*furiously*]. How dare you say such a thing!
How dare you even hint at such a desire in me, you
tumble-down, wicked woman! I do not tread the
ways of sin like you or your daughter!

Old Woman. Indeed you don't; but you could, you
know, without a risk. No harm could ever come to
you.

Bishop's Sister. I am what you never were, never can be —
a good woman!

Old Woman. Your misfortune, madam; but there's some
compensation in being a stony monument to good
conduct and virtue.

Bishop [*coming forward in front of his Sister*]. Go away, you
wretched woman, and cease from annoying a Bishop's
sister!

Old Woman [*a little confusedly*]. Oh, yes, a bishop; I
forgot. Tell me, do you, at festivals, wear a crimson
cassock and a golden cope?

Bishop. What I wear concerns you not; so go away.

Old Woman. You've been looking for a girl, haven't
you? The one with a red crescent on the hip of a
black dress, and a black one to the side of a scarlet
hat? She's my daughter.

Bishop [*somewhat sharply*]. I wasn't seeking any girl, woman. No girl at all. I once tried to help your daughter, but it was useless. So I washed my hands of her completely and for ever.

Man wearing Trilby [*coming forward*]. You've forgotten, I think, sir. Remember you asked me if I saw her, some little time ago?

Bishop [*hesitantly*]. No, no; I did not.

Bishop's Sister [*quickly*]. If he asked for anyone, it must have been I he was looking for.

Man wearing Trilby [*embarrassed and confused*]. Yes, of course, ma'am; my mistake. [*He retires again.*

Old Woman [*meditatively — to the Bishop*]. There's a hidden hum in your old voice that carries a wisp of remembrance to me. [*Suddenly*] Is your name Gilbert?

Bishop [*hastily*]. No, no; it is not. Nothing like it either.

Bishop's Sister [*quickly*]. His name is not Gilbert! [*To the world at large*] What are the police doing that undesirable persons are allowed to annoy and molest people in this way!

Bishop [*to Old Woman*]. Go away from us, woman. If our politics were what they should be, you wouldn't be permitted to wander about interfering with people enjoying the innocent pleasures of the Park!

Old Woman [*scornfully*]. Pleasures and politics! Your politics are husks that only swine will eat; your power shelters behind a battlement of hunger; your religion's as holy as a coloured garter round a whore's leg : truth's bent in two, and hope is broken. [*Mournfully*] O Jesus ! is there no wisdom to be found anywhere ! All gone with the golden life of England into the bellies of the worms !

> [*While she has been saying the last few sentences, she has been going out slowly, with tired steps, and now passes from view.*

Bishop [*turning towards the Group of Men, and trying to appear in no way affected by his scene with the Old Woman*]. Shocking example, friends, of what a woman can become ! Under the influence of drink, I'm afraid. But go on with your discussion, gentlemen — it is a fine thing to see working men trying to elevate and develop their minds.

Man wearing Cap. We've finished it, sir. We have had enough of argument for one dye. We were about to go home when the Old Woman made her appearance.

Bishop's Sister [*to the Men*]. We were going homewards, too, gentlemen, when, as you saw, the half-insane creature interfered with us. Good night to you all. Come along, Gilbert.

Bishop [*suddenly catching his Sister by the arm, and pointing away from himself — agitatedly*]. Look ! That girl going down the path there ! Is that she ? She'll be passing through the light from a lamp in a second, and my old eyes are too dim to be sure. [*A short pause.*] Now ! Quick, quick, look, can't you !

Bishop's Sister [*angrily*]. I won't, I won't look. Think of what you're trying to do, Gilbert : help and kindness are but tortures to girls of her kind and class. Please be sensible and come home !

[*He shakes off a hand she has placed on his arm, and hurries out in the direction of where he thinks he had seen the girl. His Sister remains motionless where she is for a few moments, and then, distractedly, follows him out.*

Man wearing Trilby. See, we were right after all : his name is Gilbert, en' 'e is looking for the girl. There's something curious in it all.

Man with Umbrella. May be something curious in it, but nothing strynge — you don't know bishops as well as I do.

Man wearing Bowler. Odd how, after denying it, she called him Gilbert ; en' 'e, forgetting wot 'e said a second before, called aht to 'er to tell 'im if the passing figure was the girl 'e sought.

Man wearing Cap. Aware of nothing save wot was in their minds — like a man not feeling or hearing ennything when he's unconscious.

Man with Umbrella. Nonsense, man ; 'course you can feel en' 'ear when you're unconscious. You're unconscious when you're asleep, but you still 'ave the faculty of 'earin' en' feeling.

Man wearing Cap. No, sir, no ; all the so-called senses are dormant in a styte of unconsciousness.

Man with Umbrella. Wot abaht en alawm clock agoing off first thing in the mawning ?

Man wearing Cap. You 'ear it only when you become conscious of its striking.

Man in Bowler. 'Ow does it wyeken you up, then ?

Man wearing Cap. It doesn't wyeken you up, it can't

wyeken you up till you become conscious of its sahnd. You understand thet, surely ?

Man wearing Bowler. I understand, but I don't agree. Wot I sye is, while I'm asleep, which is a styte of unconsciousness, I 'ear.

Man with Umbrella. 'Course 'e 'ears !

Man wearing Cap. The styte of unconsciousness implies a condition unaccompanied by conscious experience. We experience something when we 'ear ; 'ow then can we, when we're unconscious, pass into the experience of 'earing ?

Man with Umbrella. You're confusing the issue : let's decide first wot is 'earing : now wot do we mean when we say we 'ear ?

Man wearing Cap. The sense of 'earing exists simply as the sense of feeling exists, manifested, for instance, in pleasure or pine, though we know thet pine is nonexistent, strictly speaking.

Man wearing Bowler [*scornfully*]. Pine non-existent ? Oh, don't be silly, man !

Man with Umbrella [*with disgust*]. Aw, 'e's a giving us Christian Science now !

Man wearing Bowler. Mean to sye you carn't feel the jeb of a pin or the sting of a wasp ?

Man wearing Cap. You can, if you want to feel them.

Man with Umbrella. Can if you — but no one warnts to feel them. Aw ! We're back again at where we sterted.

Man wearing Bowler [*to the Man with Umbrella*]. Wite a

minute, wite a minute ; impatience 'll never get at the truth of things. [*To the Man wearing Cap*] Suppose you cut your finger, wouldn't you feel pine ?

Man wearing Cap. I'm not going to suppose ennything of the kind. As mind willed pine into existence, so mind c'n will pine awye again.

Man with Umbrella [*with impatience*]. Aw !

Man wearing Bowler [*to the Man with Umbrella*]. Wite a minute, wite a minute. [*To the Man wearing Cap*] You said thet if you cut your finger you wouldn't fec¹ pine ?

Man wearing Cap. I never said ennything of the kind.

Man with Umbrella. Never said ennything of the kind ? But we 'eard you syeing it just now, man !

Man wearing Cap. I argued in a general wye, en' I refuse to be refuted by a trivial particular, the genesis of which I deny : immaterially speaking, you carn't cut your finger.

Man with Umbrella [*with consternation*]. Immaterially speaking — carn't cut your finger — oh, mister, mister !

Man wearing Bowler [*suddenly interrupting*]. Hush, hush ; look — she's coming ; the girl the Bishop warnted ; coming with the Dreamer !
>[*They all cease talking, and look towards the point indicated by the Man wearing the Bowler Hat.*
>[*After a moment or two the Young Woman enters with the Dreamer. She is leaning heavily on his arm. Her breathing is quick ; her face is very pale, and in her eyes is a fixed look of fear. The lie of her clothing shows*

*that she has dressed hastily. She is dressed as before, in
black, slashed with crimson.*

[*The Dreamer wears a vivid orange scarf thrown carelessly
round his neck and shoulders. He leads the Young
Woman to a bench opposite to where the Group of Men is
standing, and gently helps her to sit down on it. There
is a hushed pause for a few moments.*]

Young Woman [*tremulously*]. I'm bad, Dreamer ; please go
and find the Bishop for me. [*She mechanically arranges
her dress.*] My clothes seem to be on me every way and
any way. [*With a wan smile*] You hurried me into them,
Dreamer, as quick as you hurried me out of them !
Things are twisting before my eyes. [*Frightened*]
Get the Bishop, go for the Bishop !

Dreamer. Aren't you safer in the arms of the Dreamer
than you are at the Bishop's feet ?

Young Woman [*tonelessly*]. While I had life — yes ; but I
feel close to death now, and I have a lot to answer for,
Dreamer.

Dreamer [*vehemently*]. Not you, fair lass ; not you ! A
few smiles bestowed on the unworthy is all that you
have to answer for. It is those who disordered your
life with their damned whims ; those who have left
a lovely thing lonely and insecure ; who have neglected
to nurture the rare : it is we, dear lass, who will have
to answer for all these things !

Young Woman. You were always kind, Dreamer, and, at
least, you led me to where I heard a song. Be kind to
me still, and bring the Bishop here.

[*The Dreamer goes over to the Group of Men who are
watching him and the Young Woman.*]

Dreamer [*to the Men*]. Have any of you seen the Bishop lately ?

Man wearing Trilby. 'E was 'ere a short time ago. [*He points at the Young Woman*.] En' 'e was looking for 'er.

Dreamer. If any of you see him, send him here — the spot where the Memorial is, near the Bird Sanctuary — please.

Man wearing Bowler. As we go 'ome, if we see 'im, we'll send 'im along.
> [*They go out by different ways, and the Dreamer goes back to the Young Woman.*

Dreamer. On their way home, if they see him, the men will send the Bishop here.

Young Woman [*agitated*]. You go, too, Dreamer — none of them might meet the Bishop. Oh, please do !

Dreamer. I don't like to leave you alone, Jannice.

Young Woman [*with a faint smile*]. You will soon have to leave me alone, whether you like it or no. I will be quite safe here. No one will bother me now.

Dreamer. Don't stir then till I come back.
> [*He takes her hand in his, gently kisses it, and goes up the slope, and out.*
> [*The Young Woman sits on the bench, staring straight before her, looking lonely and unhappy. She remains alone in the scene for a few moments ; then the Bishop's Sister comes on to the top of the slope, looking from side to side, as if in search of someone. As she appears above, the Old Woman comes in from the shadows on the left below. She is greatly bent, and walks with slow and dragging feet. She shivers as she looks about and catches sight of*

the lonely figure sitting on the bench. She shuffles over to it.

Old Woman [*peering at the figure*]. Have you seen a Bishop strolling about anywhere here recently ? He's a friend of mine. I am in sore straits, having no home now, and he may be willing to help me. [*She pauses for an answer, but gets none.*] A man, a comfortable man wearing a cassock adorned with purple buttons, with a scarlet cap on his head. Why don't you answer ? [*She peers more closely at the figure, and recognises the Young Woman.*] Oh, it's you, is it ? So here you are, looking very pale, and as if you were settling down for death. Remember now the way you treated your poor mother ! No fancy dreams in front of you now — only the last things staring you in the face !

> [*The Bishop's Sister has heard the Old Woman talking, has watched her while she spoke, and now comes down the slope towards them.*

Young Woman [*doggedly — with a vicious look at the Old Woman*]. Anyhow, if I go, I'll go game, and die dancing !

Old Woman [*with some exultation in her voice*]. Looks as if it would be me who would be dancing over your grave, my merry lady !

> [*The Young Woman rises from the bench, and walks unsteadily away from the Old Woman, meeting the Bishop's Sister, who has come down the slope. The Young Woman retreats a few steps from her, so that she is between them both, where she stands shivering.*

Bishop's Sister [*to the Young Woman*]. So I've found you just before the Bishop could come to you. Waiting for his help and pity, are you ? Be off out of the Park, and hide yourself, you shameless thing, or I'll send the police to take you out !

Old Woman [*getting in front of the Young Woman, and bowing low in mockery before the Bishop's Sister*]. Salaam, mem pukka memsahib, salaam, and pardon her and pardon me and pardon us all for getting in the way of thy greatness ; and grant us grace to have faith in thy dignity and importance, per benedicite pax hugger muggery ora pro puggery rigmarolum !

Bishop's Sister [*venomously*]. The pair of you ought to be stretched out naked on the ground so that decent women could trample the life out of you !

Old Woman [*confidently*]. Gallant men would lift us up on to our feet again.

Bishop's Sister [*violently*]. Sympathy for such as you would be a sin. The soft and gentle hand of pity must be changed to the punishing hand of bronze !

Old Woman [*remonstrating*]. Oh, sister, sister !

Bishop's Sister [*furiously*]. How dare you call me sister !

Old Woman [*reflectively*]. How savage women can be when God has been unkind and made us plain, so that no man can find a vision in our face.

    [*In the distance is heard the beat of the drum and the faint murmur of the Down-and-Out chant. The Three Women become rigid, and listen intently.*

    [*Down the slope come the tottering Attendants, followed by the Two Evangelists, bent, and with unsteady legs. All their faces are full of fear. They come into the centre, an Evangelist and an Attendant going behind the Bishop's Sister, and an Evangelist and an Attendant behind the Young Woman.*

Evangelists and Attendants [*in chorus, as they come down the slope*]. With drum-beat and chant the Down-and-Out are close upon us !

Bishop's Sister [*with merry rancour*]. Soon they will encompass you round about ; and there will be no way of escape, even for the lady of the good looks !
> [*The Bishop appears on the slope above. He stands so that the light from a lamp falls on him, a sad and dignified figure in his cassock with its purple buttons, and the scarlet biretta on his head. He stretches out an arm over those below, extending two fingers of a hand in blessing, and says in sad and low tones, almost intoning the words :*

Bishop. Benedicti vos a Domino, qui fecit coelum et terram.
> [*He comes slowly down the slope, backed by the chant, louder now, of the Down-and-Outs, and the Young Woman rushes over to him, and falls on her knees.*

Young Woman [*imploringly*]. Bless me, even me, oh ! my father !
> [*With a shiver and a quivering lip, the Bishop stretches an arm over her, extends his fingers to bless her, but his arm falls slowly to his side again, and he remains silent.*
> [*The Dreamer now appears on the slope, and stands in the light where the Bishop had stood before, looking at those below him. The Bishop walks away from the kneeling Young Woman, and stands in the centre, with a group on his right and another on his left.*

1st Evangelist. We have danced no dance, neither have we sought the beauty of any woman ; we have sung no songs, nor have we ever made merry in our hearts.

2nd Evangelist. We have honoured pain ; bound up joy

with sighing ; and multiplied sorrows that men might know Thy mercy and Thy kindness.

Bishop. Grant them pardon, O Lord, and bring them peace !

Dreamer. Let them sink into the grave, O Lord, and never let their like appear on the face of the earth again.

1st Evangelist. Stricken, we struck not back ; we blessed them that cursed us ; and prayed for them that took no note of our misery and want.

Bishop. Grant them pardon, O Lord, and bring them peace !

Dreamer. Let brambles, O Lord, grow thick where they are buried deep ; let the fox and the vixen guard their cubs in the midst of the brambles ; and let children sing and laugh and play where these have moaned in their misery !

    [*The Down-and-Outs are here now, spreading over the slope above, and making to come down ; but the Dreamer with outstretched arms bars the way. On their way, and just before coming in on to the slope, they are heard singing.*

Down-and-Outs [*chanting*] :
    Life has pass'd us by to the loud roll of her drum,
    With her waving flags of yellow and green held high,
    All starr'd with the golden, flaming names of her most mighty children.

    Oh, where shall we go when the day calls ?
    Oh, where shall we sleep when the night falls ?
    We've but a sigh for a song, and a deep sigh for a drum-beat !

[*Their chant changes into a menacing hum, like that of a swarm of wasps, to the tune of the chant, as the rest speak to each other. The Young Woman goes unsteadily over to the Bishop.*

Young Woman [*imploring*]. Let me not mingle my last moments with this marching misery !

Bishop [*to young Woman — slow, but with decision*]. You must go where they go, and their sighing shall be your song !

Down-and-Outs [*chanting*] :
   She must be merry no more ; she must walk in the
      midst of the mournful ;
   Who've but a sigh for a song, and a deep sigh for a
      drum-beat !
   [*The Young Woman has stiffened with resentment as she has listened, and now stands facing the Dreamer, looking at him for encouragement.*

Dreamer [*to Young Woman*]. Turn your back swift on the poor, purple-button'd dead-man, whose name is absent from the book of life. Offer not as incense to God the dust of your sighing, but dance to His glory, and come before His presence with a song !

Young Woman [*with reckless defiance*]. I'll go the last few steps of the way rejoicing ; I'll go, go game, and I'll die dancing !

Dreamer [*exultantly*]. Sing them silent, dance them still, and laugh them into an open shame !
   [*Faintly, as if the tune was heard only in the minds of the Dreamer and the Young Woman, the notes of a dance tune are heard, coming from the subdued playing of a flute and other instruments. The Young Woman and the*

Dreamer dance to the melody, she a little unsteadily.
They dance for about a minute, then the movements of the
Young Woman become a little uncertain ; she staggers,
recovers herself, dances again, but with faltering steps.
The music of the dance becomes fainter.

Young Woman [*frightened*]. Dreamer, Dreamer, I'm faint-
ing — I think I'm going to die.

Dreamer [*fiercely*]. Sing them silent ; dance them still ;
laugh them into an open shame !

Down-and-Outs [*chanting and coming down a little by the*
centre].
    She must be merry no more ; she must be set in the
        midst of the mournful,
    Who've but a sigh for a song, and a deep sigh for a
        drum-beat.

Dreamer [*fiercely, with his face close to the Young Woman's*].
Sing them silent ; dance them still ; laugh them into
an open shame !

Bishop [*prayerfully as they dance*]. O Lord, who taketh
pleasure in thy people, let this dance be unto thee as
a merry prayer offered by an innocent and excited
child !
    [*The tune of the dance is now mournful, and the Dreamer*
    is almost carrying the Young Woman in his arms. They
    dance in this way for a few moments, then the head of the
    Young Woman falls limp, and the Dreamer lifts her in
    his arms, carries her to a soft spot on the green sward,
    and lays her down there.

Young Woman [*almost in a whisper*]. I die, Dreamer, I die,
and there is fear in my heart.

Dreamer [*tenderly*]. Fear nothing : courage in the hearts

of men and women is what God needs most ; and
He will find room for one scarlet blossom among a
thousand white lilies !

> [*The Bishop goes unsteadily to where the Young Woman is
> lying. He kneels beside her, and takes one of her hands
> in his.*

Young Woman [*to the Bishop*]. Guide the hand you hold
into making the sign of the cross, that I may whisper
my trust in the golden mercy of God !

> [*The Bishop guides her hand as she makes the sign of the
> cross. She lies still and silent. The Down-and-Out
> come down the rest of the way, changing the waspish hum
> of their voices to the dolorous chant of their miserere.
> They spread out, enveloping the Evangelists, the Attend-
> ants, and the Old Woman.*

Down-and-Outs [*chanting*] :

> We challenge life no more, no more, with our dead
>   faith and our dead hope ;
> We carry furl'd the fainting flags of a dead hope
>   and a dead faith.
> Day sings no song, neither is there room for rest
>   beside night in her sleeping :
> We've but a sigh for a song, and a deep sigh for a
>   drum-beat !

> [*They force the Dreamer back a few paces at first ; but
> exerting his strength, he forces a way through them,
> scattering them to right and left, as he chants his vigorous
> song of defiance and resolution.*

Dreamer :

> Way for the strong and the swift and the fearless :
> Life that is stirr'd with the fear of its life, let it die ;
> Let it sink down, let it die, and pass from our vision
>   for ever.

Sorrow and pain we shall have, and struggle unend-
ing :
We shall weave courage with pain, and fight through
the struggle unending.
Way for the strong and the swift and the fearless :
Life that is stirr'd with the fear of its life let it die ;
Let it sink down, let it die, and pass from our vision
for ever !

[*The Dreamer goes up the slope. When he reaches the top,
he turns, looks down at the still form of the Young
Woman. The Bishop's Sister stands apart, and watches
the Bishop kneeling beside the form of the Young Woman.
She goes over, after a moment's pause, and gently
touches the Bishop's shoulder.*

Bishop [*looking up at his Sister*]. Go home, go home, for
Christ's sake, woman, and ask God's mercy on us all !

[*She looks at the kneeling figure for a moment, then, turning,
she goes out without a word.*

Bishop [*in low and grief-stricken tones*]. She died making the
sign of the cross !

Dreamer [*looking down to where the Young Woman is lying*].
You fought the good fight, Jannice ; and you kept the
faith : Hail and farewell, sweetheart ; for ever and
for ever, hail and farewell !

[*The Dreamer turns, and begins to go out slowly. The sky's
purple and black changes to a bright grey, pierced with
golden segments, as if the sun was rising, and a new day
about to begin. The music, sounding low, of the song
he sang to her, is heard ; in the middle of the melody the
gates begin to close slowly, coming together on the last
few notes of the tune.*

THE GATES CLOSE

Music to "WITHIN THE GATES"

Composed and adapted by

SPRING CHORUS

HERBERT HUGHES

Founded on "Haste to the Wedding"

SCENE I

life and to death as she dan - - ces a - long ___ Through the

lovely con-fus-ion of singing of birds and of blossom and bud Her thoughts are a

dance as she seeks out her bride-groom the sun Through the lovely con-fus-ion of

singing of birds and of blossom and bud Our Mother the Earth is a

maid-en a-gain ___ Young, fair and a maid-en a-gain. Our Mother the Earth is a

maiden a-gain She's young and is fair and a maiden ___ a - gain. ___

SUMMER CHORUS

Alla marcia   SCENE II

1. Ye who are hag-gard and gid-dy with care bu-sy
2. Ye who are twist-ing a pray'r from your thoughts in the
3. Ye who in sen-ates and par-lia-ments talk, Talk

count-ing your pro-fit and loss - es Showing the might of your
dim - ness and gloom of the church - es Lighting your can - dle pe-
on through the day and the night - time Talk and still talk and

name un - to God in the gay col-our'd page of a cheque book
-ti-tions a - way to chalk col-our'd vir - gins and mar - tyrs
still talk on through the hun - dreds of cen - tur-ies pass - ing

Stor - ing the best ___ of your life in a draw'r of your desk at the of - fice ___
Rack - ing your life ___ for the hope of a co - sy cor-ner in hea-ven ___
Till the wide ear of the wide ___ world is deaf - en'd with wis-dom ___

___ Bel-low good-bye ___ to the beg-gar-in' lot 'n come out To

bow down the head 'n bend down the knee to the bee 'n the bird 'n the blossom ___

233

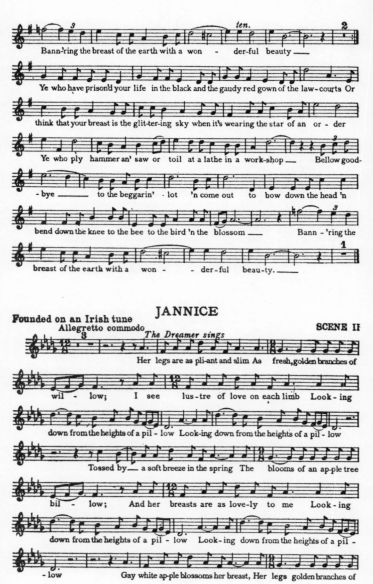

Bann-'ring the breast of the earth with a won - der-ful beauty ___

Ye who have prison'd your life in the black and the gaudy red gown of the law-courts Or

think that your breast is the glit-ter-ing sky when it's wearing the star of an or - der

Ye who ply hammer an' saw or toil at a lathe in a work-shop ___ Bellow good-

- bye ___ to the beggarin' · lot 'n come out to bow down the head 'n

bend down the knee to the bee to the bird 'n the blossom ___ Bann - 'ring the

breast of the earth with a won - - der-ful beau-ty. ___

JANNICE

Founded on an Irish tune

Allegretto commodo *The Dreamer sings*

SCENE II

Her legs are as pli-ant and slim As fresh, golden branches of

wil - low; I see lus-tre of love on each limb Look - ing

down from the heights of a pil - low Look-ing down from the heights of a pil - low

Tossed by ___ a soft breeze in the spring The blooms of an ap-ple tree

bil - low; And her breasts are as love-ly to me Look - ing

down from the heights of a pil - low Look-ing down from the heights of a pil -

- low Gay white ap-ple blossoms her breast, Her legs golden branches of

234

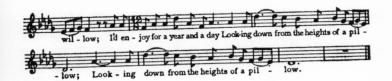

wil - low; I'd en - joy for a year and a day Look-ing down from the heights of a pil -

- low; Look - ing down from the heights of a pil - low.

SING AND DANCE

Air: **"Little Brown Jug"** *by R.A.Eastburn*

SCENE III

Allegro moderato

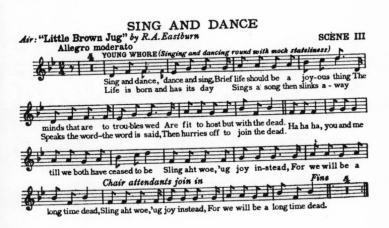

YOUNG WHORE *(Singing and dancing round with mock stateliness)*

Sing and dance, dance and sing, Brief life should be a joy-ous thing The
Life is born and has its day Sings a song then slinks a - way

minds that are to trou-bles wed Are fit to host but with the dead. Ha ha ha, you and me
Speaks the word—the word is said, Then hurries off to join the dead.

till we both have ceased to be Sling aht woe, 'ug joy in-stead, For we will be a

Chair attendants join in   *Fine*

long time dead, Sling aht woe, 'ug joy instead, For we will be a long time dead.

THE NINETY AND NINE

ELIZABETH C. CLEPHANE   IRA D. SANKEY

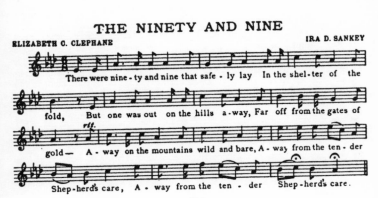

There were nine - ty and nine that safe - ly lay In the shel - ter of the

fold, But one was out on the hills a - way, Far off from the gates of

gold — A - way on the mountains wild and bare, A - way from the ten - der

Shep-herd's care, A - way from the ten - der Shep-herd's care.

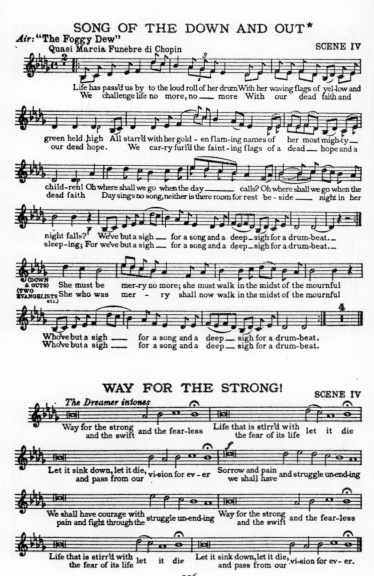

SONG OF THE DOWN AND OUT*

Air: "The Foggy Dew"

Quasi Marcia Funebre di Chopin

SCENE IV

Life has pass'd us by to the loud roll of her drum With her waving flags of yel-low and
We challenge life no more, no ___ more With our dead faith and

green held high All starr'd with her gold-en flam-ing names of her most migh-ty
our dead hope. We car-ry furl'd the faint-ing flags of a dead ___ hope and a

child-ren! Oh where shall we go when the day ___ calls? Oh where shall we go when the
dead faith Day sings no song, neither is there room for rest be-side ___ night in her

night falls? We've but a sigh ___ for a song and a deep ___ sigh for a drum-beat.
sleep-ing; For we've but a sigh ___ for a song and a deep ___ sigh for a drum-beat.

(DOWN & OUTS) She must be mer-ry no more; she must walk in the midst of the mournful
(TWO EVANGELISTS etc.) She who was mer - ry shall now walk in the midst of the mournful

Who've but a sigh ___ for a song and a deep ___ sigh for a drum-beat.
Who've but a sigh ___ for a song and a deep ___ sigh for a drum-beat.

WAY FOR THE STRONG!

SCENE IV

The Dreamer intones

Way for the strong and the fear-less Life that is stirr'd with let it die
and the swift the fear of its life

Let it sink down, let it die, vi-sion for ev - er Sorrow and pain and struggle un-end-ing
and pass from our we shall have

We shall have courage with struggle un-end-ing Way for the strong and the fear-less
pain and fight through the and the swift

Life that is stirr'd with let it die Let it sink down, let it die, vi-sion for ev - er.
the fear of its life and pass from our

GARDENER'S SONG

Air: "Moll Roone"

A fig for the blos-soms th' big-gest vase can hold, Th'
flow'rs that face the world shy the ones that face it bold; Men may
praise them and wor-ship them as some-thing fine and rare, Loung-ing
through their gor-geous per-fume so___ deft-ly hid-den there. But
I'll___ nev-er won-der though some in glee dis-close The
white of whit-est li-ly the red of red-dest rose, For I'll
fold in my arms a girl as bright as she is gay, And to-
-night the prim-rose path of love will be a won-der way!

THE IRISH DRAGOON

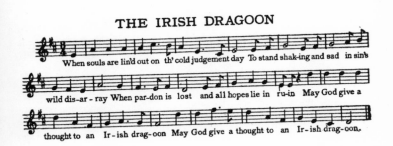

When souls are lin'd out on th' cold judgement day To stand shak-ing and sad in sin's
wild dis-ar-ray When par-don is lost and all hopes lie in ru-in May God give a
thought to an Ir-ish drag-oon May God give a thought to an Ir-ish drag-oon.

237

THE STAR TURNS RED

TO

THE MEN AND WOMEN

WHO FOUGHT

THROUGH THE GREAT DUBLIN LOCKOUT

IN NINETEEN HUNDRED AND THIRTEEN

CHARACTERS IN THE PLAY

Act I: MICHAEL
    OLD MAN
    OLD WOMAN
    JACK
    KIAN
    JULIA
    JOYBELL
    LORD MAYOR
    PURPLE PRIEST
    BROWN PRIEST
LEADER OF THE SAFFRON SHIRTS
FOUR SAFFRON SHIRT TROOPERS

Act II: PURPLE PRIEST
    BROWN PRIEST
    BRALLAIN
    CAHEER
    SHEASKER
    EGLISH
    SECRETARY
    RED JIM
    JOYBELL
    BRANNIGAN
    TWO RED GUARDS

Act III: OLD MAN
    OLD WOMAN
    MAN WITH CRUTCH
    HUNCHBACK
WOMAN WITH WITHERED CHILD
    BLIND MAN
    WELL-DRESSED MAN
YOUNG MAN WITH COUGH
    JACK
    JULIA
    FOUR RED GUARDS
    PURPLE PRIEST
    BROWN PRIEST
    RED JIM
    BRANNIGAN
    CROSS-BEARER

Act IV: LORD MAYOR
    LADY MAYORESS
    1ST WORKMAN
    2ND WORKMAN
    OLD MAN
    JOYBELL
    RED JIM
    BRANNIGAN
RED GUARD AT BUZZER
    PURPLE PRIEST
    BROWN PRIEST
    JULIA

Guests, Red Guards,
Soldiers, and Sailors

―――

The action of the play takes place during the last few hours of a Christmas Eve.

―――

TIME.—Tomorrow, or the next day.

ACT I

The home of the Old Man and the Old Woman. The walls are a vivid black, contrasting with the dark blue of the sky outside, seen through the windows. These windows (two of them), one to the right, the other to the left, at the back, are long, reaching almost to the ceiling, and beginning a foot or so from the floor. Through the window on the right can be seen the silhouette of a towering church spire, and to the left of this spire is a large, shining, silver star. Through the window on the left can be seen the silhouettes of two towering chimneys, one shorter than the other ; from these chimneys smoke is pouring, and an occasional tongue of flame shoots out. To the left of the window on the right is a sketch of a bishop's mitred head ; to the right of the window on the left, a sketch of Lenin, with his name underneath in Russian characters. Underneath these sketches, a cupboard, on the top of which is a white teapot, symbol of life's necessities (the cupboard is black). In the centre of the room, a table, black, covered with a yellow cloth bordered with white — the papal colours. Several kitchen chairs, painted white, give an indication of occasional rest. The hearth, with a cosy fire, is to the right. On the right, a door leading to the stairs and so to the street. Between the fireplace and the back is a door leading to another room. At the table, now nearly covered with newspapers, by the end nearest to the fire, the Old Man is sitting, busy studying football form to fill in a coupon. At the far end of the table the Old Woman is knitting. Between them, standing up, is Jack, their elder son, looking intently at a sheet of music propped up on the table. He has a cornet in his hand, and is practising " The Internationale ". The Old Man occasionally looks up with a glance of irritation and scorn at Jack and

his cornet. The Old Woman goes on quietly with her knitting.
Jack is twenty-three, is slim and sturdily built. He is dressed in
a light brown tweed suit, the coat buttoned over his breast. On
the right breast of his coat he wears a large red star.

The Old Man is short, but still rosy with life ; he has a
shock of grey hair and a fierce moustache.

The Old Woman is of average height, plump, and still shows
signs of the good-looking girl she once was.

Before the curtain rises, part of the hymn " O Come, All ye
Faithful ", is heard played (a few instruments only) and sung,
probably by " Waits " in the street below. The first verse is
sung before the curtain rises, and the last verse begins as the
curtain goes up. Jack takes the cornet from his lips and listens
to the tune and the hymn that disturb him ; the Old Man, too,
scowls because they interfere with the concentration necessary to
choose the right teams for entry in his football coupons. The
Old Woman goes on knitting, partly humming and partly sing-
ing softly the words of the hymn as they are sung outside in the
street.

Waits [*singing in the street*] :
     Jesu, to Thee be glory given.
     Word of the Father, now in flesh appearing.
     O come, let us adore him, O come, let us adore him,
     O come, let us adore him, Christ the lord !

     [*The sound of the singing has now moved away to a*
          distance, and can be heard but faintly. Jack places the
          cornet to his lips, and plays somewhat slowly, and at
          times jerkily, the first few bars of " The Internationale ".
          The door leading to the street flies open, and Michael
          rushes in impetuously. He is a tall man of forty-four,
          pale face, glittering eyes, long nose, and has a great
          moustache drooping over his lips. He is dressed in brown
          overalls. He runs over to Jack.

Michael [*to Jack — breathlessly*]. Jack, old son, a second ; just a second, before you start.

Jack. What is it, Mick ?

Michael. Julia. I've to go to the Hall at once. You know. I don't want her to go to a dance tonight. I want her to be near me. Tell her I'll see her in the Hall ; or [*appealingly*], you bring her down, Jack : she'll do a lot for you.

Jack. I'll tell her and I'll try, Mick.

Michael. Thanks, old son. The boys are all agog. [*Jack makes a warning movement and glances at the old couple.*] I know. A silent night that'll be sad for a lot of people.
 [*The door leading to street opens again, and Kian comes in. His dark-brown hair is cropped close to his head, and a close-cropped moustache is seen on his upper lip. He is tall, slim, and about twenty years of age. He stands at the door stiffly for a moment, then stretches out his arm in the Fascist salute. He is dressed in blue overalls.*

Kian. Hail, the Circle and the Flash !
 [*Michael's body tenses with resentment, and he is lifting his arm, but Jack catches it and stops him.*

Jack [*warningly*]. Michael !

Michael [*submissively*]. I know, Jack ; silent night.
 [*Stiffly, with a touch of the goose-step, Kian crosses the room, goes into the room on the left.*

Jack [*moving out with Michael*]. Better hurry off to the Hall — they may be waiting for you. And remember the orders, the orders, the orders : no movement to be made ; no sign to be given ; no word to be spoken till the hour strikes : remember !

Michael. I remember. Don't forget Julia, Jack. She's lonely since the mother was taken. She's all I have.

Jack. There's the Cause. I'll keep an eye on her, don't worry. I'll try to have her with me when I join you in the Hall.   [*They go out talking.*

Old Man [*with a deep sigh*]. Aaah ! It would pay a man to have a mind of his own. Once get into the mind of others, and your own is a jungle of difficulties. The opinions of all these tipsters show that the only way to win is the best way to lose. [*Murmuring*] Four away and six at home, at home ; four away and six at home ; away, away ; six away and four at home — ah, what the hell am I saying ! [*To the Old Woman*] Listen ! Chelsea did well away, and badly at home, so may do badly or well, may win or lose the match to come ; or, perhaps, it may even be a draw. Now, is that any kind of a prophecy to put before a sensible suffering man ?

Old Woman. If you ask me, it's hardly a time to be tensing yourself over football, with the workers up in arms and the Saffron Shirts and the Christian Front all aglow to down them.

Old Man. If the workers are mad enough to go against the Saffron Shirts and the Christian Front, let them ! The workers are getting like the tides now — always either coming in or going out, with their lightning strikes, stay-in strikes, stay-out strikes, sit-down strikes, and go-easy strikes. Strikes to bring war about and strikes to keep war away, till the whole land's quivering with the rush around of revolution. I'm telling you it's dangerous ; and there's a deep curse in the danger.

Old Woman [*echoing him — sadly*]. A deep curse in the danger.

Old Man. I went to work as the clock struck the first second of me fourteenth year, and for forty years I kept going gay, only slowing down for a wisp of a prayer and a tittle of rest on a Sunday. And it's often I lounged among the sleeping machinery with the other fools on strike till they came fumbling back in a lather of fear in case they wouldn't be wanted again.

Old Woman [*in a murmuring echo*]. In a lather of fear in case they wouldn't be wanted again.

Old Man. In sun and shadow, I stood by the masters, getting a rise when the others were glad to get less, even, than what they had before.

Old Woman [*echoing*]. Less, even, than what they had before.

Old Man. The masters would always be fair to the men if only the men would strive to be fair to the masters. Look at me : at the age of fifty I was ushered in before the whole Board of Directors, the Chairman commenting on how well I had done by the firm, the rest clapping agreement, all standing round me as the medal was pinned on my breast ; one of them saying, with tears in his eyes, that if employers could only get enough men like your humble servant, they'd have damn little cause for complaint ; for minds content with a little are ever the happiest. Man wants but little here below, nor wants that little long.

Old Woman [*with murmuring echo and nodding head*]. Nor wants that little long.

Old Man [*resentfully*]. Don't be chiming in on me like the ding-dong-dell of an old church bell. With your [*mimicking*] " Less than what they had before — Nor wants that little long " ! Let me do me coupons here in peace.

Old Woman [*leaning towards him*]. Peace ? Peace is it ? I suppose you don't know it's all over the city that the men in Red Jim's Union are arming ? More than an hour ago, Joybell ran in to tell me that.

Old Man [*scornfully*]. Joybell ! The lunatic that carries sensation under his arm. Arming ? I suppose the military, the police, and the Saffron Shirts 'll be too shy to say anything ?

Old Woman [*sorrowfully*]. And the peace of Christmas, too, nearly down on top of us.

Old Man [*peevishly*]. Oh, what has Christmas got to do with a stay-in strike or men arming ? [*With his nose in the coupons.*] Two away and three at home. [*Raising his head again.*] There's no use of bringing in mistletoe to stop a stay-in strike.

Old Woman. I never once mentioned the word mistletoe.

Old Man. Oh, do try to keep your ears open so that you may hear what you're saying yourself. Why don't you be honest, and admit saying the saying that's still hot on your tongue ?

Old Woman. I never once mentioned mistletoe ; never once.

Old Man [*furiously*]. Don't be so positive, woman ! The minute you mentioned the stay-in strike, you smothered it in mistletoe.

Old Woman. Don't you be so positive.

Old Man. I'm not a bit positive. I simply said that it was you and not me who mentioned the word mistletoe. And, if I hadn't checked you, you'd have brought in branches of holly and ivy too !

Old Woman. I was just trying to think of something to stem the disorder that's sowing itself everywhere.

Old Man. Well, a barrage of holly and ivy won't avail much. But we've got the military, haven't we ?
                    [*The Old Woman does not answer.*

Old Man [*peevishly*]. Why don't y'answer ? We've got the military, haven't we ?

Old Woman. Yes ; we've got the military.

Old Man. And the police, too, haven't we ?
                    [*The Old Woman does not answer.*

Old Man. Can't y'answer when you're asked a question ? We've got the police too, haven't we ?

Old Woman. Yes, I suppose so.

Old Man. There's no supposing in it. We either have or we haven't — we've got the police too, haven't we ?

Old Woman. Yes, we've got the police too.

Old Man. And the Saffron Shirts and the Christian Front as well, haven't we ?   [*The Old Woman does not answer.*

Old Man [*crossly*]. A minute ago you gave a thundering echo to every word I said ; now you can't parade even a whisper before a man. [*Furiously*] We have the Saffron Shirts and the Christian Front as well, haven't we, haven't we, haven't we ?

Old Woman. Yes, yes, yes !

Old Man. What more do you want, then ? They'll be able to preserve order, won't they ?

Old Woman. Ay ; but what kind of order ?

Old Man. What kind of order ! It won't be any of your holly and mistletoe order. Sound and sensible law and order — that's what it'll be.

Old Woman. And what's the good of order in the country if there's none in the home ? What's the good of life if you have to get the military and police to mind it for you ?

Old Man. What else are we paying them for ? You can't expect to be able to take things easy without some assistance, can you ?

Old Woman. What about our own two boys, always at each other's throats for the sake of a slogan ? What with the Saffron Shirts prodding us on one side, and the Communists pouncing at us on the other, life's lost everything but its name.

Old Man. Ask your Communist son, Jack, and he'll tell you that, to the workers, life is nothing but a name.

Old Woman. What about your Fascist son, Kian, going about as if he was the deputy of God Almighty ?

Old Man [*shouting*]. I never held with either of them ! I never held with either of them !

Old Woman [*warningly*]. Hush !
> [*Jack comes back in a thoughtful mood, goes back to his place at the table, rearranges the music, and plays a few bars of " The Internationale " on the cornet.*

Old Man [*annoyed — with his nose in the coupons*]. Dtch, dtch, dtch !

Old Woman [*nervously — to Jack*]. I shouldn't go on playing that, Jack, till Kian goes out. Let him go off quiet to his Fascist meeting, and then you can blow to your heart's content.

Old Man. And what about quiet for me and me calculations ?

Jack [*doggedly*]. He that hath ears to hear, let him hear what the workers say to the world.

Old Woman [*going over and placing her hand persuadingly on Jack's shoulder*]. For my sake, Jack ; for your mother's sake, let us have a little peace.

Jack [*gently removing her hand from his shoulder*]. Kian must learn to sing what we sing, for that will bring him life ; or close his ears till the hour comes when the sound of the song will bring him face to face with death.

Old Woman. Jack, Jack, he is your brother.

Jack. I have brothers everywhere, Mother ; but I have none in this house.

Old Woman. He is my son ; you are my son : therefore you are his brother.

Jack. He is dead ; I see him not, I hear him not, I touch him not — he is dead.

Old Man. He's bone of your bone, isn't he ? He's flesh of your flesh, isn't he ? Trout in the same stream ; birds in the same nest ; deer in the same wood, cropping the same grass, and couched in the same glade. Ay, and thinking the same thoughts too ; for he's as ready to murder you as you are ready to murder him.

Old Woman [*warningly*]. Hush !

[*Kian comes from the room on the left. He is now wearing a vivid saffron-coloured shirt, black breeches, jack-boots, and a beret. On his right arm is a black piece of cloth ; on the piece of cloth is a white circle, and inside the circle, a flash. A pistol in a holster hangs at his hip. He looks contemptuously at Jack as he crosses the room to the other door.*]

Kian [*to Old Woman*]. I don't know when I'll be back, so don't wait up ; don't worry, and don't fuss. [*He looks across at Jack for a moment, in silence.*] We march tonight. [*A pause.*] The Saffron Shirts march tonight ; they will lead the great procession that is to declare, once for all, once for all, once for all, the end, the utter end, of Communism. [*Jack is silent ; there is a pause.*]

Kian. The end, the utter end, of Communism.

[*Quietly, but clearly, Jack begins to chant a Communist song.*]

Jack [*chanting*] :

The wor-kers are march-ing, men, wo-men and chil-dren, Sing-ing men o'er the wide world close com-rades shall be; Th' red flag fly-ing

o - ver   field,   fact-'ry,   and   work-shop, And

steel-heart-ed   ships   go-ing   down   to   the   sea.

The workers are marching, men, women, and chil-
    dren,
Singing, men o'er the wide world close comrades
    shall be ;
Th' red flag flying over field, fact'ry, and workshop,
And steel-hearted ships going down to the sea.

I love thee, red soldier, red soldier, red soldier,
Standing between us and our bold enemie,
Thy hand on a rifle, red star in thy helmet,
And th' workers' red flag flying high over thee.

Kian. Your red soldier's day is done ; his teeth are
broken in his mouth ; the bayonets of the brave are
searching out his bowels ; he runs hither and thither,
knowing no way out of the blaze that is melting him
as a snail melts in a forest fire ! Our Leader's new
order will overwhelm the living world !

Jack [*chanting*] :
    Down with all flags that defend but the mighty,
    Leaving the workers the dole and the dree ;
    Not this flag, nor that flag, blue, green, or bright
        gold flag,
    But only the one flag, the red flag for me !

Kian [*bitterly*]. Your damned flag is falling. It is being
driven from the world of men to take refuge with the

wolves. The few hands that still hold it, hold it tight — ay, as tight as the stiffening hands of death can hold anything ! [*He gives the Fascist salute.*] Hail, the Circle and the Flash !

[*As he is giving the salute. Julia rushes in. She is a pretty and vigorous girl of nineteen. She is dressed in petticoat, bodice, shoes, and stockings, and carries a green and black pierrette costume over her arm. Kian lets his arm drop, looks at Julia for a moment, then goes out.*]

Julia. It's the bitter heart that flaunts the bitter word.

Jack :

I'd rather be a doll, with waxen face and sawdust body,
From a dull and dusty window tapping
A duller message, with mechanic finger,
For ever to an empty street,
Than have a heart like that.

Old Woman [*briskly to the Old Man*]. Here, you, make way for Julia to iron her fancy-dress costume for the fancy-dress dance.

[*She bustles the Old Man's papers out of the way off the table, so that Julia may have room to iron her costume. The Old Man, stuck near the fire, goes on looking at some of the papers.*]

Old Woman [*with a sigh*]. There's one torment gone, anyway, and peace can steal into the room for a minute or two.

Julia. There'll be a red core in the night before it closes. The Purple Priest of the politicians is patrolling the streets, cursing with book and bell and candle any who have cried or murmured a welcome to Communism ; and he's dragging the Brown Priest of the poor at his

heels, afraid to let him out of his sight, the way he'll
be kept from mixing or sympathising with the people ;
while, with a silent march, dotted with drum-beats,
the Saffron Shirts are shooing the people into a wary
stillness. [*Vehemently*] But we'll face them and fight
them and make them flee before us !

Jack [*putting an arm round her*]. Face them and fight them
and make them flee before us, curly head, silken
cheek, and velvet thighs.

Old Man [*contemptuously*]. A squib, a flash in the pan,
will-o'-the-wisp, the fight of the hornless cows, march
of the wooden soldiers — bah ! And it's near time
that the Brown Priest of the poor should be harnessed
to common sense, and kept from spouting queer and
dangerous Rerum Novarum Quadragesimo Anno
nonsense, trying to make the people uneasy in the state
of life they have to live in.

Old Woman. But the Brown Priest of the poor says that
the Rerum Novarum's the charter of the workers,
and that it's not him, but the holy Pope himself that
said it.

Old Man. What if he did aself ? The Rerum Novarum's
not a question of faith and morals, is it, woman ? And
on any other question the Pope's as infallible as me-
self ! Nice thing for a holy Pope to fix a red fringe on
the Papal banner.

Old Woman. Everyone loves the Brown Priest, anyway,
and so there must be something in what he says.

Old Man [*fiercely*]. It's facts we have to face now, woman,
and not fancies ! The Brown Priest's only making

things worse. Even if he's right, what good is he doing? Bah! He's only a faint sigh in the heart of a clap of thunder!

Jack [thoughtfully]. Ah, if the Brown Priest would only step to the fore and cry out with a loud voice, a host would follow him!

Julia [with a little irritation]. Let's talk of something else, Jack. The dance tonight and the dress that goes with it — look! [She holds up the dress for Jack to see.

Jack [admiringly]. There's not a note of mockery in its gaiety and charm, for it'll slip over the finest figure the gods have ever seen. But not tonight.

Julia. Not tonight? Why not tonight?

Jack. Tonight you and I, and all good Communists, must go full fast from anything that would keep us an inch away from the Red Front.

Julia. And miss the dance? Oh, Jack, I've looked forward to it for months. I've saved up to get the dress, and, at the last minute, I'm asked to forget about it! I can't. I've worked for the Cause as well as you, and it's only fair I should have an hour of forgetfulness tonight.

Old Woman [who has been looking out of the window, through which the star and church spire are seen]. I wonder, now, if that is the east out there?

Julia [facing towards the window]. East? I never bothered to know whether it was east or west.

Old Man [facing towards window]. Nor me either; no, nor north or south either.

Julia [*to Old Woman*]. Why, Old Woman?

Old Woman [*in a reverie*]. If only that wonderful and wondering light, watching our movements, happened, now, to be the star.

Old Man. Which star?

Julia. What star?

Jack [*interested*]. Whose star, Mother?

Old Woman. The star which led the three kings to where the little child lay.

Old Man. Which kings?

Julia. What child?

Jack. Whose star, Mother?

Old Woman [*in a reverie*]. The star of Him who is called Wonderful, Counsellor, Everlasting Father, the Prince of Peace.

> [*From the moment the Old Woman asks if the window be facing east, the Waits can be faintly heard singing " O Come, All ye Faithful ", a little more clearly as she is talking of the star and the kings (as if the hymn was shyly revealing the thoughts of their minds), faintly again while Jack is speaking, and fading away when the Old Man tells those in the room to think of serious things.*

Old Man [*disappointed*]. Oh, Him!

Julia [*turning away her gaze from the window*]. Time has made that story a little stale.

Jack [*still interested*]. How does the star shine, Mother?

Old Woman. It shines as purest silver shines, all brightened by a useful and a loving hand.

Jack [*turning away from looking at his mother*]. So it shone when it led the kings ; so shall it not shine when it leads the people. It leads no more, and never shall till its silver turns to red.

Old Man [*disgustedly*]. Oh, let's think of serious things, and not be disturbing our heads about stars and kings and never-present princes of peace !
[*He plunges his head into the football coupons. The Old Woman comes slowly away from the window to the table, and silently helps Julia to spread out the costume so that it may be smooth under the iron. Julia begins to iron, Jack watching her with a longing look in his eyes.*

Jack [*to Julia*]. Leave the dress and dance alone tonight, dear Julia, and come with me.

Julia [*obstinately*]. I can't ; I won't.

Jack. Remember what you said : We'll face them and fight them and make then flee before us. The Saffron Shirts are marching, Julia.

Julia. Let them march. A few hours of merriment can make small difference.

Jack. An hour may mean the difference between life and death. Come — the Red Star leads.

Julia. Let the Red Star stand still in the heavens for one lone night.

Jack [*going over to the door, and turning towards Julia*]. The Red Star waits for no one. Julia, come.

Julia [*with a catch in her voice — doggedly*]. No !

Jack [*after a pause*]. Goodbye.
[*He waits a moment. Julia says nothing. Then he goes out.*

Julia [*bitterly*]. Asking me to give up everything ! I'm as good a Communist as he is ; better, for where I'm working it's harder for a girl than a man to be one.

Old Woman. Don't fret, dear. He'll be running back at the last minute to kick up a row because you aren't ready.

Old Man. It was the Brown Priest of the poor who started all this nonsense with Jack. He got the chap to cry out for the terms of the Rerum Novarum, and now Jack wants the Brown Priest to cry out in the terms of the Communist Manifesto !

Julia. I'm as good a Communist as Jack is, any day.

Old Woman. 'Course, you are, dear.

Old Man. Ay, or as bad.

> [*The door opens and Joybell comes into the room. He is dressed in a Confraternity robe of rich blue reaching to his heels. A short black cape, attached to the robe, hangs from his shoulders. His waist is girdled by a thick white cord from which hangs a black cross. Big, heavy, clumsy boots peep from underneath the hem of his rich robe ; Joybell is a young fellow of twenty or so, small but tough. He bubbles over with good-will to everybody : yet, essentially, is ever only thinking of himself. His eyes are big, staring, and inclined to bulge a little. He has plump legs, plump arms, and a plump head. He has bushy hair, making his head look plumper still. Sometimes he talks so quickly that he trips over his thoughts, fails to find a word, and repeats the last one several times. At times a doleful note sounds queer in the midst of merry sentences. He is a Catholic flag-wagger.*

Joybell [*in bubbling talk*]. How are you, Mr. — eh — ah —

oh — and you, Mrs. — oh — ah — eh ?   Very well ?
Yes — yes ;   good — good.   Splendid.   All very well ;
splendid.   Very good, so it is ;   good thing to be —
be — be well ;   good, isn't it ?   Quite well, all well,
and on the baker's list.   And how's Mrs. What's-her-
name's baby you take an interest in ?   All right again,
eh, what ?   Yes.

Old Woman.   No, she's not all right.

Joybell.   No, isn't well ?   Isn't she, she well ?   No ?
None of us well, if you come to think of it :   dying
every day, each of us, all of us, every — every day.
She'll be all right soon, never fear.

Old Woman [*getting a word in edgeways*].   No, she won't ;
Doctor says she's too far gone in consumption.

Joybell [*hardly hearing or heeding*].   No !   Nothing to trouble
about, really though.   We've all got it, one way or
another.   Lovely night, tonight, bright night, isn't it ?
Touch of frost out, just a touch ;   nothing more,
nothing else.   Healthy weather ;   seasonable.   Holly
going about, packed — packed with berries, packed !
Bad sign ;   red as blood, all in clusters.   Sign of a hard
winter ;   but a — but a — but a typical, yes, typical
Christmas ;   sparkling frost on Christmas morning, eh,
what ?   Look lovely, wouldn't it ?   To be sure, to be
sure it would.   Nearly here too, Christmas — only a
few hours you might say ;   just a few more, not more,
not many.   Grand festival ;   best of all ;   dearest, too ;
jolly times — God rest you merry, gentlemen, you
know, and all that ;   Immanuel, God with us.   Everybody at their best.   Holly and ivy ;   peace and good-
will, and plenty ;   Early Mass, the crib, holy night,
and — and — and shepherds watching their flocks —

flocks by night and — and — and all eyes turned towards the star — your star, my star, his and her star, their star !

Old Woman. Everybody's star.

Joybell. Yes ; everybody's star ; yes, eh, what ?

Old Man [*roguishly indicating Julia*]. What do you think of that little star, eh ?

    [*Joybell has been disturbed by Julia's undress. From time to time he has been throwing quick, frightened, desiring glances at her pretty legs and bare shoulders, Julia smiling mischievously when she catches him glancing at her ; but, most of the time, Joybell averts his eyes and tries to keep them fixed on the ceiling.*

Old Woman [*roguishly — to Julia*]. Slip something over your bare shoulders, Julia ; you're disturbing poor Joybell.

Julia. Joybell's having a good look and getting a great thrill out of it all — aren't you, Joybell ?

Joybell [*with his eyes to the ceiling*]. You all should have heard Father Fabian's sermon last Sunday, and he telling of a poor man tried for stealing a few loaves. " How many children have you ? " asked the magistrate. " Eight, and another coming," says the poor man. " Shame for a man of your means to have so many," says the magistrate. " The impudence of that magistrate," says Father Fabian ; " why couldn't he have been content to fine the poor man ten shillings, and be done with it ? "

Old Man [*with a sad shake of his head*]. His poor mind's wandering !

Julia [*dancing lightly round the room*]. Joybell can see the good points of a girl's figure as well as anyone — can't you, dear ?

Old Woman. Light of God to us, did he ever even untie a lassie's shoe?

Old Man [*enthusiastically*]. Kiss her, man; go'n; now's your chance, Joybell!

Joybell [*embarrassed, but still holding his gaze towards the ceiling*]. You'll all have to come to the unrolling of our new Guild banner, so you will. Presented by the head of the Christian Front who did so much to help the cause of Christ in Sp — Sp — Spain, and — and — and — you know him — him who was a Saffron Shirt and left them to lead the Christian Front.

Old Man. He took off his shirt to show his Christian front.

Joybell. Yes, yes; eh, what?

Julia [*recklessly — very close to Joybell*]. How would you like to be with me in a lonely wood, and the darkness falling?

Old Woman. He'd run all the way home as fast as his legs could carry him — wouldn't you, Joybell?

Joybell [*pretending not to hear*]. The United Confraternities'll all be there, and, and three bishops, and — and — and three bishops, and——

Old Man. Why don't you listen to what the girl's saying to you?

Joybell [*desperate*]. Which girl — girl, what girl?

Old Man. Julia there.

Joybell. Julia? [*Glancing at her.*] Oh yes, Julia. Didn't notice her till now. Never knew she was there. Didn't know she was speaking to anyone. What did she say?

[Julia suddenly pounces on him, puts her arms round him, and gives him a hug. Frightened, he staggers back while she holds on to him.

Julia. How would you like to cuddle me in a lonely wood with the darkness falling?

Joybell [frantic]. Yes, yes; no, no. Let go — let me go, or you'll do some damage.

Julia. Go on — hug me! Give me a kiss hot enough to melt the bones in a girlie's body!

Old Man [jubilantly]. Go on, Joybell, be a man; now's your chance.

Joybell. Oh, please do let me go! Whist! is that someone calling me? Let a fellow go, can't you!

Old Woman. Call out for help, Joybell!

Julia [pressing herself to him]. Give me a squeeze, a tight one, and make me giddy!

[Joybell suddenly clasps her fiercely to him and kisses her madly till she is breathless and frightened.

Joybell [with mad passion]. I'll make you giddy, you pretty little bitch! I'll press you till you break in two! I'll tear off every stitch you ever had on, so I will!

Julia [frightened]. Let me go, let me go, you ape! Get hold of him and pull him away from me, someone!

Old Woman [angry and frightened — running over and pulling Joybell from Julia]. Here, what d'ye think you are doing, you slippery scut! Couldn't you stand a little harmless joke? Get to hell out of this, you misbegotten worm!

[Joybell, ashamed and panting, leans against the wall : Julia, a little hysterical and frightened, sinks down on a chair.

Julia [*tearful and angry*]. Now you see, now you all see the kind of boyo he is ! Bruising a girl black and blue, without a hint of provocation from anyone. No decent girl's safe with him !

Old Woman. This is a quare eye-opener against the innocent look of holy habiliments.

Old Man [*indignantly — to Joybell*]. You are a nice thing to let run round innocent girls !

Joybell [*piteously*]. It was her fault : she ran at me and — and hugged me, and — and goaded me, and — and — and made me lose me senses !

Old Man. Get out of this house ! What'll the poor clergy think, now, of the boyo who's always looking up into their eyes and leaning on their arm ?

Joybell [*to Old Man*]. Listen, can't you ? It was the streel herself that plucked me into misbehaviour.

Old Man [*sarcastically*]. It's always the poor girl that does the harm. Get out of here, and never darken the door again.

Joybell. Can't you see fair, and try to listen to what I'm saying ?

Old Man [*going over threateningly to Joybell — with a shout*]. Get out, before I fling you out !
[*Joybell, half mad with rage and shame, suddenly lets fly and swipes the Old Man over the eye with his fist.*

Joybell [*striking Old Man*]. Yah, you old coffin-fac'd get !
[*He runs out.*

Old Man [*clapping a hand to the stricken eye and staggering back*]. God Almighty, he's nearly smashed me eye in ! Took me unawares, the litany-lit bowsey !

Old Woman [*going over to him*]. Show me ; let's have a look at it.
  [*She looks closely at the stricken eye and presses her finger on it.*

Old Man [*protestingly*]. Eh, there, eh ; don't push the eyeball out ! He got home on me while I was winking. And neither of you made the slightest stir to stop him !

Old Woman. It's only a little red ; it'll be all right before the morning.

Old Man [*sarcastically*]. Oh, will it, now ? Gone in the morning, eh ? That's grand news ! Before the sun comes up, I suppose. Gone with the wind. [*Vehemently*] Can't you see, woman, it's swelling and puffed and black and blue ? Why do you always try to hide things ? I never yet met a woman fit to face facts.

Julia [*who is ironing her dress again*]. Oh, for goodness' sake don't make such a fuss over a little tap on the eye.

Old Man [*almost stupefied with rage — turning angrily on Julia*]. Here, there, clear out of this you, too ! You've no right to be breaking in on the harmony here. It's the like of you, flaunting your flimsy nakedness before the eyes of innocent men, that causes trouble to sprout and has the clergy running round wild and ferocious against all that doesn't touch the edge of an act of contrition ! Go on, off you go !

Julia [*defiantly*]. I'll finish my dress first.

Old Woman. Let her finish her dress first.

Old Man. Skedaddle off out of here. I'm not going to

have any half-naked hussy jigging round our little respectable home.

Julia. Who's a half-naked hussy !

Old Woman. Julia's a fully respectable girl, without a glimmer of guile in her.

Julia [to the Old Man]. If even the back of the truth was known, you yourself can't keep your fading old eyes from roving over every trim-looking girl that passes ; and, on the stairs, you're always seeking to fortify your good-morning or good-evening with an abiding pinch on a girl's backside !

Old Man [taken aback]. Oh, listen to the dangerous lies that's flowing fast from her now !

Old Woman [deprecatingly — to Julia]. You shouldn't resort to lies, Julia, when my husband's only quietly trying to mend your manners.

Julia [fiercely — to the Old Woman]. If you only opened your eyes, you'd see it too.

Old Woman [losing her temper]. You better go about your business, Julia, and don't be trying to malefy my poor husband. Putting dresses on and taking dresses off is about all you are fit for. I'd have to strain myself to find any good in you. If you can't listen to the truth, then keep your distance and leave the peace of the family alone.

Julia [taking up her dress and going towards the door — bitterly]. Truth ? If either of you saw truth in the street you'd take her for a tramp.

[As Julia is going out the Old Woman goes over to the door and shuts it, giving Julia a helping push out as she does so.

Julia [*outside — beating a tattoo on the door*]. Let that old withered stick of yours wrap himself up in caution when he's passing me again on the stairs — mind, I'm giving you fair warning.

Old Man [*quickly and warningly*]. Don't answer ; keep still ; let her rave.

Old Woman [*at the closed door — loudly*]. Go home quietly to your own place, with your dressed-up indecency. If you don't, I'll leave the mark of my fingers on your paint-patterned face ! [*She swings the door open.*] Mother of God, it's the Lord Mayor !

> [*The Lord Mayor is now seen in the doorway. He is a short man, with a thick torso and thin legs. He puffs out his chest a little as he walks and talks. He has a thin dark moustache, and looks like a cross between a robin redbreast and a snipe. Some of his words have a faint touch of a lisp on them, and his manner is usually of one eager, if not able, to please everybody. He is dressed in morning dress, tall hat, and wears a thick gold chain of office round his neck.*

Lord Mayor [*effusively — as he comes in*]. Good morning, good evening, my very deah friends !

Old Woman [*in confusion*]. Come in, come in, Julia — no, no — me Lord Mayor, won't you come in, no, no, me and me husband were just giving that gadabout, Julia, the Lord Mayor — good God, what am I saying ? — that Julia was about to sit down here and there, after always running round after boys in face of the clergy's warning to keep calm and collected in the pursuit of a girl by a boy, or a boy by a girl, remembering to keep a tight hold up and down on the excitement experienced in dallying away a sweet hour over the trying time of a girl gone on a boy or a boy gone on a girl !

Lord Mayor [*puzzled*]. Exactly !

Old Man [*in confusion — with a chair in his hand for the Lord Mayor*]. As I was saying to my good missus before you hopped in, me Lord Mayor, is that life as it is and isn't and seems to be something more and something less, if you know what I mean, than a simple problem to be solved, by a mere hem here and a mere haw there, and a How are you, Mrs. So-and-so ? bowing and scraping before you know where you are in a matter of this kind of such consideration, more or less, if you know what I mean.

Lord Mayor [*more puzzled than ever*]. Exactly !

Old Woman [*with a chair in her hand*]
Old Man [*carrying a chair*] [*together*]: Won't you sit down, me Lord Mayor ?

[*They plank the two chairs on the floor beside the Lord Mayor, and he sits down — half on one and half on the other, as if he sat on a minor throne.*

Lord Mayor [*gleefully*]. I have good news, my deah friends, I have good news.

Old Man [*nodding to the Old Woman*]. He has good news.

Old Woman [*nodding to the Old Man*]. Good news.

Lord Mayor [*jubilantly*]. Isn't it grand, isn't it lovely, isn't it wonderful ! Christ, the Prince of Peace, has conquered. The stay-in strike, arranged to begin tonight, is stopped before it started. The Bishops have spoken ; the Saffron Shirts are marching ; the Christian Front is holding a rally ; the soldiers are under arms ; the respectable workers have denounced the Reds ; the Trades Congress have voted for peace, and are going to fling Red Jim from the Central Council. Christ, the King, has conquered. Isn't it grand, isn't it lovely, isn't it wonderful !

Old Man. It's time Communism was curbed, anyhow.

Lord Mayor. Or a full-blown detriment would cover every sacred thing in the country.

Old Man. We'd have free love without fee or licence introducing smash-and-grab methods into the holy solicitation of marriage.

Old Woman. The quiet loveliness and grand quality of family life would go for ever.

Lord Mayor. The security of the banks would be shaken badly.

Old Woman. The Lord deliver us from all harm.

Old Man. Amen to that.

Lord Mayor [*seriously*]. I've some bad news to tell you too.

Old Man [*nodding to Old Woman*]. Oh, some bad news to tell us, too.

Old Woman [*nodding to Old Man*]. To tell us, too.

Lord Mayor [*bending forward towards the old couple*]. The Saffron Shirts are coming here to speak to your son, Jack.
  [*The old couple are silent, looking at the Mayor.   A pause.*

Lord Mayor [*almost in a whisper*]. You must get your son Jack to join in with the Christian Front tonight.
  [*The old couple are silent, looking at the Mayor.   A pause.*

Lord Mayor [*emphatically*]. You must get your son Jack to join in with the Christian Front tonight.

Old Woman [*to Old Man*]. You must get Jack to join in with the Christian Front tonight.

Old Man [*vehemently*]. Amn't I tired telling you he'll take no notice of me !

Lord Mayor [*solemnly*]. If he doesn't abjure Communism he will lose his job [*slowly and with emphasis*] and, maybe, lose his life.

Old Woman [*to Old Man*]. How do you know he won't take notice, if you don't try.

Old Man [*furiously*]. Didn't I try before, didn't I try a hundred times before !

Old Woman. It won't do you any harm to try again.

Old Man. You try for a change.

Old Woman. You're his father.

Old Man. And aren't you his mother ?

Old Woman. A father's head of the house, and ought to be able to exert his authority.

Old Man [*fiercely*]. I'm exerting it now by ordering you to try yourself, and it doesn't seem to have much effect !

Old Woman. The Purple Priest has told you often that as a practising Catholic, and a member of the Bona Mors Confraternity, it was your bounden duty to comb your son out of Communism and lead him back to the faith.

Old Man [*furiously*]. Let the Purple Priest do it himself then ! What are we paying him his dues for ? Or, for a change [*indicating the Mayor*], let his eminence, there, have a shot at it !

[*In the distance the very faint sound of a drum-beat, like the sound of a tom-tom leading marching men, is heard.*

Lord Mayor [*with awe in his voice*]. Listen ! [*A pause, while they listen.*] The Saffron Shirts are marching. The Flash in the Circle is driving out the discontented. Get your son to see reason, even if you have to go down on your knees to do it.

[*The door from the street opens, and Jack comes in. He glances at the Lord Mayor and turns away with a look of contempt.*

Jack [*to the old couple*]. Where's Julia ?

Old Woman. She's gone.

Lord Mayor [*standing up to meet Jack — beamingly*]. Ah, how iss my young friend, how iss my deah young friend ?

Jack [*viciously*]. Your friend ? I'd as lief be the friend of Dermot of the curses, who sold his country, or of Judas, who sold his Master !

Lord Mayor [*blandly*]. Now, now, now. You are my friend all the same ; yeth, you are, in spite of thinking that you hate me.

Jack [*venomously*]. So I do, you hopabout little bugger ! Flight, and the hatred of men to you ; bothering and blasting winds blow on you ! And when your last sigh asks for mercy, may the pardon of Christ be lost in the loud curses of the crowd !

[*The door again flies open, and Julia, dressed now in her bright green and black pierrette costume, short-skirted and barebacked, runs into the room and goes over to Jack.*

Julia [*running to Jack and flinging her arms round him excitedly*]. Jack, dear, I'm not going to the dance. I'll stay with you. I'll go to the Hall. Misery came over me while I was dressing, and I fought against going to joy when there was work to be done. And when I was all ready, I saw the Star, and came flying up to you. I'll stay with you, I'll follow the Star. The Saffron Shirts are raiding the houses of all who have even a single wish against them. And the Purple Priest of the politicians is busy preparing a safe and wide way before them, commanding from all the people a bent knee and a curse on the Communists. Together we'll face them.

Jack. And fight them.

Julia. And make them flee before us !

Jack [*putting an arm round Julia*]. Keep close to me. Do as I do : say nothing ; hear nothing ; see nothing ; and they will not strike tonight.

[*In the doorway — left open by Julia — the Purple Priest and the Brown Priest are seen on the threshold, the Brown Priest a little behind the other. The Purple Priest is clad in a violet cassock, girdled with a black cord. A cowl hides all but the front of his face, which is pale, fixed like a mask in lines of cold severity. The Brown Priest wears a brown cassock ; the cowl lies on his shoulders, and his head is partly covered by a black skull-cap. The Brown Priest's cassock is girdled by a white cord. His face is gentle and kind, marred by a look of bewilderment. The Purple Priest wears a black cross on his breast ; the Brown Priest a white one. There are a few moments of tense silence, broken by the drum-beats of the marching Saffron Shirts, while those in the room stare at the two priests.   They come a little way into the room, and the Brown Priest gently closes the door.*

Purple Priest [*with a hand extended in blessing*]. The peace of God that passeth all understanding be close to all and dwell in the hearts of all who are in this house tonight.

Brown Priest [*fervently*]. Tonight, and for ever more. Amen !

Purple Priest [*in cold and level tones*]. Peace to all but those who would mar the peace of this holy season with the hate of a deadly idea ; who would rouse brother against brother, with Christ's own Mass but a short night's sleep ahead of us, and his holy star high in the sky of the evening !

Brown Priest. Let it not be a tale with thee, O Lord, that there is to be no peace for us.

Purple Priest. I see before me a poor daughter of Eve dressed for a folly that will fondle sin with a busy finger ; I see before me a son of God wearing the badge of the enemy, man's enemy, the Church's enemy, God's own enemy. The one must strip off the dress of folly and put on a garment meet for penance and prayer ; the other must cast away a badge that insults the soul of a child of God.

Brown Priest [*to Julia*]. Do what the Church commands, my daughter ; [*To Jack*] Do what the Church commands, my son.

Jack. The Star stays where it is.

Julia. And I stay with the Star.

Purple Priest. Let your hearts be humble and contrite

before God starts with His sore wounding, before His
anger sears you with pain and lamentation, when bitter
calling out will bring no help.

Jack. The Star stays where it is.

Julia. And I stay with the Star.
> [*The drums of the marching Saffron Shirts, after a slight
> pause, are now outside the house. The drums give a roll,
> which is followed by a shout of " Hail the Circle and
> the Flash ! " As soon as the shout ends, two sharp
> knocks are given on the door. A short pause.*

Voice of Leader of the Saffron Shirts [*outside the door*]. Let the
door open ; in the name of the new power, the great
power, the one and only power — let the door open !
> [*The Old Man opens the door and stands back. The Leader
> of the Saffron Shirts, followed by Kian and some of his
> troopers, enters. He is a man of about thirty-two,
> middle-sized and stiff in his bearing. He is dressed in
> a Saffron Shirt (a vivid, dark, rich yellow) and has a
> badge on his right arm of a white circle enclosing a flash
> on a black ground ; his black breeches are thrust into
> top-boots. His head is covered with a black beret. He
> carries a riding-whip in his hand. Two of his troopers
> turn smartly, one to the right, the other to the left, and
> extend their arms in salute of their Leader. The two
> priests join in the salute. For a few moments the
> Leader stares at Jack. Kian stands beside the Leader.*

Leader [*to Julia, who has moved protectively in front of Jack*].
Out of the light, vain doll, till we see more clearly
the poor fool who would shove the sun out of the
heavens with a push of his shoulder !
> [*Jack tries gently to set Julia aside. but she resists, and
> remains standing in front of him.*

Leader [*more sternly — to Julia*]. Out of the light, you painted pansy, till we fix our eyes on him whose ignorant hand would try to stop a thunderbolt !
    [*Julia suddenly runs over to the Leader, stares him full in the face for a second, then slaps him across the face.*

Julia [*scornfully*]. Take from a vain doll an immortal salute to your business and your banner !
    [*The Leader stands still and silent for a moment, then tosses his whip to a trooper.*

Leader [*quietly, but malignantly*]. Take the painted pansy away, and teach her manners.
    [*Several troopers seize Julia and drag her from the room.*

Julia [*as she is being dragged out*]. Stick to the Star, Jack, stick to the Star ! [*A pause.*

Old Woman [*to the Purple Priest*]. Father, Father, let not this savage violence be done to this poor girl.

Brown Priest. What she did was done but in a burst of anger, and may be pardoned, Father.

Purple Priest [*coldly*]. Let what is to do be done. A passing pain will take some glitter out of the dress and dream of seduction. It is good that the little immodest wretch should have the lash laid on her back, lest worse befall her.

Old Woman [*turning to Kian — appealingly*]. Kian, Kian, let them not do this dark, damned thing to Julia ! You love her ; I know you do. For the sake of that love speak a word, raise a hand to save her !

Kian. The Flash strikes those who strike at the rim of the Circle.

Leader. Hail to the Circle and the Flash !

Kian. Hail !

Brown Priest [*to Purple Priest — pleadingly*]. Let not this be done, dear Father, to this poor worker. The workers will remember. It goes against the grain and is against the spirit of the sacred Rerum Novarum.

Purple Priest [*coldly — to Brown Priest*]. Keep silence. I ask you to keep silence, and I order you to obey. To a priest, the first step to heaven is obedience, the second step is obedience, and the third step is obedience. Let what is to do be done.

Jack [*who has remained tense and still — to the Purple Priest*]. This shall be remembered unto you, dead-hearted priest, when the hour strikes for the workers to will the way to power !

S.S. Leader [*to Jack*]. Take that Star from your coat.

Jack [*sullenly*]. The Star stays where it is.

Brown Priest. Do what the State commands, my son.

Jack. The Star stays where it is.

Leader [*to Jack*]. For the sake of the brother who serves within the Circle, we wait to warn you. We warn you once, and once only. The State can have no enemies within its Circle. We root them out, thousand by thousand, ten by ten, and one by one. If the warning isn't heeded, we come again. Neither drum nor trumpet tell of our second coming : we come silently, like a thief in the night : we come silently, and we strike at once !

> [*Michael, Julia's father, pale and frantic, pushes into the room, knocking troopers aside who try to check him.*

Michael [*furiously*]. Where's Julia ? I'm told the yellow-shirted scum are lashing her. If they are, they'll pay for it ! [*To Leader*] It isn't true, you dog ? Where's Julia ? where's my daughter ?

Leader [*calmly*]. She's where she's being taught obedience to the State.

Old Woman [*to Michael*]. She slapped him across the face, Mick ; right across the face.

Michael. She did, did she ? Slapped the scum across the face, did she ? [*To the Leader*] So you're finding out that, in spite of your uniform, your outstretched paw saluting cruelty, that the workers are getting the guts to fight !

Jack [*catching Michael's arm*]. Your orders, man, remember ; silence !

Michael [*shaking his arm free*]. To hell with orders — I want my daughter !

Leader [*coldly*]. Yet but a little while, and we shall skim the scum from the State : the gaping mouth shall be shut tight ; the feet that run in the way of riot shall be tied together ; the violent shall be made meek ; and the stubborn back shall be bent or broken.

Michael [*losing all control of himself*]. You damned, slug-soul'd renegade, there'll be one brute less when that time comes !

> [*Michael rushes at the Leader, and Kian shoots him down. There is a tense silence for a moment ; then the Old Woman rushes over to Kian.*

Old Woman [*frantically — to Kian*]. What have you done, what have you done, Kian ? my Kian, my poor Kian, my dear son Kian !

Kian [*doggedly*]. The Flash strikes those who strike at the rim of the Circle.

Old Woman. Oh, Kian, my son, my poor, sense-forsaken son, what have you done !

Leader [*looking at Michael lying on the floor*]. The gaping mouth shall be shut tight ; the violent shall be made meek.

[*The Brown Priest goes over and bends down over the dying Michael.*

Michael [*gently setting aside the Brown Priest*]. Not that now. [*To Jack*] Jack, Jack, comrade.

[*Jack goes over and kneels beside him.*

Michael [*raising himself a little*]. Jack, comrade, keep little Julia near you. She's all I've got, and all I've got I give to you. Now, my fist — close it. [*Jack does so.*] Now, my arm — raise it, lift it high. [*Jack does so.*] Lift it up, lift it up in the face of these murdering bastards — the Clenched Fist !

CURTAIN

ACT II

A room in the headquarters of the General Workers' Union. The background is the same as the scene before, except that, instead of black, the dominant colour here is green, a bright green, the colour of new grass or the opening of fresh leaves on the trees in advancing spring. Through the window on the right, the church seems a little farther away — though the star is as near and as bright as ever — and through the other window the foundry chimneys seem to be nearer and more massive. Instead of the sketches between the windows, there is a black poster, having on it a white cross on which a red hammer and sickle are imposed. Over this poster and over the two windows is a streamer having on it the words " An Injury to One is the Concern of All ". There is a door, left, leading to the other parts of the building. To the right, a table-desk with writing materials and a telephone. There is a stove higher up from the door on the left, some chairs, a bookcase filled with books having bright bindings, and a few filing cabinets. Against the desk a picture of a man (that of Sheasker) in a grand gilt frame is leaning. All the furniture is black — so that the colours here are black and bright green. Between the door and the stove some overcoats hang on the wall. When the scene is shown, the Secretary is standing beside his desk ; the Brown Priest, with bent head, is standing before the window showing the church spire ; the Purple Priest in centre, right in front of the poster ; Caheer stands beside a chair before the stove ; Brallain by a chair to the right ; and Eglish stands at back, right in front of the window showing the foundry chimneys.

The Secretary is a long, thin man of about thirty-five. The front of his head is bald, giving him the look of a man with a very high brow. On the tip of each cheek is a pink patch, telling, perhaps, of a tendency to consumption. He has a habit of sinking his head on his breast when he is nervous and undecided — which is often ; and he is inclined to be cautious and evasive in his answers to questions.

Brallain is a man of forty, shifty and ambitious, with a foxy face.

Eglish is about thirty, gathered up in the shoulders, has a closely cropped moustache, and likes to take things quietly.

Caheer is about thirty-five, thin and mean-looking, giving, sometimes, a little cough of hesitation before he speaks. He is keen, seeking authority rather than power, serving his own conceit.

Purple Priest. We confirm all we decided this morning. Now, more than ever, we must face him ; face him and frighten him. He will create whatever anger and rage he can among the workers out of the shooting and the just punishment given to an impudent and seductive hussy. His efforts here must be met, checked, and brought to nothing. To deprive Red Jim of his chance of a demonstration we will have the body brought to the church. You must do your part here without a taint of hesitation. Separate Red Jim from the workers, and he is but an arrowhead without a shaft ; a blank cartridge — noisy, but not dangerous. In our church tonight we will sanctify our resolution against the curse of Communism. You have all done well. [*He looks at Caheer.*] You stand for the Wood-workers. [*He glances at Brallain.*] You for the Railway-men. [*He glances at Eglish.*] You for the Agricultural Workers. And Sheasker — [*he glances at the Secretary*] — you say, is sure of the Metal-workers ?

Secretary. Yes, Father.

Purple Priest. Then the tale is told : Red Jim is finished.
[*He stands to his full height, and all stiffen their bodies
with resolution except the Brown Priest, who still stands
with his head bent on his breast.*

Purple Priest [*in a droning voice*]. Before God, for Whom
we act, and in Whose name we speak :

Brown Priest [*very softly and slowly*]. Amen.

Purple Priest :
  To save dire and everlasting havoc,
  To save the frightened souls tied to his terror,
  To deliver them from the error of their present way,
  To give them back the hope and patience of the
    children of God,
  We condemn and join together against the body and
    soul and all the influences of Red Jim ;
  Against his words, his work, and his savage teaching ;
  We banish his desire and most dangerous doctrines,
    that are burning up the sweet souls of the faithful ;
  We banish him and them to far-away airs, to mists of
    high mountains man's eyes never see ;
  To the lonely, wild, wandering waters, uncharted by
    man, forgotten by God,
  In the Name of the Lord !

Caheer :
  The Shapers of Wood and the Moulders of Metal.

Eglish :
  The Tillers who dig for the fruits of the earth.

Brallain. The Railwaymen bringing far distances near.

Purple Priest :
  Deny him the right to make of them foes
  To the Church, to the State, or to property sacred,

Handed down through the ages from father to son ;
So one with the Church, with the State, and with
   Owners,
We mark Red Jim down as a wolf to be worried,
Wounded and worried away from the core of the
   flock ;
To be hurried away from the fringe of the flock ;
To be hunted when merry day's dancing around,
To be hunted when silent night's hush'd her to
   sleep,
Till his flight is as far from the fringe of the flock
As the dead are from all the dear murmurs of
   morning !   [*He pauses.*
Remember, remember, remember :
No merit peeps from him ;
No twinge for a comrade shall hinder our hunting ;
No cozening service shall shorten our curse on him.
He goes and none go with him.
So shall it be.   [*He glances at Eglish.*

Eglish. In the name of the Lord.

Caheer [*as the Purple Priest glances at him*]. In the name of
   the Lord.

Secretary [*as the Purple Priest glances at him*]. In the name
   of the Lord.

Brallain [*as the Purple Priest looks at him*]. In the name of
   the Lord.
   [*Then the Purple Priest moves slowly towards the door,
   followed by the Brown Priest, with his head bent on his
   breast. The others move with them to show them to the
   door, smiling and reverent.*

Purple Priest [*moving towards the door*]. This menace shall

be but a forgotten mist ere the holy feast of Christmas
ends.

Brallain. Never fear, Father ; his leadership's a shroud
already. We, the men in the Unions, you with the
people in their homes, will stamp on his dying stir ;
and the Saffron Shirts can deal with any armed rabble
hanging at his heels.

Purple Priest [*at the door*]. God be with you all. Goodbye.
[*He goes, followed by the Brown Priest. The others come
back and resume their places. There is a silence for a
few moments.*

Caheer. Did you notice that the Brown Priest kept his
head down the whole of the time ?

Brallain. He doesn't count.

Caheer. We're left to do the dirty and the dangerous
work.

Secretary. Gain or loss, now, we must go on with it.

Brallain. Oh, let's forget it till Red Jim's here.

Eglish [*dubiously*]. If we can.

Caheer. Let's have another look at Sheasker's presenta-
tion portrait.
[*The Secretary brings forward the picture that has been
standing by the desk, props it up, and they all stare at it
for a few moments in silence. The picture is an enlarged
coloured photograph in a massive gilt frame, and shows,
from the waist up, the well-paunched, smug-looking
figure of a man of forty, well dressed, with gloves in a fat
hand, a broad gold watch-chain across his belly, and a
bowler on a table beside him.*

Eglish. What a concentrated, conceited-looking, snobbish gob he has !

Caheer. He says his face is the dead spit of the face of Julius Caesar.

Eglish. Jasus !

Caheer. He must have a very humble mind, mustn't he ? Doesn't think much of himself, does he ? More like a face you'd see in a bad dream, if you ask me. He's a little more like Caesar than a woman's spit, and that's about all !

Eglish. He should have been here to help us with the Purple Priest — dodging everything but the soft jobs.

Secretary. With this crisis due, he should never have taken the suite of furniture, thrown in with this perfect portrait, from the Fireiron and Fendermakers' Union.

Eglish. If he deserved it, what matter ; but it was Red Jim's Union keeping the strike clear of scabs that allowed the men to win.

Caheer. Fighting the employers for an increase of five shillings and then down on his knees thanking them for an increase of sixpence !

Eglish. And thanking them on behalf of himself for a cheque, if the truth was known.

Secretary. To give Red Jim his due, if it hadn't been for him the men would have had to creep back with their caps in their hands.

Brallain [*swiftly, and with tense coldness*]. There's no merit in Red Jim — remember that, all of you. He and his Union's a danger and a curse to us all. He's a bully, a blind Boanerges, a big noise ! Let no tint of merit mingle with the mention of him or his Union. [*To the Secretary*] Fix that in your mind, you.

Caheer. Anyway, Sheasker wouldn't hurt his little finger for God Almighty. If he could, he'd spend his life toasting his fat arse before a fire.

Eglish. He can sit cushy at home, now, in one of the soft chairs he got for nothing.

Caheer. Sheasker's got no principle : criticizing the clergy here, but, anywhere else, when he gets a chance, flinging himself headlong down to kiss a Bishop's ring.

Eglish. If he thought he'd curry favour he'd kiss a Bishop's backside, without consent of canonical law.

Caheer. Remember the time when he thought he'd said too much, going to Rome and carrying a banner at the head of the parade of pilgrims.

Eglish. Jasus !

Brallain. In this fight he's with us, see ? When Red Jim's down we can deal with Sheasker.

Secretary. I wish it was all over.

Eglish. Well, it's *jacta alea est* now, and we'll have to stick together.

Secretary [*warningly*]. Hush ! There's somebody coming. [*Sheasker comes in, looking something like his picture, though he now carries a neatly folded umbrella in his hand, and is wearing a nice grey overcoat. He pauses to stand and admire the picture of himself.*

Sheasker [*proud of the picture*]. Well, what do you think of it, boys — any kind of a likeness ?

Eglish [*enthusiastically*]. Spit of you, I'd say ; and the frame is beau-ti-ful !

Sheasker. Real gold leaf — worth a lot. [*To the Secretary*] What do you think of it, Ned ?

Secretary [*with a hesitating cough*]. Um, um, classic piece of work, I'd say.

Caheer. The face is particularly well done.

Sheasker. Think so ? The Lord Mayor thinks the face has a distinct resemblance to the face of Julius Caesar — the nose, eyes, brow, chin, and cheeks especially.

Eglish. Now that you mention it, I see the likeness myself.

Caheer. Put a laurel round the head, and the likeness would be startling !

Eglish [*going a little distance away*]. Look at it from here, now — first-class work. Julius Caesar looking at things with a glittering eye !

Sheasker [*trying to control his vanity*]. Makes me out a little too young, what ?

Caheer. No, no ; I shouldn't say so.

Sheasker. Red Jim 'll be jealous when he sees it.

Brallain [*quickly and keenly*]. Don't let him see it ; and, what's more, don't let him hear about the presented furniture either.

Sheasker [*angrily*]. What's it to do with him ? Didn't I earn it — working night and day to get the men an increase ? Are you all afraid of him, or what ?

Brallain. No more than you are — maybe less ; but we don't want to put any weapon in his hand, just now.

Sheasker [*truculently*]. We've settled him, once for all, haven't we ? We're only waiting here now to tell him where he stands. It's no longer us who'll have to obey him, but him who'll have to obey us. Me, Brallain, and the Purple Priest, are now, or will be, first day of the New Year, Trustees of the Union. The Church is against him ; the authorities are itching to lay hands on him ; the Saffron Shirts are hard on his heels ; decent Union men are full of hatred of him, under their fear — only the genuine bowseys of the movement cling to him — so what, in the name of God, have we to fear ?

Brallain [*quietly*]. We've got to tell him all this yet, haven't we ?

Caheer [*hopefully*]. When he knows everything, he'll cave in — I'm sure of it !

Eglish. There won't be much else for him to do.

Secretary [*dubiously*]. Uuuuum, I'm not so sure.

Caheer [*nervously and testily*]. Why aren't you sure, man ?

Secretary. He'll fight, I'm sure, he'll fight. That's all left for him to do. Take it from me, he won't swoon — he'll fight.

Caheer [*impatiently*]. How can he fight, and the ground cut from under his feet ? How can he fight, with the Bishops and the Saffron Shirts against him ?

Eglish. And the Christian Front — don't forget the Christian Front ; they may be on the make, but they are a power.

Secretary. What about the armed men in the Union? They'll fight too.

Eglish [*mockingly — to the Secretary*]. You're getting a little pale at the gills. Don't be afraid of a few wooden soldiers.

Caheer [*angrily — to Secretary*]. For God's sake try to stiffen your spine for one lone hour in your life!

Secretary. None of you, if you ask me, is looking in the best of health at the moment.

Brallain. Oh, no quarrelling now. We must all stand or fall together.

Caheer. How much went out of the Funds last year?

Secretary. Nearly a thousand pounds.

Caheer. Good God! If that went on we'd shortly be without a penny wages.

Secretary. And a rumour going round that it all went in arms. And thousands before that too.

Brallain. That's ended now, anyhow.

Sheasker [*looking at his gold watch*]. He's late. Wish he'd come. The Lord Mayor has asked me to act Father Christmas at the giving out of tea and sugar to the poor.

Caheer. Another little cunning, little all-for-meself little bastard!

Secretary [*warningly*]. Hush. Somebody's coming!
    [*They all stiffen in expectation of seeing Red Jim come in;
    but it is Brannigan who shoves the door open and surges in
    on top of them. He is a big brawny fellow with a red*

face, big hands, big heart, and a husky voice. His eyes are glittering and he has a few drinks taken. He is dressed in a faded blue coat, corduroy trousers, and heavy boots. A faded grey trilby hat, too small for him, is crushed on his head. He is wearing a bandolier, and a bayonet in a frog hangs at his hip.

Brannigan [*roughly*]. Where's Jim ? where's he ? wasn't he to be here tonight ? About this time, wasn't he ?

Brallain [*angry and dignified*]. What do you mean by bursting into a private room where a Council Meeting's being held ? Get out, and get out quick !

Brannigan [*ignoring Brallain — to Secretary*]. Where's Jim — hasn't he been here ?

Secretary. Red Jim isn't here ; you're not blind, are you ?

Brannigan. No, not blind, boy ; I see more'n many see — see ? [*After a pause*] I wonder what you four bastards are plotting about now.

Brallain [*coming closer to Brannigan*]. You've no business here ; get out quick !

Brannigan [*looking him straight in the eyes*]. Yessir, yessir, yessir ; I go, sir ; at once, sir. [*He spits splendidly in Brallain's eye.*] You envy-stippled titivated toad !
    [*He waits a second to see if Brallain will offer resentment or show resistance, then turns and goes out.*

Brallain [*wiping his eye*]. There's one of his troopers for you ; one of his Old Guard ; one of his right-of-the-line lowsers ; a ripe, red, drunken ruffian !

Secretary. And armed too. You can't stir now without bumping into an armed fool somewhere or other.

Brallain [*viciously*]. When we've got Red Jim silent and sorrowful we'll brush the Union free from these runabout ruffians !

Sheasker. We'll make them beg for what they snatch at now.

Eglish. By written permission ; standing with hats off, and fair, respectful mien, begging the advice and help they need.

Secretary [*with a sigh*]. Soon may that sweet time come, say I, for now the slightest thing they think is wrong sends them in on top of us, blowing their hot breath in our patient faces, cannonading us with curses, and trying to trample on us with their muddy boots.

Brallain [*listening*]. Hush ; what's happening now ?
   [*A noise of someone hammering at another door in the building is heard.*

Secretary. Another of them asking quietly for something.
   [*The door suddenly flies open and Brannigan rushes in again.*

Brannigan [*violently*]. Where the hell's everyone ? Why's the Insurance Office shut ? Who's responsible for this non-attention to the members' needs ? I want me maternity money. Do you hear me, you tied-up pack of employers' silk and shiny-coloured dressing gowns !

Brallain [*angrily — to Secretary*]. Order this fellow out, will you ? Pack him off about his business. Who lets this roaring rowdy burst in on responsible men deep in responsible business ?

Secretary [*severely — to Brannigan*]. Get out, Brannigan, or I'll report you to the Committee. Go to the proper place and come at the proper hour, and you'll get whatever may be due to you.

Brannigan [*wrathfully*]. Report till your tongue dries, you long, lingering hinderer of honest men ! A man just after having a kid's entitled to his due and some civility, isn't he ?

Secretary. Please go away at once, Brannigan.

Brannigan [*passionately*]. I want me maternity money, I'm telling you ! I've paid me dues to the last tick of the clock, and I've been looking forward to the money for months. There'll be bloodshed if it's not forthcoming.

Sheasker [*rising to his feet*]. Get out !

Brallain [*standing beside Sheasker — both now a little nearer to Brannigan*]. Go on, get out !

Caheer [*rising and standing beside them*]. Go on ; off with you when you're ordered !

Eglish [*grabbing a ruler from the desk and joining them*]. Go on — make yourself scarce !
    [*The light of battle gleams in Brannigan's eyes. He glares at the four of them for a moment ; then, with a yell, he whips out his bayonet and draws it back for a lunge. The four fall over each other to get clear, and rush round to the further end of the desk.*

Brannigan [*with a yell*]. Yah, I'll do for yous ! I'll let daylight through yous, one be one ! I'll skewer the four of you together ! I'll let some of the arrogance escape out of you. Come on out here, in front of me, you golden-snouted snails !

Brallain [*appealingly*]. Now, now, Brannigan, please ; that's enough, like a good man. Please, please put up that bayonet. We're only for your own good. We meant no harm.

Eglish. We're comrades, after all, don't forget that, Brannigan.

Brannigan [*furiously*]. Comrades ? I'll leave yous fidgeting about in fragments if you dare to call me comrade !

Caheer. For God's sake, Brannigan, keep cool ! We're only too eager to do all we can for you. You've only got to say what you want and we'll do the rest — honest to God, Brannigan !

Sheasker [*searching a pocket and taking out a shilling*]. Here you are, Brannigan, me son, a shilling for a drink.

Brannigan [*eyeing the shilling with scorn*]. Put that back for fear it'll catch cold. [*With quiet rancour — to Brallain*] A ten-shilling note from you, and five shillings each from your coadjutors ; and over here with you all to present the tribute money, kneeling down on one knee in a fit and tidy fashion to receive the honour of a proletarian knighthood.

 [*Brallain, Eglish, Sheasker and Caheer come over hesitatingly, and kneel on one knee before the delighted Brannigan.*

Brannigan [*tapping Brallain on the head with the bayonet*]. Rise up, you ready-ripened son of serve-yourself. [*Tapping Eglish on the head with the bayonet*] Rise up, you shattered idea of a man made backwards. [*Tapping Sheasker on the head with the bayonet*] Rise up, you silky sulky slow-worm. [*Tapping Caheer on the head with the bayonet*] Rise up, you tattered tail-end of a false beginning. [*To them as they stand in a row before him*]

Now fork out the fees for the honours given. [*He collects the ten shillings from Brallain and five shillings from each of the others.*] I'll teach yous manners. I'll civilize the four of you. I'll show you it's dangerous to be safe in this world. Now back to your seats and take your ease while honest men are doing useful work in the world.

[*They go back and sit down. Brannigan gives them a contemptuous look, and then goes.*

Eglish [*bitterly*]. Not one of you lifted a hand to help when I took the ruler to him — a pack of runaways !

Caheer. You were first at the back of the desk yourself.

Brallain. Showed us the right way, led the van there.

Caheer [*sneering to Eglish*]. I thought you were going to do something fine when you whipped up the ruler.

Secretary [*with a half-suppressed titter*]. I'll teach yous, he says ; I'll civilize the four of you !

Sheasker [*bitterly — to Secretary*]. The telephone was at your elbow, and you didn't think to call the police.

Secretary [*still tittering*]. I'll skewer the four of yous, he says — and he looked as if he'd do it, too !

Caheer [*fiercely*]. Damn your tittering tongue, man !

Brallain [*sharply*]. Lock the door, or he'll be bursting in on us again.

Eglish [*about to lock the door*]. Here's the Brown Priest hurrying up the corridor.

[*The Brown Priest comes in panting. He sits down on a chair, breathless.*

Brown Priest [*between pants*]. Jim, Red Jim, I want to see Red Jim — at once. I've news for Red Jim ; a warning — he must hide somewhere at once ! Oh dear, I'm not so young as I was. I ran all the way ; I'm puffed, I'm puffed ! Where's he, where's Red Jim ?

Sheasker [*looking at his watch*]. He should be here. He's late. I wish he'd come, for the Lord Mayor wants me to do Father Christmas for him.

Eglish [*jealous*]. And help him afterwards at the ball to eat and drink the good things going.

Sheasker [*angrily*]. You're fond of a few of them yourself !

Brallain [*who has been staring at the priest*]. Yes, yes, Father ; you say you've news for Red Jim : a warning — what is it ?

Brown Priest [*easier, but still panting a little*]. Yes, a warning. The Purple Priest let it out a while ago. I slipped away to run here. I shouldn't, I know, but I felt I had to come. It is deceit, disobedience, but I had to come. Oh dear, I am puffed ! He must hide, Red Jim must hide. [*All are intensely interested.*

Eglish. Hide ? How hide ?

Caheer. Hide ? For what ?

Sheasker. Hide ? Why ? Where ?

Brallain [*silencing the others with a gesture — to the Brown Priest*]. Take it easy, Father. Now why must Red Jim be warned and why must he hide ?

Brown Priest. The Saffron Shirts are out to seize him, and hold him fast. [*A silent pause.*

Brallain [*coldly*]. And you hurried here all the way to tell us that ?

Brown Priest. He must be warned ; he must hide !

Brallain [*coldly*]. He mustn't be warned, Father.

Brown Priest [*surprised*]. No ? Mustn't be warned ?

Brallain. To warn him may make it harder for the authorities to lay hands on him. The easier we make it for them to lay hands on him the easier it will be for us to carry out things we have arranged to do.

Sheasker [*excitedly*]. By God, his sudden disappearance 'll come in damn handy !

Eglish [*rubbing his hands gleefully*]. It's providential, so it is !

Caheer. It'll give us time to fix ourselves too tight for him to move us !

Brown Priest [*shocked, but quiet*]. I see. My news is good news. I might have saved myself the trouble of coming here. But think a little : would Red Jim act like this were one of you in the same danger ?

Eglish. That's different.

Caheer. Of course it's different — Red Jim's a danger to everyone.

Brown Priest. I suppose you know what may happen to him if they get him in their power ?

Brallain. We don't know, and we don't care. We must think first of the men in our Unions.

Brown Priest. I'm afraid you are thinking of yourselves

only. Oh, I am almost persuaded that Red Jim is right when such as you go all against him !

Brallain [*with cold passion*]. I seem to remember a Brown Priest standing with us a short while ago in the desire and determination to destroy him ! I suppose you know that he is busy now using the shooting of his henchman by the Saffron Shirts to change an orderly agitation into an orgy of battle, murder, and sudden death. Believe me, Father, the Purple Priest knows more about these things than you do. Will you answer for this man ? Will you, will you ? Is there even one ready to answer for what this big bully is ready to do ?

> [*Red Jim is now seen standing at the door. He is tall and strongly built. His eyes are grey and brilliant. His hair is raven black. His nose is long, thick, and combative. He walks with a slight seaman's lurch. He is dressed in a dark-green coat, faded blue trousers, and his head is covered by a wide-brimmed black slouch hat. On the right breast of the dark-green coat is a Red Star. When he speaks, one hears a touch of hoarseness in his voice, due to constant speaking in the open to large crowds. He smiles when the Brown Priest sees him — it is a smile of welcome and affection. There is a tense silence when he is seen, and when he looks at the uneasy Delegates.*

Red Jim. There's one will answer for what Red Jim is doing — Red Jim himself ! [*To the Brown Priest*] Will you not answer for me too, Brown Priest of the poor ?

Brown Priest [*agitated*]. For some of the things you do, Red Jim ; for most of the things you do.

Red Jim [*calmly*]. But not for all ?

Brown Priest [*in a low voice*]. But not for all.

Red Jim :

    Stretch not a timid finger towards the holy fire of
        Revolution ;

    But step into the midst of it, man, or flee away.

    Flee from the fire that brings rebellion's beam to
        the darken'd eye,

    That burns corroding deafness from the indiff'rent
        ear,

    And stirs to hefty action the fast withering arm !

    Stretch not a timid finger towards the holy fire,

    Lest the life behind the finger perish in its coldness.

    Step into the midst of the fire, or flee away !

Brown Priest [*uneasy — with bent head*]. I'm going now. I
hurried here to warn you.

Red Jim. To warn me ?

Brown Priest. The Saffron Shirts have planned to seize
you sudden !

Red Jim [*calmly*]. They have, have they ? [*He glances at the
Delegates.*] So that's why all my comrades seem so
sorrowful ! They won't know what to do without me.

Brown Priest [*staring steadily at Red Jim*]. Maybe they're
not so sorrowful as they look.

Red Jim. Aha, you've put your prying finger on their
pulse, have you ? So you don't think they love me,
Brown Priest of the poor ? At times I've actually
thought so myself. Maybe you are right. They're
not all I have, anyhow. So I'm to be taken away and
hid in a dark corner ?

Brown Priest [*going close to Red Jim*]. Sent to a concentration,
and, maybe — killed !

Red Jim [*pretending concern*]. Poor Red Jim ! [*Indicating Delegates*] And I selected these to be my bodyguard — [*indicating Sheasker*] — with Julius Caesar, there, to lead them. That's Sheasker, you know — he thinks he's the spit of Caesar.

Brown Priest [*anxious to go away*]. You know all now, and I have served my turn. Goodbye.   [*A pause.*

Red Jim. Stay with us, comrade.

Brown Priest [*a little frightened at the very thought*]. Stay with you ? How ? why ?

Red Jim. To be with us when the star turns red ; to help us to carry the fiery cross. Join with us. March with us in the midst of the holy fire.

Brown Priest [*frightened*]. No, no, not yet ; not yet. I must go, I must go. Goodbye.

Red Jim [*offering his hand*]. Goodbye, comrade.
          [*The Brown Priest hesitates for a moment, then takes the offered hand of Red Jim.*

Brown Priest. If I have done wrong, may God forgive me !

Red Jim [*grimly*]. He's forgiven worse !

Brown Priest [*with a sigh*]. He has. Goodbye, comrade !
          [*He goes out slowly. Red Jim turns to the Delegates.*

Red Jim [*briskly*]. Bit late, boys, but I had a lot of work to do. [*He stares at them.*] Anything wrong ? You are all looking as if you were about to be sick. Where's the rest of the Committee ? Didn't they all know we were to meet here to decide on what we ought to do about the killing of our comrade ?

Secretary [*having waited for someone else to answer —
mumblingly*]. They knew, but I don't think they're
coming.

Red Jim. Not coming ? Why aren't they coming ?

Secretary [*hesitatingly*]. They — they 'phoned me some
time ago.

Red Jim [*impatiently*]. Yes, yes ; go on, man.

Secretary [*awkwardly*]. They were all, each of them, most
of them, as far as I know, every one of them said
almost the same thing.

Red Jim. Go on, man, spit it out ; don't be afraid to
speak.

Secretary [*with simulated courage*]. Who's afraid? I'm no
more afraid than anyone else here.

Red Jim. That's no sign of undiluted courage. Now tell
us why the rest of the Committee aren't coming? I
can answer for one — Michael, who has a Saffron Shirt
bullet in his brain. Now what about the others ?

Secretary. They aren't coming.

Red Jim. You said so before. Now tell me why.

Secretary [*sullenly*]. They said there was no necessity for
one, after the meeting held this morning.

Red Jim. This morning ? What meeting ? The only one
arranged for is the one to be held here and now.

Secretary. There was one held this morning to decide
certain questions.

Red Jim. Where was it held ? [*The Secretary does not
answer.*] Where was it held ?

Secretary [*as if the answer was being dragged from him*]. In the Purple Priest's Presbytery.

Red Jim. Ah ! Was Michael there ?

Secretary and Brallain [*together*]. {No.
{Yes.

Red Jim [*savagely — to Brallain*]. So you wouldn't stop even to defame a dead comrade ! But the Secretary's " no " was as quick as your " yes ". Michael wasn't there, for he was with me, you reptilian schemer ! [*To the Secretary*] Why wasn't I sommoned ?

Secretary. I was ordered not to summon you.

Red Jim. Whose orders ? Come on, quick, man ! — whose orders ?

Secretary [*roused*]. The orders of the whole Committee, if you want to know !

Red Jim. Bar Michael — a man among a bunch of barking mongrels ! [*He glares at the group.*] Now, out with what was decided at that meeting. [*Loudly*] Out with it !

Secretary [*pale and frightened — to the others*]. Isn't it time for one of you to answer some of these questions ?

Brallain [*as truculently as he can — getting to his feet*]. You may as well know, first as last, that we have deposed you ! The Purple Priest's our President and our Patron. We've too much love for the men to let you wreck the Unions by your savage and ceaseless opposition to the Church and the Christian Front.

Red Jim [*quickly*]. And the Saffron Shirts. [*Ironically*] And my senseless opposition to the employers — you forgot to mention that.

Brallain [*coldly*]. We can fight the employers as well as you can.

Eglish. Ay, and best them too with their own weapons — common sense and reason.

Brallain [*mockingly*]. And we want no toy soldiers to help us either.

Red Jim [*resignedly — with a touch of mockery*]. It seems everything is settled, eh? Well, we'll have a last little ceremonial at the wake of our dead comrade Michael, anyway.

Caheer. Not even that : the Church is doing the needful there too.

Red Jim. Even that is settled to your liking too. Everything's arranged according to plan. [*He goes over to where the topcoats are hanging and puts a hand in a pocket.*] Oh well, we'll pinch a fill of tobacco. [*He takes out a gold case filled with choice cigars.*] Good God, who owns this property ? [*He looks at the labels on the cigars.*] The best that money can buy. What's this name on them ? [*He reads*] Sir Jake Jester. The bastard who was honoured for his work in keeping the workers down ! [*To the Delegates*] Who owns this coat ?

                 [*There is a long, rather silent pause.*

Red Jim. Who — owns — this — coat ?

Secretary. I don't know ; 'tisn't mine.

Brallain [*indicating his coat*]. That's mine, there.

Caheer [*sullenly*]. It's mine, if you are so eager to know.

Red Jim. First-class cigars in a gold case for the soul of

Caheer : well, old Jake Jester has paid rather a heavy price for it.

[*A worker, belted and pouched, carrying a rifle, enters hurriedly.*

Worker. Comrade Jim, Brannigan's amok in a pub down the street, driving everyone out and drinking their beer !

Red Jim [*angrily*]. Send a picket to the pub ; put him under arrest and bring him back here.

[*The Delegates snigger, titter.*

Caheer. A nice rascal, muddying the whole Labour Movement with his dirty habits !

Red Jim [*sarcastically*]. He hasn't defiled his dirty habits by taking fine cigars from Sir Jake Jester. [*To Sheasker*] Nor is he furnishing his house with presents filched from the workers. The lot of you, joined together and multiplied a hundredfold, wouldn't make a Brannigan !

[*Joybell comes hurrying in. He is wearing a snowy apron over his Confraternity Robe, and he has a chef's hat on his head.*

Joybell [*briskly*]. God rest you merry, gentlemen, let nothing you dismay. Hallo, Jim ! How's the mother and the missus ? Well ? Yes, of course — well. How's everybody ? All fit, well, and smiling, eh ? But fading flowers, fading flowers, waiting for our little day to end. *Lapsus annus est*, you know — the hour is gone. The Lord Mayor's waiting for Mr. Sheasker to get ready for the part of Father Christmas, and give out our little gifts of tea and sugar to the deserving poor. I'll be serving, and the Lord Mayor 'll be serving himself : Him who is greatest among you, let him be your servant — you know. Good deeds against the day of wrath — *Dies Irae* — of wrath, see, understand ? What's all the silence for ?

Red Jim [*with a shout*]. Get out !

Joybell [*astonished*]. Eh ? When ? what ?

Red Jim. Get out, you pale hypothesis of a needless life !

Joybell. Oh yes ; no, no. I'm off. Goodbye — God bless you all !

> [*Joybell goes. Red Jim goes over to the Secretary.*

Red Jim [*to the Secretary*]. Give us the keys of the safe. Michael's daughter Julia'll want something to keep her going for a while.

Secretary [*mumbling*]. Ummmm ; I'm afraid I can't, Jim.

Red Jim. Can't ? What are you talking about ? Come on — don't keep me waiting.

Secretary. It's the Committee's orders — no money to be given without written permission.

> [*Brannigan now is brought in between an escort of armed workers. They move to the back of the room ; the workers standing stiff ; Brannigan between them, trying to look defiant and careless but really ashamed and a little anxious. Red Jim glances at them, then turns again to the Secretary.*

Red Jim. No money without written permission, eh ? Whose permission ? The Saffron Shirts' or Sir Jake Jester's ? This one of your new rules ?

Brallain [*with cold tenseness*]. Ay, one of them. It was time to nick the hand that tries to thin out the assets of the Union to nothing. Last Christmas, when the reserve was good, you poured away half on hams and geese for needy members. It's the Committee's order, and you'd best obey it.

Red Jim [*tensely*]. Committee ? What Committee ? Sir Jake Jester's ?

Brallain. The Union Committee ; our Committee.

Red Jim [*more tensely still*]. I'm the Committee now ; I'm the Union ! I march with th' men and women.

Brallain [*with cold fury*]. Take it or leave it ! Obey us or take the alternative that sits beside obedience.

Red Jim. And what's that ?

Brallain [*rising to his feet — pale and rigid*]. To drive you to the smallest power there is in the Labour Movement, and, when you're down there, drive you out of that little power too !

Red Jim [*hoarse and raging*]. You gang of daws ! Don't you see me obeying you, you eel-policy'd pickers and stealers of the workers' courage ! [*To Sheasker*] Who lifted you, you hearseman's get, from the job of worrying the poor to pay for their plywood coffins ? [*Sheasker glares silently at him.*] I did ! [*To Caheer*] To whom did you run when, as an insurance agent, your boss found you dipping too deep into the money satchel ? Who got a solicitor to fight your case ? Who saved you from jail and, for a time, turned you from a picaroon into a man ? I did ! [*To Brallain*] Who found you with hardly a boot on your foot, a ragged shirt flaunting a way out of a breach in your britches ? Who took you up because he thought he saw a glimmer

of a man in you, and made you into an Alderman? I
did! The Union chose you, did it? The men elected
you, did they? Who made the Union? Who made
the men men? Who gave you the power you have?
I did, you gang of daws! [*To the Secretary*] Hand out
the keys!

   [*The Secretary does so, and then Jim turns towards
   Brannigan.*

Red Jim [*to Brannigan*]. Well, what the hell have you got
to say for yourself — tearing the decency of our great
movement into drunken shreds!

Brannigan [*loudly and defiantly*]. Is it any wonder, when I
called here, quiet, and couldn't get my maternity
money!

Red Jim [*calmly*]. Don't raise your voice here. There's
no maternity money due to you.

Brannigan. And who the hell else is it due to then?

Red Jim. To your wife : she has the only right to it. She's
got it, and I sent word that you weren't to get a penny
of it.

Brannigan [*reproachfully*]. That's hitting below the belt,
Jim.

Red Jim. When you're sober, Brannigan, you're the
Union's finest member ; when you're drunk, you're a
swine !   [*Brannigan hangs his head but says nothing.*

Red Jim [*putting a hand affectionately on Brannigan's shoulder*].
Brannigan, dear comrade, I want you to do something
for me.

Brannigan [*eagerly*]. Anything, Jim, anything!

Red Jim. Give up the drink !

Brannigan [*frightened*]. Oh, for God's sake, Jim, I couldn't !
One of the walls at home is covered with printed
pledges taken from priests, but I wasn't able to keep
one of them.

Red Jim. You'll keep this one for me, and sign nothing.
I want you, Brannigan, I want you. We've enemies
everywhere — even here. [*He indicates the Delegates.*]
There's a brazen bunch of them ! I can't trust you if
you drink — sober, I'd trust you with my life eternal !

Brannigan [*after a long pause — enthusiastically*]. I'll do it,
Jim ; no drink ; not once ; no more ; never again —
so help me God !

Red Jim [*gripping Brannigan's hand*]. My comrade was dead,
and is alive again ; he was lost, and is found ! [*To the
escort*] Bring forth his side-arms and put them on
him.
   [*One of the escort fixes Brannigan's belt and side-arms on
   him ; then he joins the other member of the escort who
   is standing near the door. The Delegates put on their
   top-coats and move towards the door.*

Red Jim [*to the Delegates*]. Where are you going ?

Sheasker. We've no reason for remaining here longer.

Red Jim. Stay a little longer with us, won't you ? We'll
feel rather lonely without you.
   [*The Delegates do not answer and make to go out, but the
   escort blocks the way.*

Sheasker [*to Red Jim*]. Ask your troops to stand aside and let
us out, please.

Red Jim [*mockingly*]. They're but toy soldiers — knock them down and force your way out.

Sheasker [*angrily*]. We want no more of this tomfoolery ! I have to act the part of Father Christmas for the Lord Mayor and I'm late already.

Red Jim. Then the deserving poor 'll be disappointed, for you can't go ! You must all stay here for your own good. If the workers get a grip on you there'll be no holding them back. [*To Brannigan*] Brannigan, me boy, keep these things [*indicating the Delegates*] quiet here till you get written permission from me to let them go.

Brannigan [*joyfully*]. Till their backs bend and their hair grows grey, Jim, if you don't send word.

Red Jim [*to the Delegates*]. Don't worry too much. Everything will be all right. You're safe here. Only, don't do anything to get on Captain Brannigan's nerves !

    [*Red Jim goes out. The Delegates go back sullenly to their chairs. Brannigan goes over to Caheer, evicts him from his place by the fire, and sits down himself. One of the Guards stands beneath the poster, the other at the door. The Delegates and the Secretary look uncomfortable and uneasy.*

Brannigan [*to the Secretary and Delegates*]. Sit up, there, and don't be downhearted. You're kept here for your own good. We're all comrades, aren't we ? Show your joy and delight in the holy star shining in the heavens. [*To the Guards*] What about a carol, boys ?

Guards. Yes, yes ; let's have a carol !

Brannigan. Us and Sir Jakey Jester's jewels together, eh ? No sooner said than done ! [*To the Delegates*] Let us try to pass the time pleasantly. Up on your feet, and do something for your living. [*To Caheer, whose hand is on the telephone*] That's no use — it's cut ! Now for the carol !

> [*The Secretary and the Delegates take no notice.*

Brannigan [*fiercely — putting his hand to his bayonet*]. Up on your feet, you buggers, and do homage to the time that's in it !

> [*The Delegates and the Secretary rise to their feet slowly and reluctantly.*

Brannigan. Now, first, " God Rest You Merry, Gentlemen ". [*To the Secretary and the Delegates*] And let us hear you all singing, or we won't be pleased. Ready, all ? The Delegates and the Secretary are to sing the verse, and we the chorus. Steady ; now, boys, go !

Delegates and Secretary [*singing self-consciously*] :

> God rest you merry, gentlemen, let nothing you dismay,
> Remember Christ, our Saviour, was born on Christmas Day,
> To save poor souls from Satan's power, which had long time gone astray.

Brannigan and Guards [*lustily*] :

> And it's tidings of comfort and joy, comfort and joy,
> And it's tidings of comfort and joy !

> [*The curtain comes down while the second verse is being sung.*

CURTAIN

ACT III

*The same as Act I. The church spire, flanked by the shining
star, appears through one window, the foundry chimneys through
the other. Under the window showing the church spire, on a
bier placed on a platform, wtih some steps leading to it, lies the
body of Julia's father, Michael. The body is covered with a
black pall, on the side of which, facing the front, is a crucifix.
The face of the dead man is visible, and has on it a stylised look
of steady determination. Over the head of the body is a spread-
out Red Banner having on it, in white, the Hammer and Sickle.
At the foot of the bier, near the sketch of the Bishop, is a lighted
candle in a tall candlestick resting on the floor. The rest of the
room is as it was in Act I. The Old Man is sitting by the fire,
with his back turned as much as possible towards the body on the
bier ; he has a very worried look on his face. The Old Woman
is sitting by the table uneasily, rising to look at the body, going
to one of the windows to look out, coming back to the table, and
then wandering over to poke the fire. She is restless and worried.
It is about two hours after the First Act.*

Old Woman [*half to herself, half to Old Man*]. Kian will
never be able to live here, or hold his head up again,
never. Poor boy — his mind must be tense with
sorrow. He didn't mean, he didn't mean to shoot
poor Michael. Oh no ; that's certain. All done in
the heat of the moment. [*Over to the Old Man*] Wasn't
it ? [*He does not answer.*] Of course it was. And the
holy Purple Priest said it couldn't be helped. [*Over to
the Old Man*] Didn't he ? [*He does not answer.*] Everybody heard him say it. Kian wanted only to frighten

307

poor Michael, that was all ; an accident ; just that ; Michael was half to blame himself, rushing at Kian like a — like a——

Old Man. Like a wild bull of Bashan !

Old Woman. Poor Kian just had to protect himself ; so he drew his gun——

Old Man. And the gun went off !

Old Woman. And downed poor Michael before all our eyes, God rest his poor soul ; and poor Kian's too.

Old Man [*testily — to Old Woman, who is now poking the fire*]. Oh, leave the fire as it is, woman — you're poking the heart out of it !

Old Woman. The room's cold and creepy, and needs as big a glow as the fire can give.

Old Man. Well, you're doing your best to comb the glow out of it !

Old Woman. Julia's a long time gone to the Union Hall, but I hope she'll be longer, for I don't know what to say when she's here, seeing the way it all happened.

Old Man. By the time she makes a proper martyr of herself, showing her back to everyone willing to look, she'll be gone longer.

Old Woman. You shouldn't say anything against the living daughter, with the dead father lying stiff and stark before us.

Old Man [*with a shiver*]. I know he's lying behind me ; if I can't see it, I feel it. And I bet it's going round like wildfire that a member of the Workers' Committee's been shot by one batch of the Saffron Shirts while another batch was busy flogging his daughter. We should never have sanctioned Jack leaving the body here in this house.

Old Woman. Julia's Jack's girl, and the dead man was her father, and, seeing how it happened, he could do no less. [*She looks uneasily out of one of the windows.*] The church over the street's ablaze with lights, packed with a mighty gathering shying away from Communism, and getting nearer to the safe side of God. It'll soon be over now, and some of the neighbours 'll be coming up to see the last of Michael.

Old Man [*gloomily*]. Red Jim 'll make all he can out of the shooting, parading the body from here to the Union Hall, with Julia marching behind the bier, showing her reddened back to the gaping crowd. The Saffron Shirts 'll have it in for us for letting the demonstration start from our door.

Old Woman. Well, I warned you to prevent Jack from having anything to do with it when the deed was done. You should have insisted that it was all the clergy's business, and none of his.

Old Man [*jeeringly*]. You're a brave one, you are ! If the clergy came, you'd be all for him being near the saints ; but if the Communists came, you'd want him to have the last honour of a wake among the workers !

Old Woman. Yes ; and you'd be posturing in front of the clergy, with your "Yes, your reverence, No, your reverence " till a body would think it was raining reverences, while, in your heart, you'd be pining for bands playing sturdy marches instead of having to listen to the De Profundis !

Old Man. I'm not going to start a row in front of the dead.

Old Woman. You always say you're not going to start a row when it's nearly ended.

Old Man. I'd soon make up my mind if I got a chance.

Old Woman. Make it up, then ; for I've made all arrangements for the clergy to come when the service is over and take the body to the church, so that poor Julia's poor father can be given a fair and fortunate Christian burial ; and the wise clergy themselves are only too anxious to quell anything in the nature of a demonstration.

Old Man [*quickly*]. And how are we going to act if the Communists come first with bands and banners to take the body to the Union Hall ?

Old Woman [*snappily*]. I thought your mind was made up ?

Old Man. I have made up my mind ; of course I've made up my mind ; and, once I've made up my mind, I've made it up, haven't I ?

Old Woman. The ground trembles when you're making up your mind. It frightened me at first, till I remembered it was only a man's mind moving.

Old Man [*anxiously*]. I hope the clergy 'll come quick, for you know I have to go to the Mansion House to help the Lord Mayor to dish out the tea to the very deserving poor that he's giving, before the grandees have their ball.

Old Woman [*looking out of the window*]. You needn't fear, and can go now if you like ; for here are the crowds streaming out of the church, and the clergy will soon follow.

Old Man [*hurriedly putting on his hat*]. Well, then, I'll be off ; and don't forget to be firm if the Communists come first. If Jack would only open his eyes he'd see we're doing it all for his own good.

Old Woman. And Julia's too.

Old Man. To keep them out of further trouble.

Old Woman. That's all.

Old Man. What else ?

Old Woman [*anxiously*]. Slip into the church as you're passing and hurry the clergy up. If they'd only clap Red Jim into jail — God forgive me for wishing that to anyone !

Old Man [*defensively*]. You're wishing it only for the man's own good, woman ; for jail's the safest place for the poor man while the Saffron Shirts are marching.

Old Woman. If you're going, go, and get the clergy to come, best foot foremost.

Old Man. Don't forget to be strictly adamant if the Communists come first.

    [*The Old Man goes. The Old Woman stirs the fire, goes over to the window, looks out and listens ; then, going over to the door, she opens it to let in a number of neighbours. A few are comfortably clad, but the most of them are wretched-looking, and several are the picture of misery. One man has a crutch ; another man is blind, and is led in by a young man with a cough ; a young woman has a withered baby in her arms ; a hunchback follows. They file round the bier, looking at the face of the dead man, and, after some time, group themselves round the room, some near the fire, the blind man by himself in a corner.*

Young Man with Cough. Nearly the same as he was when he was alive ; nose a little thinner, maybe ; no, not really though, when you look into it. [*He coughs.*] Oh, this cough !

Hunchback. Where's his " Workers of the world, unite ! " now ? Hid in the dust of his mouth and lost in the still pool of his darken'd eyes.

Woman with Baby. I often warned him that his Communist commotions would furnish him, sooner or later, with a sudden death.

Old Woman. Didn't even give him a chance to say farewell to his friends.

Man with Crutch. We all get what's coming to us.

Woman with Baby [*peering into its face*]. Jasus, me baby's withering worse every hour. Born without vital force, the doctor says.

Most Respectable Man. They couldn't be let carry on for ever ; there wouldn't be a thing of value left standing.

Young Man with Cough. 'Course they couldn't — oh, this cough !

Man with Crutch. Look at what they did in Spain.

Woman with Baby. The blessed child's slowly dying in my arms !

Blind Man. They burned and pillaged the homes of all who couldn't see eye to eye with them.

Man with Crutch. Singing a song, they sawed a priest in two, fair in the open air, and the blessed sun shining.

Blind Man. With a weapon as long as my arm and as thick as my little finger, they knifed a priest, and he murmuring the Mass.

Young Man with Cough. Looka here, if I'd been taken care of I shouldn't be the way I am.

Blind Man. It's easy to see how we'd fare if they once got the upper hand here.

Hunchback. We've a world to gain, says they, and nothing to lose but our chains.

Woman with Baby. A world to gain ! Let them throw in the sun, moon, and stars as a tilly, and we'll be talking !

Blind Man. Not content with that, putting holy nuns, like mannequins, without a stitch of clothes on them, in the shop windows, only a thin veil of glass between their shrinking nakedness and the giggling crowd.

Young Man with Cough. Me poor mouth's often a little well of red blood lately !

Hunchback. A world to gain ! Ay, and, at the same time, lose the dignity and loveliness that priests say poverty gives the poor.

Old Woman. They haven't got these things themselves, and they want to snap them from us.

Man with Crutch. What greater can we be than what the holy Purple Priest said we were, and he preaching on the twenty-seventh Sunday after Pentecost, during the holy communion of Reparation.

Woman with Baby. Kings and priests unto God, Who has called us out of darkness into His marvellous light !

Blind Man. " In the doze and drab of life ", says he, " we are as pearls quietly aglow with a great beauty."

Young Man with Cough. Could the Communists say more than that — the bowseys !

Hunchback [*proudly*]. The Purple Priest patted me on the head, saying, " You're all the more beautiful in the sight of God because of the hump on your back."

Blind Man. Look at that now !

Woman with Baby. Could the Communists say more than that — the bastards !

Young Man with Cough. " In God's sight ", he says, says he, " the poor and wretched are all clad in gold."

Old Woman. The clergy are a long time coming.

Man with Crutch. They'll be here any minute now.

Most Respectable Man [*looking at the Red Flag over the bier*]. Before they come, we should take that symbol down and toss it far from the sense of our seeing.

Man with Crutch. That the dead man's soul may steal away from a dark reminder.

Blind Man. And go on his way, with a light foot wending.

Hunchback. Through the dangerous dark to the house of the weighing.

[*At the first mention of the Red Flag by the Most Respectable Man, they have all become tense, and move, while they are speaking, slowly nearer and nearer to the bier and the*

*Red Flag. When they are close to the bier, Julia appears
in the doorway, watching them. She is still dressed in
her fancy costume, now a little disordered, and her bare
back is covered with linen bandages. She is now wearing a Red Star in the side of her hair. She gets between
the crowd and the bier, facing them fixedly. They
slowly go back to their places ; Julia goes to the head of
the bier, bending over a little to look at the face of her
father.*

Hunchback. When the clergy come, we'll move with the
benediction of authority.

Julia [*after a short pause*]. You had a rich death, Da.
Together, we'll never feel the wind in our faces again
going gladly to the pictures ; nor shall we eat together,
or laugh together ; or wander away into a gossip about
our neighbour's good or our neighbour's evil. Nor
will the hand, so clever with the hammer, ever be
lifted again to knit two boards together ! The eye is
closed, the mouth is shut, the voice is silent, and the
hand is still ! May the eternal curse of Jesus wither
the hand that fired the shot that killed you ! Listen,
Da, listen. Your last dying sigh is swelling into the
great chant of " The Internationale ". You will hear
it voiced by the workers of the world ere you wither
into the clay that will shortly hold you tight ! And
the priests that sanctioned your shooting shall fall
and shall be dust and shall be priests no longer !
[*She glances at the crucifix.*] Against you, dear one,
we have no grudge ; but those of your ministers
who sit like gobbling cormorants in the market-place
shall fall and shall be dust, and shall be priests no
longer.

Most Respectable Man. Shocking ! Shame on you ! A

woman of the lowest order.   Your hands are claws and
your nose a snout !

Old Woman [*roughly pushing him away*]. Away, and shout
in silence, fool, and leave the girl alone.   Let her
harden all the air with anger and soften all her own,
till she shall feel less full of venom brewed by her poor
father's sharp and sudden death.   [*She stretches out her
hands to Julia.*]   Dear child, forgive the worker's hand
that brought a hurried death to thy poor father.

> [*Julia, after a moment's hesitation, stretches out her hands,
> and clasps those of the Old Woman.   Then they slowly
> let each other's hands go, and the Old Woman returns to
> her place by the fire.*

Most Respectable Man. He shouldn't have gone against
them who knew better.

Blind Man. Here's somebody now.

Woman with Withered Baby. Here they come — the clergy !
Open the door to them who come in the name of
Christ the king !

> [*The Hunchback opens the door wide.   The sound of steps
> are heard, and then Jack, followed by four of Red Jim's
> followers, comes into the room.   One of the followers is
> dressed as a clerk might be in his off time ; the second
> in blue overalls ;   the third in moleskin trousers and
> cardigan jacket ;   the fourth in postman's uniform, but
> wearing a slouch hat.   They are belted and carry
> rifles.   They go over and take their places, one at each
> corner of the bier, standing, not stiffly, but at ease there.
> Jack, with a belt round his waist and a revolver at his
> hip, goes over to Julia and lays a gentle and comforting
> hand on her head.   The crowd go back and gather at the
> other end of the room.*

Jack [*affectionately — to Julia*]. The comrades will soon be here, Julia ; they are mustering in their thousands.

> [*Julia catches Jack's hand in hers, presses it, but remains silent.*

Jack [*to the crowd*]. What do ye here ? This is no place for those whose knees are ever ready to press the ground.

Woman with Baby. We came but to pay a last respect to a fallen neighbour.

Hunchback. And wish him well on his last long journey.

Young Man with Cough. And murmur a prayer for the repose of his soul.

Jack. Well, have you done all these things ?

The Crowd. We have done them all.

Jack. Then go ; go, you dead, and bury your dead : the living sleep here.

Julia. He hath walked in the vigour of life ; he hath disquieted himself for the people ; he hath heaped up the riches of comradeship, and his children shall gather them, and live greatly.

Jack. We are the resurrection and the life ; whoso worketh and believeth in the people shall never die !

> [*The crowd, led by the Hunchback, has moved slowly towards the door while Jack and Julia have been speaking. There they pause, and go back slowly to the places they had come from, listening to a soft chant sung by the Purple and Brown Priests. They are soon seen coming into the room, followed by some Confraternity men, one of them carrying a cross. These remain at the door, the Cross-Bearer a little inside.*

Purple Priest [*coming up the stairs*]. De profundis clamavi ad te, Domine ; Domine, exaudi vocem meam ; Fiant aures tuae intendentes, in vocem deprecationis meae. Si Iniquitates observaveris, Domine, Domine, quis sustinebit ?

Hunchback. Prepare ye the way for them that cometh in the name of the Lord !

Blind Man. Who will deliver us from the way of the evil men.

Young Man with Cough. And teach us to ponder the path of our feet.

Purple Priest. The peace of the Holy Birth be with all here present — [*after a pause — to Jack*] — and with you, my son — [*after a pause — to Julia*] — and with you, my daughter.

Jack [*sullenly*]. Your peace is not our peace : we seek a peace of our own — a peace abiding and a peace that's sure.

Purple Priest. That peace God has given to the Church to be offered to all men ; and we offer it to you.

Jack. It is the peace of crying out, and no one heareth ; of secret and open hunger, and no one cometh with food ; of cold and nakedness, and no one giveth a covering : put that peace back in your bosom and go !

Julia [*angrily — to Red Guards*]. Make then go. Drive them out !
[*But the Guards have sagged a little on their feet, have become uneasy, and stand with heads bent, without moving.*

Jack [*to the Red Guards — indicating the Purple Priest*]. This

is he, comrades, who sanctioned the lash on this girl's
back, and sanctioned the shot that killed her father !

Most Respectable Man. There's no reason to be rough-
spoken — after all, priests are priests.
          [*The crowd gives a murmuring assent to this remark.*

Purple Priest. The hand that fired the shot was hot and
hasty ; but it was, at least, the hand of authority ;
and God grant the lash may teach the girl the danger
of indecent dress and immodest manners.

Woman with Baby. Trying to raise up evil thoughts in
the mind of every man who sees her, with her dress
low down at the neck and high up over the knees.
The clergy are out to save any sensible man from
trusting himself to the danger of walking on a country
road with a sex-hilarious lassie eager to pillage him
bare of all his holy hesitation !

Most Respectable Man. If the way of a maid with a man
can't be controlled, it'll have to be stopped altogether.

Purple Priest. If the foolish young hearken not to the voice
of the Church warning against the pleasure of a sinful
love, then the lash should be laid on their backs to
turn them away from the lust of the flesh.

Jack [*boldly to the threatening priests — with his arm around
Julia*]. The young in each other's arms shall go on
confirming the vigour of life. They shall go on listening to the stars thronging the roof of a country lane ;
their eyes shall see bright joys strolling the streets of the
shadowy city ; a foggy sky shall be golden, and the
hardy pavement shall lift a thick-piled velvet to their
passing feet !

Man with Crutch [*droning sleepily*] :

> Youth, all heedless of tomorrow, ever gazing up at the skies,
> Bring your thoughts to the earth, and listen,
> For we are Christian souls and wise.

Julia [*brightly — to Jack*]. Young man, seek a young maid early, ere the flame of your manhood dies.

Jack [*brightly — to Julia*] :

> Young maid, seek a young man early, ere the song in your bosom sighs,
> The life-bringing song in your bosom sighs.

Purple Priest [*droning sleepily*] :

> Listen, heedless youth, oh, listen : the lore of sages in sorrow cries,
> That sex is but a golden madness, and youth the majesty of lies.

Crowd [*droning sleepily*] :

> If you want to wisdom foster, listen to our pater-noster :
> Sex is madness, youth is lies,
> Laughter's a silly exchange for sighs,
> Health and strength and gladness dies ;
> Listen, listen while we tell you
> Youth and all its thoughts are lies !

Jack [*scornfully*]. Put your damned wisdom back in your bosom, and go !

Julia [*defiantly*]. And go !

Purple Priest [*turning his back on Julia and Jack*]. We turn our back on these two pride-bound souls, leaving them to God's best and bitter judgment ; and turn our face, bright with blessing, to the dearer souls safely housed in the core of God's great mercy and love. [*He indicates the Brown Priest.*] Our Brother here, in the heat of the day, in the cool of the evening, and when all but the stars were sleeping, prayed and toiled for you without a single sigh. Your sorrow is his sorrow ; your joy his only pleasure. Let him speak now, for me, for holy Church, and in the dear name of God !

Jack [*doggedly*]. We've no grudge against the Brown Priest.

Brown Priest. My dear children, let us be patient for a little longer. Do you think that the shout of the world for the workers goes quicker and closer to the ear of God than the self-answering appeal of " Give us this day our daily bread " ? From the Quadra-gesimo Anno will spring an abundant and a golden life for all the workers.

Jack [*violently*]. Where's the bread we've prayed so long for ? The golden grain of the world's a bonefire, and the bidders of the Corn Exchange dance a jig around it ! I tell you that the clenched fist alone can gather the corn that the earth can give !

Well-dressed Man [*to Jack*]. Shut your big mouth and give the holy fathers a chance to speak !

Crowd [*menacingly*]. Give the holy fathers a chance to speak !

Purple Priest. Communism would banish God from your altars : it would change your holy churches into places where bats hang by day and owls hoot by night ; it would soil the sacrament of marriage with lust ; it would hack in sunder the holy union of the family ; street gutters would run with the blood of your pastors ; and all holy thoughts and deeds would sink down into a weary heap of blackened ashes !

Blind Man. It's the sacred truth he's saying — I seen it all and more in the papers.

Purple Priest. In the name of God, let us cease to think of Communism ! It is the bugle-call of the powers of darkness ; it is the fire of hell flaming in its energy !

Crowd [*violently*]. Burn, maim, kill all that dare to touch it !

Purple Priest [*holding up a hand*]. Let us pray.
    [*The crowd bend their heads low. The Red Guards look on, intent and suspicious. Julia and Jack stand stiff and straight. The Brown Priest bends his head on his breast. The Purple Priest stands erect and proud. Members of the Confraternity, dressed like Joybell, stand at the head of the crowd.*

Purple Priest [*in cold and level tones*]. Let those, our working brothers, see, O Lord, clear and plain, that the happiness of the toiling masses is hidden only in the bosom of the holy Church.

Crowd. In the deep bosom of our holy Church.

Jack [*scornfully*]. Ay, too deep for them to get at it.

Purple Priest. Let the fair greeting given to Communism by virtuous men be the greeting of ball and bayonet; that we may sit safe and high over this oozy scum of the world's wickedness ; that we may be delivered from these racketeers of the souls of the faithful ; that we may be free from these restless red rats who seize a high holy day for the loudest slaughter and the richest rape !

Crowd. Save us from the curse of Communism !

Purple Priest. Ye shall not speak with them, nor eat with them ; ye shall not play nor plead with them ; ye shall not pray nor protest with them ; neither shall ye live nor die with them !

Crowd. None of these things, God helping us, shall we do.

Purple Priest. World without end, amen. [*He turns towards the bier.*] Now we bring our dead brother with us to where he may lie nearer to the joy of offered mercy. But, first, take down that red and rowdy emblem from over the dead man's head.

            [*The crowd stirs slowly to do what he says.*

Purple Priest [*impatiently*]. Tear it down, I say !
    [*Jack stretches his right arm before the flag ; Julia stretches her left one, and both hands meet, protecting the flag. In the distance the sound of many marching men is heard. The crowd, who have moved to obey the Purple Priest, stand still, undecided and a little afraid. Jack and Julia listen till the sound is very near. The Priests are still and silent too.*

Julia [*as the sound of the march comes near — joyously*]. The People's Church has come to claim him now !

Jack [*exultantly*]. Long live the march of the militant workers !
    [*When the sound of the marching is at its loudest a commanding voice outside shouts " Halt ! " and this " Halt " is echoed till it dies away in the distance. The Red Guards stand stiff and expectant. There is a tense stillness for a few moments. Then Red Jim comes in, followed by Brannigan. Red Jim looks around, taking in all that has happened, and he smiles a little grimly.*

Red Jim. Have I come too late ?

Purple Priest. You have come too late. Our dead brother's soul has found forgiveness in the Church, and we are now going to bring his dear body to where it will receive its last handling by Christian priests and Christian brethren.

Red Jim [*grimly*]. 'Twere better he had received Christian handling when he was living than to receive it now when he is dead.

Purple Priest. Go, vain and turbulent man ; go, and leave us to carry out our last office of charity in peace ! [*He turns to the crowd and the Confraternity men.*] Take up the body.   [*They do not stir.*

Red Jim. Our comrade comes with us. His quiet shall not be disturbed by the wail of the virtuous vagabonds. The chant of his own comrades and the melody of his own class shall go with him for some of the way he's wending. [*He turns to Brannigan.*] Take up your comrade's body and let the drums strike !

Purple Priest [*quickly and fiercely*]. Let the man who first moves to obey this order be cut for ever from all attachment to eternal salvation !

> [*There is a tense pause, and again no one stirs.*

Brown Priest [*appealingly*]. My children, my children, let the holy star shine on a moment of peace ! Hear, I beseech you, and obey the voice that gives, not the violent orders of foolhardy men, but the orders of the everlasting Church : hear, and obey that we may be made meet for the heritage of heaven !

Red Jim [*passionately*]. If the heritage of heaven be the heritage here of shame and rags and the dead puzzle of poverty, then we turn our backs on it ! If your God stands for one child to be born in a hovel and another in a palace, then we declare against him. If your God declares that one child shall be clad in silks and another in sores, then we declare against him. If your God declares that it takes a sack of sovereigns to keep one child and a handful of pence to keep another, then we declare against him. If your God declares that one child shall dwell in the glory of knowledge and another shall die in the poverty of ignorance, then we declare against him : once and for all and for ever we declare against your God, who hath filled the wealthy with good things and hath sent the poor empty away ! [*He turns to Brannigan.*] Take up our comrade and strike up the drums !

Purple Priest [*rapidly*]. From all promises, from all affirmations, and from any oath made to this man, and from all obedience to the sin-slushed cause he stands for, we absolve you, each and every one of you ; and we give our blessing, here and now, to him or them who will lay restraining hands on him, seize him, and hold him tight prisoner till he be handed over to the civil power for just and lasting punishment ! [*He speaks directly to the Red Guards.*] He who is on the side of God and His saints, of mercy and of truth — strike him down !

> [*There is a pause as Red Jim waits silently and calmly for any sign of a hostile movement from the Red Guards. But they stand silent, motionless, to attention.*

Red Jim [*with fierce confidence*]. Prating priest, peradventure my comrades are deaf and did not hear you. And, outside, there are many thousands as deaf as these. We have turned aside from you. The life we have lived is coming to an end : life rotten in the ear that it

could not hear ; life rotten in the eye that it could
not see ; in the limbs that they could not move ; in
the mind that it could not think ; and in the heart
that it could not love ! We have bothered the ear of
your God till our tongues were dry ; we have crept flat
on our bellies to where 'twas said we'd find him, and
for our meekness the whip of hunger stung us. The
sign of fear ever flamed from our foreheads ; and we
sang our praises to the pomp of fools. Now we stand
up, we turn, and go our own way, the bent back
changing to the massed majesty of the Clenched Fist !

[*He raises his clenched fist ; so do Jack, Julia, and the Red
Guards ; and a mass of clenched fists is seen through the
windows.*

Red Jim [*to Brannigan*]. Take up your comrade and strike
up the drums !

Brannigan [*at the door — shouting*]. Strike up the drums !

Voices outside and in the street. Strike up the drums !

[*A steady drum-roll is heard in the street below. The Red
Guards lift the bier and begin to carry it from the room.
The priests move back to the end of the room with those
loyal to them. One of the Red Guards leads in the song
"Our Comrade's Gone", and all Red Jim's followers,
inside and outside, join in the refrain as the bier is carried
out of the room.*

Our com-rade's gone, but there's no weep-ing, A - way, the drums are

beat-ing! The   Cause he lov'd   is   in   safe

keep - ing,   A   -   ha,   Red   Star,   a -

rise,   the ——   wide   world   o -   ver!

Leader :

     Our comrade's gone, but there's no weeping,

Rest :

     Away, the drums are beating !

Leader :

     The Cause he lov'd is in safe keeping,

Rest :

     Aha, Red Star, arise, the wide world over !

Leader :

     Our comrade's gone ; he's soundly sleeping,

Rest :

     Away, the drums are beating !

Leader :

     The workers all to arms are leaping.

Rest :

     Aha, Red Star, arise, the wide world over !

Leader :

     He died that men might quell their creeping,

Rest :
    Away, the drums are beating !

Leader :
    That where they sow'd, they'd find a reaping,

Rest :
    Aha, Red Star, arise, the wide world over !

CURTAIN

Act IV

Lounge room in the residence of the Lord Mayor. The background is the same as in the previous Acts, but the walls here are pompous with purple and gold. Through the window on the right the church spire is farther away than it was before ; and the foundry chimneys loom larger through the window on the left. The star that shone beside the church spire now shines beside the chimneys. Between the windows is a large black shield having on it a white circle enclosing a white flash. Below this the motto " Ora Et Labora ". Easy-chairs, a settee, all covered with brown material edged with purple, a small desk carrying a telephone, make up the furniture of the room. Festoons of flowers and tiny flags run from corner to corner of the ceiling, and a coloured lantern hangs from the centre. All the festoons are not yet fixed, and two workmen are doing the finishing touches to the decorations. Two ladders lean against the wall, one at each end of the room, where the festoons are still to be fixed. There are two entrances. One, wide and arched, closed with heavy purple curtains which are now pulled back to each side, is on the right, and leads to the dance hall ; to the left, a much smaller arched doorway leads to another part of the building. Just now the two workmen are standing idle, listening, holding the ends of festoons in their hands.

The Lord Mayor appears through the smaller arched entrance. He is dressed in a sky-blue coat, cut evening fashion, flowered waistcoat, and white satin knee-breeches. His heavy gold chain of office still hangs round his little neck. His costume is partly hidden by a white apron. Across his breast is a yellow-and-white sash with a green cross in the middle — The Order of Saint Mulgarius. He trips across in a hurry, stopping for a moment to speak a word or two to the workmen.

Lord Mayor. Geth a move on, boyth, geth a move on. They'll be flooding in any minute now.

> [*He hurries away.*

1st Workman. J'ever see such a half-got, dull-grown, hell-bent little shower-off than that in your life, Bill ? Now did you, honest ?

2nd Workman [*mimicking the Mayor*]. Geth a moveth on, boyth, geth a moveth on. He little knows the move-on he's going to get before he's much older — the little under-sized scut, scattering his seeds of kindness, singing a bit of everybody's song, and feathering his own nest with the finest of fine feathers.

1st Workman. And all the time he isn't fit to become, even with the help of the saints, a flea in a hidden feather of a mighty angel's wing.

2nd Workman. Let us take our ease and wait in comfort for what we know is going to come soon.

> [*They settle themselves into easy-chairs ; one takes out a pipe, the other a fag, and both begin to smoke. The Lord Mayor trots in again, sees them, stops, and stands before them.*

Lord Mayor. Oh, boyth, boyth, there's a lot to be done yet.

1st Workman. Go and do it then.

2nd Workman. We're tired.

Lord Mayor. Tired ! Look at me — I'm never tired ! And remember, we'll soon be singing " Christians, awake, salute the happy morn, whereon the Saviour of the world was born ". Oh, boyth, for shame — the thar is looking at you !

1st Workman. Let it look.

2nd Workman. It's time the workers began putting their bums into soft places, isn't it ?

1st Workman. My oath !

Lord Mayor. Yeth, yeth, boyth ; but remember what the Purple Priest said : an honest day's work for an honest day's pay.

1st Workman. To hell with the Purple Priest.

Lord Mayor. Remember the example of our ancient warrior forefathers : strength in their arms, truth on their lips, and purity in their hearts.

1st Workman. Well, we're the young warriors, and we're different.

2nd Workman. A helluva lot different.

Lord Mayor [*smilingly*]. When I come back you'll be hard at it, yeth ?   [*He hurries out again.*

1st Workman. They can't abide seeing a worker sitting in an easy-chair.

2nd Workman. Doesn't look a natural sight to them.

1st Workman [*mimicking Lord Mayor*]. Remember what the Purple Priest said !   I remember him damn well telling us one day of hearing a rustle in church, and of creeping down to see what it was. [*He attempts to mimic an ecclesiastical voice.*]   And there, brethren, kneeling before the altar, was a wee girl, clad only in rags and tatters, busy mumbling, " Thank God for everything " !

2nd Workman. Ending up with the grand finale of us having nothing, yet possessing all things.

1st Workman. Well, we're no longer going to thank God for the empty belly and the shivering back !

2nd Workman. Or drift, unmarked, through the wide and lonely sea of unemployment.

1st Workman. Life isn't life without what life can give.

2nd Workman. So we'll seize all that life can give : no more, no less.

1st Workman. So Red Jim orders.

2nd Workman. And we obey.

1st Workman. Ours is the kingdom, the power, and the glory.

2nd Workman. So Red Jim says.

1st Workman. And we agree.

2nd Workman. Workers of the world, unite ; advance ; and the fight is won.

1st Workman. So thinks Red Jim.

2nd Workman. As we think too.

1st Workman. They're all full-fortuned that are stirring now.

2nd Workman. Our time to sit still will soon end now.
  [*The Old Man, followed by Joybell, comes in through the lesser entrance. Each is carrying a large watering-can with a long spout. Both are wearing aprons and modified chefs' caps, Joybell's apron is over his Confraternity robe. The Old Man sinks down wearily on a settee and wipes sweat from his face.*

Old Man. Oh, take the weight off your legs for a second or two.

Joybell. But the poor people may be waiting for more tea.

Old Man. Well, let them wait. We can't be eternally thinking of others, can we?

Joybell. We can. We must. Do unto others — you know the rest. Keep going, and keep gay. It'll all soon end, won't it? Soon we must through darkness go, to inherit bliss unending, or eternity of woe. So keep gay, and keep going!

1st Workman. What's in the cans?

Joybell. Lovely boiling tea in this one.

Old Man. And beautiful boiling water in this to stretch out the lovely tea.

2nd Workman. That's a nice way to dish out tea to the poor.

Old Man. Aren't they glad to get it? And what does anyone want more than what they're damn well glad to get?

  [*The Lady Mayoress enters from the hall. She is about forty-five, brisk, sharp, sure of herself, and quick in her speech. She is wearing a widely flowing yellow dress, and has a red rose in her hair. The Old Man tries to jump up from the settee, falls back, slidders, but keeps struggling till he gets to his feet.*

Lady Mayoress. Oh, here the pair of you are, are you? We've been looking for the two of you everywhere. You know you can't expect any reward if you sink down under your duties like this.

Old Man [*in confusion*]. Yis, ma'am; no, ma'am.

Lady Mayoress. You know we must get the poor people away before the gentry come. I guessed, I told the

Lord Mayor, you wouldn't be spry enough; felt certain you wouldn't be spry.

Old Man. I am spry, me lady, ma'am. I am spry, oh, quite spry, when it comes to the push.

Lady Mayoress. Well, it's come to the push now, for if Mr. Sheasker doesn't come within the next few minutes, you'll have to take the part of Father Christmas for us.

Old Man [*frightened*]. Is it me, ma'am? Oh no, no, ma'am.

Lady Mayoress [*pushing him off*]. Oh, but, yes, yes, ma'am. Go on — they're waiting for the cans of tea.
   [*The Old Man goes off, followed by Joybell. The two workmen have risen from their chairs while the Lady Mayoress was speaking.*

Lady Mayoress [*to the workmen*]. And what are you two doing?

1st Workman [*a little in awe of the vivid yellow dress*]. Just putting the finishing touches to the decorations, ma'am.

Lady Mayoress [*effusively*]. You're making the place look beautiful. Strikes the eye. Now, finish it off as quick as you can, like dear men.

2nd Workman. Lord Mayor said, ma'am, we might have a smoke.

Lady Mayoress. Of course, of course; you can smoke your fill when it's done; but put on a spurt now, please.

1st Workman. Yes, of course, ma'am.

Lady Mayoress. I know you will ! I'm half a Socialist myself, you know. The Lord Mayor does be quite angry with me at times, quite angry. But workers have their rights, I tell him quite calmly. They are so kind, so honest, and so good. Real children of their forefathers, with strength in their arms, truth on their lips, and purity in their hearts. God bless them ! [*She pushes them towards the ladders.*] Now, up you go !

    [*They mount up a step or two. The Lady Mayoress runs off through the smaller archway, kissing her hand to them as she goes.*

2nd Workman [*to his mate*]. What sort of a man are you to let her get the upper hand of you like that ?

1st Workman [*tartly*]. Simply because I saw you were itching to please her.

2nd Workman. I can never understand why some workers are ready to fall on their knees the minute a well-dressed cow flits in front of them.

    [*Joybell runs in from the hall, excited and elated.*

Joybell [*loudly, as he crosses over*]. Where's the Lord Mayor ? I've news for him — grand news, great news, good news ! [*As he hurries away through the lesser arched entrance*] Me Lord Mayor, me Lord Mayor !

1st Workman. What news has he got, I wonder ? Did you hear him ? " Great news," says he, " grand news, good news."

2nd Workman. We should have laid hold of the little bastard, and got it out of him. I hope it's got nothing to do with what's going to happen soon.

    [*Joybell comes running in again, excited and elated.*

Joybell [*to the workmen*]. Where's the Lord Mayor ? Did yous see the Lord Mayor ?

1st Workman [*getting down off the ladder and gripping Joybell*]. What news have you got, you praying compound of fear and favour ?

Joybell [*truculently*]. Now, maybe, we'll have peace for a space. Now, maybe, you'll realise we can't live without the help of better men than ourselves.

1st Workman. What news, you sly circumstance of life ?

Joybell. What news ? Good news ! The police, mounted and on foot, have gone down to the Union Hall to arrest Red Jim !

1st Workman. It's a God-damn lie !

Joybell [*exultantly*]. Well, if you like a lie, believe it's a lie. Fifty mounted men, with carbine and sword, have gone to get him. The Purple Priest's coming here to arrange with the Lord Mayor for a procession to Midnight Mass, where a special Te Deum's to be sung in honour of the star of peace. Now yessir and nosir 'll be flicked about from mouth to mouth, instead of comrade this and comrade that. [*Vehemently*] I hope it'll be for ever !

> [*Joybell breaks away from the workman, and runs off through the greater archway on the right, leaving the two workmen standing by the ladders, silent and unhappy.*

1st Workman [*mournfully*]. The people have failed again. The workers must sleep again ; must sing sad and slow, and sleep again.

2nd Workman. I don't believe it. What ! give up without even knocking a chair about ?

1st Workman. Oh, can't you see, man, that it must be after the time for the call to go.

2nd Workman. We can only wait and wonder now.

1st Workman. And we thinking that the star was about to turn red.

2nd Workman. And the kings change into shepherds, and the shepherds become kings.

1st Workman. That the holders-down of men would wax old as doth a garment, and be folded up as a vesture is folded and put away, and burned as a worn-out thing and useless.

2nd Workman. That their pomp would be brought down to the grave, and the music of their viols, and that the worms would cover them from the sight of men.

    [*The Lord Mayor, with Joybell and the Old Man, come in through the smaller archway, all of them in a joyous mood. The Old Man is now dressed up as Father Christmas — scarlet robe and hood, top-boots, long white beard and moustache, but his face is as the face of a fool. The Old Man is on the Lord Mayor's right hand and Joybell is on his left.*

Old Man [*conceitedly — to Lord Mayor*]. I told you so, didn't I, me Lord Mayor ? Long ago, ages ago, time and time again : a furious fake it was — nothing else.

Joybell. I said and knew it too ; didn't I, me Lord Mayor ? Said it often and said it early.

Lord Mayor [*with calm complacency*]. Yeth, yeth, boyth. Noding could really stand long against the Church, the Christian Front, and the Saffron Shirts. [*To Joy-*

bell] Run and bring the Lady Mayoress here, and say noding to anyone.

> [*Joybell runs out through the entrance to the hall.*

Lord Mayor. Poor Red Jim ! We mustn't rejoice too much over it, though.

Old Man. No, oh, no, no. It shouldn't be fair, wouldn't be charitable.

Lord Mayor. I'm really sorry for him — mithled, mithled ! It's just as well, for the sake of the poor mithled workers.

> [*The Lady Mayoress, with Joybell, comes running in to the Lord Mayor.*

Lady Mayoress. Isn't it good news, Albert ?

Lord Mayor. It's great news !

Joybell and Old Man [*together*]. It's grand news !

Lady Mayoress. Now that the disturber, Red Jim, is soon to be out of the way, we can look around quietly. [*She sinks into a chair*]. The place is looking lovely, isn't it ?

Old Man [*rapturously*]. It's a lovely dream, that's what it is, so it is, ma'am !

Joybell [*as rapturously*]. It'll be a nine-days wonder, me lady !

Lady Mayoress. Strikes the eye. Oh, it does look artistic — I'll say that of it.

Lord Mayor. Berry, berry artistic.

Old Man. A welter of colour, me lady, ma'am.

Lady Mayoress. And to think that only yesterday we

thought our enterprise would have to be given up on the head of the Labour trouble. [*She speaks louder — for the benefit of the workmen.*] But the Church and the authorities put an end to that !

Old Man. Yes, indeed, ma'am.

Lord Mayor [*gently reproachful*]. We mustn't crow too loud, darling.

Lady Mayoress. Oh, we don't mind the workers organizing ; we like them to organize ; we encourage them to organize.

Old Man. Oh yes, indeed we do, me lady, ma'am.

Lady Mayoress. But only in safe and sensible and secure and Christian and Catholic Unions. [*To the Old Man*] You agree with that, don't you ?

Old Man. Agree ?   Oh yes, indeed, ma'am ; indeed yes, ma'am.
    [*They are startled by hearing the " Assembly " blown on a bugle in the distance. The workmen stiffen and clench their fists. The rest stand, intently listening.*

Lady Mayoress [*as the call is ending*]. What's that ?
    [*The workmen come down from the ladders, fling down the festoons they have been holding, and start to go away.*

Lady Mayoress [*to the workmen*]. Where are you two going ?

1st Workman [*as they go out*]. The clock has struck !

Lady Mayoress. What clock ?   Which clock ?   Whose clock ?   [*To the Old Man*] What clock were they talking about ?

Joybell. Must have been the bugle-call they meant.

Old Man [*clicking his tongue — irritably*]. Dtch, dtch, dtch ! They didn't refer to a bugle-call — they mentioned a clock.

Joybell. There must be something up still, then.

Old Man. There's nothing up still or down still. It's just that they are simply gone trembling in their boots to see what's to be done when Red Jim's clapped into jail.

Lady Mayoress [*relieved*]. And they left these two festoons hanging round, and the ladders in the way, too. These workers need a firm hand over them.

Old Man [*all alert*]. Don't you fret, ma'am ; we two — me and Joybell — can manage the little left to be done — can't we, Joybell ?

Joybell [*confidently*]. Yehess, of course we can, *deo volente*.

Old Man [*to the Lord Mayor*]. Just you and your lady pop off and leave the rest to us !

Lord Mayor. You are a pair of useful men. [*To Lady Mayoress*] Come along, dear, till we see how the place is shaping for the ball. [*As they go out*] I wonder, now, what they meant by " the clock has struck " ?

Old Man [*left to themselves — to Joybell*]. Now to business, boy.
　　[*The Old Man and Joybell finger the festoons, stare at the ladders, and then look up to where the ends are to be fixed.*

Old Man. Slip up, Joybell, as a preliminary, and fix your end first.

Joybell. No ; you slip up first and see how your end'll hang.

Old Man. How my end'll hang ? Don't you know well
enough how my end'll hang ? My end'll hang just the
same as your end'll hang !

Joybell. My eye is younger than yours, and I'll be able to
see if your end is hanging at the right angle.

Old Man [*viciously*]. Right angle ! This is a matter of
pluck and hammer and nails, and not a question of
aljaybra ! There's only one angle to hang it be — the
right angle.

Joybell. That's just what I'm after saying.

Old Man. Just what are you just after saying ?

Joybell. That if you hang it at all, you must hang it at a
right angle.

Old Man [*shouting*]. Good God, man, isn't that just what
I'm just after saying !

Joybell. No you didn't ; you just said that if you wanted
to hang it at a right angle you'd have to know aljaybra.

Old Man [*shouting*]. And what has aljaybra got to do
with it ?

Joybell. Isn't that just what I'm after asking you ?

Old Man [*shouting*]. What are you after asking me, for
God's sake ?

Joybell. I'm after asking you what has aljaybra got to do
with it ?

Old Man [*furiously*]. Got to do with what, man ?

Joybell. Got to do with hanging this strip of decoration
at a right angle ?

Old Man. Amn't I hoarse shouting out that aljaybra has nothing to do with it !

Joybell. There you are, you see.

Old Man. There I am, I see, what ?

Joybell. At the end of your argument you have to admit that aljaybra has nothing to do with hanging festoons at a right angle.

Old Man [*in anguish*]. Oh, isn't an intelligent man nicely tested when he's fronted with a fool !

Joybell. In any case, I don't know why they want to be putting up so many of these coloured vanities at a time like this.

Old Man [*with conviction*]. Now you're talking. No more do I. It's overpowering. [*Mimicking the Lady Mayoress.*] It looks artistic — I'll say that of it, says she — a surging shame of a show-off, I call it !

Joybell [*mimicking her too*]. It strikes the eye, says she. It does, right enough — knocks the eye out of you, if you look at it long enough.

Old Man [*sarcastically*]. Pity you didn't say that in front of her old wizened face instead of crowing out of you that it was a nine-days wonder.

Joybell. I fancy I heard someone saying that it all looked like a lovely dream.

Old Man. A man's a man only when he says what he thinks.

Joybell. Why, man, when she was here, wasn't the whole place lit up, light as day, with the sparkle of all your glittering " yes, ma'ams " !

[*They have now mounted about six rungs of the ladders, each clasping the ladder he is on as if he was embracing a woman. The ends of the festoons are wound round their necks so as to leave their arms free to clasp the ladders tightly.*

Old Man. What are we going to do now? I don't like ladders.

Joybell. I was never on one before in me life. Pray to God and His blessed saints that we won't fall!

Old Man. Oh, talk sense, man. And supposing, only supposing, mind you, that we get to the top, how are we going to disentangle these arrangements from around our necks?

Joybell. I never once thought of that.

Old Man [*viciously*]. Well, think of it twice now! You and your *deo volentes* — your *deo volentes* aren't doing much for us now!

Joybell. We haven't fallen off yet, have we?

Old Man. The worst has yet to come, hasn't it? We're only at the start of our pilgrimage, aren't we? And how are we going to get our hands going when we do get to the top?

Joybell. Oh, let's get to the top first before we tax our brains with the question of what we'll do when we get there. We'll simply have to keep hugging the ladders while we're fixing the festoons.

Old Man. How the hell can we hug the ladders and fix the festoons at the same time?

Joybell. We'll have to think out some way of doing it, that's all.

Old Man [*explosively*]. Oh, will we ? Well, I'm not going to let myself go cantering down through space with nothing definite but the air to stand on !

Joybell. You should have thought of that before you started.

Old Man. Well, I'm thinking of it now before I'm ended

Joybell. What else can we do but risk going up ?

Old Man. We can risk going down, can't we ?
 [*The Lord Mayor suddenly appears at the larger arched entrance.*

Lord Mayor [*over to Joybell and the Old Man*]. Eh, you two there : don't do any hammering for a few moments. We're all going to sing a carol before we start to dance.
          [*He goes away.*

Old Man [*in disgust*]. Always some interference when a man has something to do. How are we going to go on if they're always wanting us to stop !
 [*From the hall the carol " Silent Night " floats into their ears.*

   Silent night, holy night,
   Earth is hushed, heaven alight,
   Angels throng the starlit sky,
   Whispering low their lullaby,
   Sleep, my baby, sleep, they softly sing.

 [*In the far distance, outside, can be faintly heard the playing of " The Internationale " ; then, cutting in on these two airs, is heard the sound of galloping horses, getting louder and louder till they gallop right by the windows. Joybell and the Old Man get down from the ladders, run over to the windows, and look out.*

Joybell [*excitedly*]. The mounted police flying hell for leather down the street !

Old Man. And five of them toppling from their saddles !
  [*Several sirens, one from the foundry whose chimney can be seen through the window, blow shrill and loud, those farther away less loud than the siren from the foundry seen through the window. The moment the sirens start sounding, the star turns red. There is a pause as the Old Man and Joybell stand listening.*

Old Man [*looking out of the window*]. Look ! oh, look ! — they're firing at the police from the foundry windows !

Joybell. Lord have mercy on us ! We're no sooner out of one trouble than we're pitching into another.

Old Man. Where are we going to go ?

Joybell. What are we going to do ?

Old Man. Where are we going to hide ?

Joybell [*panic-stricken*]. Get the Lord Mayor — ask the Lord Mayor — find the Lord Mayor !
  [*The two of them rush for the entrance to the hall, and are nearly knocked down by the Lord Mayor and Lady Mayoress running out of it, followed by a group of guests who crowd the entrance. The Lord Mayor is now without his apron. He rushes over to the telephone and picks up the receiver.*

Lord Mayor [*frantic with fright — fumbling with the telephone*] Keep calm, the lot of you ! There's no reason to be excited ! Damn this thing, I can't get it right. Everybody keep perfectly — this is the time to show your nerve !

Lady Mayoress [*angrily*]. You show your nerve and get the Exchange, and don't faint, you fool !

Lord Mayor [*speaking into the 'phone*]. That the Exchange ? Yes ? Oh, this is the Lord Mayor speaking. Put me through to . the Saffron Shirt Headquarters, please. Yes, at once ! What ?
> [*He drops the receiver and is very close to a swoon.*

Lady Mayoress. What did they say, what did they say, you damned fool ?

Lord Mayor. They called me a terrible, oh, a terrible name !

Lady Mayoress [*stiff and pale*]. The Reds must have taken the Exchange.
> [*The Old Man catches the Lord Mayor's right arm and Joybell catches the left one.*

Joybell and Old Man [*together*]. Where can we go ? what shall we do ? where can we hide ?

Lord Mayor [*shaking them off — violently*]. Go and hide in hell, you fools, with your great news and grand news and good news !
> [*Red Guards come in through the smaller arched entrance and commence to sandbag the windows.*

Lord Mayor [*to the first Red Guard that passes him*]. What do you want, please ? What can I do for you ? [*To a second as he passes*] You've made some mistake — this is the Lord Mayor's residence. [*To a third as he passes by*] Please, listen ; you really have made some silly mistake, and have come to the wrong place.
> [*The Red Guards take no notice, but go on with their work.*

Lord Mayor [*to Lady Mayoress*]. You speak to them, darling.

[*A Red Guard settles himself at the desk with headphone and wire, to send and take messages. Red Jim, followed by Brannigan and Red Guards, comes in. The Lord Mayor and Lady Mayoress back towards the entrance, where the frightened guests are grouped. There they face Red Jim — from a distance.*]

Lord Mayor [*over to Red Jim*]. What is this ? what is this ? oh, what does all this mean ?

Red Jim [*grimly*]. Can't you guess ?

Lady Mayoress [*indignantly — over to Red Jim*]. How dare you and your gang invade the privacy of the city's first citizen !

Lord Mayor [*deprecatingly — pushing in front of the Lady Mayoress*]. Easy, darling, easy, dear ; it's all simply due to a mistake.

Lady Mayoress [*angrily pulling the Lord Mayor behind her*]. This is no time for civility, man. [*To Red Jim*] Take away your rough-and-ready men at once, for there are honoured and even titled guests in the Lord Mayor's residence tonight !

Red Jim :
    A silken gown's no refuge now, me lady.
    Tell your beads and smite your bosom, woman, for
       your gilded day is dying.
    The trumpet of God, unblown in the hand of a
       crawler,
    Will ring its news out now from the lips of the
       young men.
    The sound shall shrill in the drowsy ears of the
       guildhall diners,
    Chattering the teeth of the big-pursed pagans,

Hiding in the shade of a safely measur'd alms ;
Given on the handy holy days of the helping saints,
To any puling pet that will kneel and bless their
   bounty.
The thinkers, poets, and brave men say with us :
No more shall the frantic, wakeful mother watch
Her child's new body shrink away from freshness ;
First marked by calm canonical hands with the cross
   of Christ,
Then blazon'd with the stigma of tuberculosis.
No more shall the big-nam'd beggars crave over the
   eager air,
A coin or two from a mounting heap, to give
A rotting child a minute's glimpse of the healing
   sea :
The flame in the eyes that see will burn
This useless chaff of charity to ashes !

Lady Mayoress. What, in the name of God, do you want ?

Red Jim. The world !

Brannigan [*who has been bending over the Red Guard at the buzzer — to Red Jim*]. Comrade chief, the Saffron Shirts are ready to advance.

Red Jim. And we are here to welcome them ! [*He indicates Lord Mayor, Lady Mayoress, and guests.*] Get these down to where there may be wailing and gnashing of teeth, but a safer place than this.

Brannigan [*pushing them all out*]. Away, away, you silken dead men ! Down to the cellars, and lullaby each other there !
   [*He pushes them out. In the distance a bugle blows the "Advance". This is followed by a cheer, and the fight*

begins. The Red Guards go through the movements of firing and loading their rifles, and some do the same with machine-guns. Occasionally one of them slides over, wounded or dead, while Glazounov's Preamble to his " Scènes de Ballet ", Op. 52, is played to represent the heat, the firing, and the stress of battle. Then the curtain goes down, to represent the passing of a few hours. When it rises again, the scene is disordered ; a number of stiff forms lie around, each with a stiffened clenched fist held high. Jim has his arm in a sling. The buzzer is sounding fiercely.

Red Guard [*at buzzer*]. Commandant Jack reports that he is hard pressed.

Red Jim. Tell him to hold out till the last !

Red Guard [*at buzzer*]. Captain Murray reports a rumour that the Carrickfergus Fusiliers have refused to fire on the workers.

Red Jim [*excited*]. I guessed it ; I knew they would.

Red Guard [*at buzzer*]. Captain reports, too, that half of his men are down and he can't hold out much longer.

Red Jim. Tell him to hold out till they're all down !
    [*There is a lull and Brannigan comes in, begrimed and sweating.*

Brannigan. A flag of truce, comrade Jim, a flag of truce !

Red Jim. Who comes with the flag of truce ?

Brannigan. Kian, comrade Jack's brother, and the damned Purple Priest of the politicians. And, Jim, the Brown Priest's with the boys — he came climbing over the barricades in the midst of the firing.   [*A pause.*

Brannigan [*slowly*]. And, Jim, Jack's gone west. Got it in

the heart.   The Brown Priest and Julia were with him
— they're bringing him here.   [*A pause.*

Red Jim. We fight for life ; for life is all and death is
   nothing.   Pass the flag of truce on.
   [*The word " Pass " is shouted and echoed outside. From one
   side the Purple Priest, followed by Kian, who is carrying a white flag, enters.   From the other side the body of
   Jack is borne in, followed by Julia, weeping softly.   She
   is still dressed in her fancy costume, but it is partly
   covered by a man's waterproof coat.   She is followed by
   the Brown Priest.   The Purple Priest, Kian, the dead
   man, Julia, and the Brown Priest meet in the centre of
   the room.   The Purple Priest fixes a cold look on the
   Brown Priest.   Kian looks steadfastly at the body.*

Brannigan [*to Kian*]. Do you recognize him ?   He was
   your brother, your own brother.

Red Jim. More than that ; more than brother, Comrade
   Brannigan — he was a comrade worker.

Brown Priest. Grant him eternal rest, O God !

'*Kian* [*making the sign of the cross*]. And let perpetual light
   shine upon him !
   [*Kian turns away his head, stares in front of him, and
   tries to stiffen himself against showing any sentiment.*

Purple Priest [*to Brown Priest*] :
   Brother, brother,
   God is grieved to see you here ;
   Here, where shouting words drive off the voice of
      wisdom,
   And reason changes murder to a holy duty.
   Come out of these curses, and be blessed.

Brown Priest [*in a low voice*] :

    I serve my Master here.
    In the loud clamour made by war-mad men
    The voice of God may still be heard ;
    And, in a storm of curses, God can bless.
    The star turned red is still the star
    Of him who came as man's pure prince of peace ;
    And so I serve him here.

Purple Priest :

    Behind us, only, is the rose of Sharon —
    There's nothing here but hemlock !

Red Jim :

    The flaming hemlock here will burn to ashes
    The rose that sucked its power from men's dejection ;
    And from the flaming hemlock, dying here,
    The tree of life shall grow.
    So jet into our ear your holy message ;
    Then go,
    And let us fight in peace.

Kian. The Saffron Shirts have stormed your first and second trenches.

Red Jim. That much we know.   Our heart is here — they haven't taken that !

Purple Priest. I call upon you, in the name of God, to lay down your arms, to send your poor, misguided soldiers home and end this brazen butchery, that this holy night, at least, may end in peace !

Red Jim. Look at the star, look at the star, man !   The crescent has come, and the crescent has gone ; the cross has come, and the cross is going !   [*To the Red Guards*] What is left to take their place, comrades ?

Red Guards [*loudly and in chorus*]. The Red Star is rising !
The Red Star will take their place and burn in the
heavens over our heads for ever !

Red Jim :

We fight on ; we suffer ; we die ; but we fight on.
Our altar is the spinning earth, chanting reveille to
the newborn, sounding the Last Post over those
sinking back into her bosom when the day's well-
done work is over.
Our saints are those who fall beating a roll on the
drum of revolution.
We fight on ; we suffer ; we die ; but we fight on.
Till brave-breasted women and men, terrac'd with
strength,
Shall live and die together, co-equal in all things ;
And romping, living children, anointed with joy,
shall be banners and banneroles of this moving
world !
In all that great minds give, we share ;
And unto man be all might, majesty, dominion, and
power !

Red Guards [*in chorus*]. Now and for evermore !

Red Jim [*to the Purple Priest*]. You have heard the answer.
You can go back now, silent and soft.

Purple Priest. We go, and take all signs of mercy with us.
The power you battle for will soon be but a flaming
flaw. The vexed wind of law shall sweep down upon
you, scattering the last few petals of the bloody flower
that tries to blossom here. [*To Kian*] Come on, my son.
[*Kian, staring down at the face of his dead brother, takes no
notice. The Purple Priest touches his arm.*

Purple Priest. My son, your brother's dead. As well to

die today as die tomorrow. Come, and sink your
sorrow in the greater good that we will crown today.

Kian [*leaning on the staff of the white flag, and staring down at
his dead brother — murmuringly*]. I stay where I am. He
was my brother, my own brother. Tumble your shot
and shell in on us here, and let me pass away beside
him.

Red Jim [*to Brannigan*]. Pass the Purple Priest out.

Brannigan [*loudly*]. Pass out the Purple Priest of the
politicians !
    [*The Purple Priest touches Kian's arm again, hesitates for
    a moment, and then goes out.*

Voice Outside [*at some distance*]. Pass out the Purple Priest
of the politicians !
    [*The music of Glazounov plays softly for a moment or two.*

Red Guard [*at buzzer*]. Jim, Jim, oh comrade Jim !

Red Jim [*tense too*]. What — what is it, man ?

Red Guard [*at buzzer — tense and jubilant*]. The soldiers
are joining the workers ! Listen — listen, Jim !
    [*In the far distance great cheering is heard, mingling with
    the singing of " The Internationale ".*

Jim [*to the silently crying Julia*]. He's not too far away
to hear what's happening. You'll nurse, now, a far
greater thing than a darling dead man. Up, young
woman, and join in the glowing hour your lover died
to fashion. He fought for life, for life is all ; and
death is nothing !
    [*Julia stands up with her right fist clenched. The playing
    and singing of " The Internationale " grow louder.*

Soldiers and sailors appear at the windows, and all join in the singing. The Red Star glows, and seems to grow bigger as the curtain falls. Kian alone — the one disconsolate figure in the crowd — stands, sad, gazing down on the stiff face of his dead brother.

THE END